George Harwood

Disestablishment; or a Defence of the Principle of a National Church

George Harwood

Disestablishment; or a Defence of the Principle of a National Church

ISBN/EAN: 9783337162436

Printed in Europe, USA, Canada, Australia, Japan

Cover: Foto ©ninafisch / pixelio.de

More available books at **www.hansebooks.com**

DISESTABLISHMENT;

OR,

A DEFENCE OF THE PRINCIPLE OF A

NATIONAL CHURCH.

BY

GEORGE HARWOOD, M.A.

London:

MACMILLAN AND CO.

1876.

[*The Right of Translation and Reproduction is Reserved.*]

PREFACE.

The following pages, written by a young business-man in his leisure, are offered with the simple hope that they may help the English nation a little to get at the truth about a most important matter. The writer, whilst himself thoroughly upholding the principle of a National Church, trusts that he is not incapable of understanding the arguments or of sympathising with the feelings of its opponents, for he was born and bred amongst the Dissenters, and has always been favoured with the intimate friendship of many of them.

CONTENTS.

CHAPTER I.
INTRODUCTION . . . . PAGE 1

CHAPTER II.
SKETCH OF THE HISTORY OF THE CONNECTION BETWEEN CHURCH AND STATE IN ENGLAND 15

CHAPTER III.
SKETCH OF THE HISTORY OF DISSENT . . . 93

CHAPTER IV.
WHAT IS A NATIONAL CHURCH? 141

CHAPTER V.
RELIGIOUS OBJECTIONS TO THE PRINCIPLE OF A NATIONAL CHURCH CONSIDERED 162

BIBLICAL 164
    Inferences from the Primitive Church . 173
    Quotations from the Bible 186

GENERAL 196
    1. It puts the State in the Place of Christ . . . 196
    2. It Violates the Rights of Conscience 197
    3. It Implies a Distrust of the Intrinsic Power of Religion . 198
    4. It Prevents the Spread of Truth 200
    5. It is Degrading to the Church 205
    6. It is Lowering to the Clergy 220
    7. A National Church cannot Uphold a Definite Religion . 245

CHAPTER VI.

SOCIAL OBJECTIONS CONSIDERED 257

1. The State has no Right to Pay towards the Support of one Religious Body 257
2. It Promotes Social Dissensions 280
3. It Places Dissenters in an Inferior Social Position . . 284
4. It Represses Individual Generosity 288
5. Its System is not Adaptable to Changes of Population . . 290
6. It does not Draw the Laity Socially together . . . 291
7. Its Clergy have not Sufficient Intercourse with their Congregations 294
8. It does not Allow the Congregations to Choose their own Ministers 299
9. It makes the Clergy too Independent 304
10. The Salaries of the Clergy are not Proportioned to their Congregations 308
11. The Church of England has ceased to be the Church of the Majority of the Nation 316

CHAPTER VII.

POLITICAL OBJECTIONS CONSIDERED 318

1. The State has no Right to Choose what Religion the Nation shall Follow 321
2. Religion has no Right to be Subservient to the State . . 322
3. It makes Religious Men Political 323
4. It makes the Clergy Political Conservatives . . . 326
5. It is not the Business of the State to Meddle with Religion . 328
6. It is Contrary to the Rights of Citizenship . . . 338
7. It Obstructs the Business of the State 344
8. It Arrays Religion against Political Reform . . . 346
9. It Lowers the Dignity of the State 354
10. It Endangers the Safety of the State 363

CHAPTER VIII.

CONCLUSION . 373

ERRATUM.

Page 59, line 17 from bottom, *for* "Licensed" *read* "Learned."

DISESTABLISHMENT.

CHAPTER I.

INTRODUCTION.

THE question of the Disestablishment of the Church of England has recently come into prominence and it seems probable that before long it will have to be more fully discussed.

It is said that in these days of inquiry and scepticism no institution can expect to endure which cannot show good reasons for its existence; we seem to have come to a point on the national journey at which the tickets are examined and all those are turned out who are not found properly provided. Such examinations are undoubtedly very beneficial at times for they clear away many useless encumbrances and make room for many desirable additions. But it must be remembered that it is not well for a nation to be always, or too frequently, in the critical temper. A people inheriting a political constitution which is the product of a long and continuous development is like a man coming by ancient descent into the possession of large and varied estates. If such a man is determined to go through all the title-deeds, and make himself acquainted with all the grounds upon which he holds his property, he will be able to do little else, and although he may be thought a conscientious heir he will certainly be found a useless one, for he will be spending that time in examining his power which ought to be given to using it. So unless a nation such as ours is prepared to relapse into political unproductiveness it must be content to accept most of its inheritance on trust if it means to make proper use of it and be worthy of the position and opportunities to which it has been born. And indeed there seems something ungrateful, if not presumptuous, in any one generation taking upon itself to overhaul the work of all its forefathers, for although much of that work may only have been adapted to changing circumstances, much of it must also have been based upon those fixed principles which are necessarily the chief foundation of any durable political constitution. The richness of the inheritance which has been prepared for us ought of itself to give us at least so much confidence in those who have gone before that we may be willing to accept some of the institutions which they have handed down to us without much examination, and even to be careful about destroying those for which sufficient reasons are not apparent to us, from a feeling that our forefathers knew something, if not as much as ourselves, and that perhaps their accumulated experience may be worth more in some respects than our new sagacity.

These remarks seem to apply to the National Church, which is the oldest part of our constitution and has received for a longer time, and more continuously and generally than any other institution, the approval of our forefathers. Thus in ordinary times it is a sufficient defence of the National Church, in the absence of any convincing argument against it, simply to say that it has existed well so long. There will generally be much sounder reasoning in such a defence than in any specific arguments, for it is the condensed result of a multitude of such arguments. Therefore we utterly deny the reasonableness of sneering at those who allege no other ground for adhering to the Church than that it is a venerable institution. Fidelity to a thing because it is ancient is not to be put down as mere sentimentalism, for it has in its favour the chief arguments of experimental philosophy, the only difference being that whilst this philosophy, now so popular, often bases its conclusions upon the knowledge of a single individual or generation, this sentiment, as it is called, has the accumulated experience of ages at its back, and it is well known that the wider are the observations the greater is the probability that the conclusion is true.

But although this spirit of trust may do very well as a general rule there are times when it is not sufficient. Such a time has now come for the Church of England, and those who are its confident friends may be glad of it. For as long as this institution was accepted and worked as a matter of course, it was unnecessary, and would have been superfluous, to bring forth specific arguments in its behalf. One result of a continuance of such a state is that many people come to suppose that since no such arguments are brought forward there are none to bring, and that the Church may be adhered to because it is an ancient institution but for no other reason which would be satisfactory to sensible men. Thus we are told again and again that it may be all right to hold by the Church since we have it, and it is bound up with so many associations, but that no one would think of erecting such an institution in these days or can now offer any satisfactory theoretical defence for it.

Instead of being frightened, we venture to say that the friends of the Church need have no hesitation in boldly taking up such a challenge. The onus of bringing on the fight does not rest with them; they were quite contented to stay behind the ramparts of sentiment, as they may be called, but since they are summoned out into the open plain of reason they are nothing loth to come, indeed they are very glad to have the opportunity of showing that the Church is quite able to beat her enemies with their own weapons.

Thus, since this question of Disestablishment is now

properly raised we would strongly hope that it may be thoroughly argued out, feeling fully confident that the Church will come forth from it the gainer, for if its enemies are not convinced at least the confidence of its friends will be strengthened.

And another advantage will be that this question, after having been thoroughly gone into, will probably be set at rest for a time, so that the energy of the nation may be turned into some more profitable direction. We may not be glad that Disestablishment is now the lion in the path, but since it is there our first duty is to clear it away; there may be doubts as to the wisdom of raising this question but there can be none as to that of trying to consider it thoroughly when it has been properly raised.

There are special reasons why we should now speak plainly respecting Disestablishment and say all that we think worth saying about it, for our nation is at present in a peculiar political condition. We are in a state of quiescent expectancy; one more volume of our political history has been finished and we have not yet opened the next. We are confidently told that this next volume will have Disestablishment for its principal subject, and that by this subject before long the fortunes of political parties and the fate of the nation will be determined. It is said that one of the great political parties has exhausted the catalogue of objects drawn up by its prophetic founders and accepted by this generation as the charter of its existence, and that unless some other subject is found round which its supporters may rally that party will fall to pieces, for gratitude is more than usually evanescent when it is political, and the war-standards of parties, unlike those of armies, must be emblazoned with the names of future achievements and not of past victories. Such a subject, such a name, we are told, is Disestablishment, and that as the soldiers of Gideon were chosen by their methods of drinking so their attitudes towards Disestablishment will one day determine between those who are to be the heroes of progress and those who are to be the inglorious defenders of doomed abuses. Its friends firmly believe that Disestablishment is to be the question of the future.

In one respect it is well fitted for such a position, and that is in its essential greatness, for undoubtedly the issues involved in this question are of the utmost importance. There is no corner of the realm of politics which is out of the reach of religion and its most important parts are those which are most subject to its influence. The majority, at least, of those who study human nature and past history will acknowledge that of all the forces of which political action is the resultant effect religion is, and always has been, and always must be, by far the strongest, including in the term not merely its positive but also its negative forms. Greece, and Grecian character, decayed with the decay of the national religion, and great as were the achievements of Rome, they fell far short of what they ought to have been, and began to fail as the old gods retreated before the new Mammon and no religion was left capable of preserving brotherly sympathy between classes and of inspiring a high national ideal. And so through the middle ages on to our own time religion has been the chief formative force of politics and the knowledge of its movements is the only key which can unlock and lay open to us the mysterious chambers of European history. And instead of its influence being now nearly spent those who may be supposed to have most of the prophetic gift believe that a time is quickly coming when religion will again become paramount in politics and hold in its fingers the fortunes of parties and the fates of nations. Anything therefore which greatly affects religion must be of primary importance politically and that Disestablishment must so affect it cannot but be acknowledged both by its supporters and opponents.

But the intrinsic importance of Disestablishment is no argument for its adoption, although it furnishes the strongest reason why the question when once properly raised should then be properly argued out and disposed of. For the more important a principle is the more necessary is it that there should be no vacillation in the public mind about it; there is no safe resting-place on the misty moor of doubt which divides the valley of unquestioning faith from that of experienced conviction.

But as the importance of the proposal for Disestablishment is no reason for its adoption neither does the comparative newness of its prominence afford any ground for the belief that it will be adopted. We must protest against that sort of logic, now so influential over some minds, which infers that because several new proposals have been recently adopted therefore their newness is of itself a reason for believing that other proposals will ultimately win the same fate. Because some true things are new it does not follow that all new things are true, neither does it follow that since Free Trade and Parliamentary Reform and other measures have become almost universally approved of, although met at first with general opposition, therefore Disestablishment will be ultimately adopted simply because it is now strongly opposed. Many people have laughed at ideas which have turned out to be true, but politics will become even duller than they now are if our laughter is to be taken as in itself a proof of the truth of what we laugh at.

If we wish to establish a new institution we must offer positive arguments in its favour but if our object is merely to maintain an old one it is sufficient for us to answer the objections which are raised against it. So since the proposal for Disestablishment means the abolition of the Established Church of England, in attempting to show why this proposal ought not to be adopted it is not necessary, and indeed it would be presumptuous, for us to attempt to give a positive vindication of this Church, to explain the causes of its coming into being and to show the reasons why it should continue.

The simple facts that such a Church has existed so long and does exist now are in themselves arguments sufficiently strong why it should remain unless stronger arguments can be produced on the other side. Our task, therefore, is confined to dealing with the objections raised by those upon whom lies the burden of proof and if we can show that these objections are not sufficiently strong to warrant the abolition of the Church we have a right to conclude that the proposal for Disestablishment is, until at least some stronger reasons can be offered in its favour, one which ought to be rejected. Since, however, such objections cannot be properly appreciated unless we understand the nature of the institution against which they are raised and have some acquaintance with its history—for the present is chiefly the result of the past—we have attempted to explain the meaning of that national principle which is the foundation upon which the Established Church rests, and likewise to give a short sketch of the history, in respect to that principle, of the Church and of Dissent, that is of those who have followed that principle and those who have not.

The persons who may more or less be considered as enemies to the continuance of the Established Church may be roughly divided into four classes, the first two consisting of those whose opposition is based upon religious grounds, and the second two upon political grounds. The first class comprises those who do not believe in religion at all. With these we can here have nothing to do, for it is plainly quite out of our scope to treat of religion itself. We must take for granted not only the truth of the religion inculcated by the Established Church but also the necessity for that religion to be inculcated by this or some other instrumentality. We may assume that those who do not believe in religion must of necessity be opposed to an Established Church, although it is possible to suppose that some of these may think that it is for the benefit of social order that the masses should be attached to some superstition in spite of their being themselves superior to such a weakness, as it is supposed that Socrates, as especially indicated in his last request to Crito to pay the cock he owed to Æsculapius, believed in the maintenance amongst the people of adherence to religious rites in the truth of which he himself could have no faith. But an Established Church could only exist on such a basis amongst a nation falling into the decay of hypocrisy and those who are most in favour of the national principle would be the first to reject such an institution. If a religion has ceased to be believed in it is much the best to face the fact boldly, for to retain an institution whose spirit is gone is only like trying to persuade ourselves that our friends are not dead by keeping their embalmed corpses by us. No surer method can be adopted to kill any life there may still be left in religion and to demoralise the nation than the keeping up of an Established Church which rests upon a sham. Therefore all those who are opposed to religion are, or ought to be, opposed to the Established Church, and as it would be out of place here to open any discussion respecting the truth or necessity of religion we cannot reason with such but must take them for granted as opponents. *Argument is impossible when there are no common premises and useless when there is no chance of reconciliation.

Whilst the first class consists of those who will have no religion at all, the second class consists of those who will have nothing but religion, and who reject all interference of the State as a violation of the fundamental rights of religion. Such persons believe that a Church which submits to the authority of the State becomes desecrated and is thereby convicted of faithlessness to its high trusts; the State may help the Church, may fight its battles, and pay its expenses, and carry out its persecutions, but must not on any account be allowed to exercise any control over it.

We might suggest that an arrangement which can be proved to be for the general good of religion cannot possibly be derogatory to its real dignity, but it is better to confess at once that we do not believe any good can come from attempts to reason with those who constitute this class. For when once a belief of this sort becomes a primary matter of conscience it is put out of the reach of argument, at least when directly applied. Those who put the Pope's health before the Queen's indicate by that apparently trifling action a spirit which is radically at enmity with the national principle. Between those who are possessed by this spirit and those who are in favour of a National Church there can be no relationship but, in this respect, one of such antagonism as argument is powerless against, and which must be left to be subdued by the slow operation of time.

The third class consists of those who are opposed to the Church simply for political reasons. These are indifferent about religion; they have no active feeling against it, and certainly none in its favour, and to express plainly their condition we must say that they care very little about it. Therefore if the Established Church was merely a religious institution they would have no desire to concern themselves with it, but they are its opponents because they believe that it is an enemy to political progress and a friend to the unjust predominance of the aristocratic and rich, and that at any rate its existence is a theoretical injustice. This class, although at present comparatively small, is potentially the largest of all, for there is in England an immense store of heathenism and ignorance from which it may possibly be recruited. We cannot shut our eyes to the fact that great multitudes of our people, if not absolutely indifferent about religion, have for it a feeling so vague and slight that it would count for nothing if strong political or mercenary motives were brought into action. And great exertions are now being made to stir up such motives, for whilst the National Church is represented to such people as the natural enemy to those political objects which they most desire to obtain, its property is held out as a bait to induce them to help to the overthrow of the Church so that thereby they may lighten their own proper burdens. If Disestablishment is ever carried out here it must be by its gaining the alliance of ignorance and cupidity, therefore it is our duty to try to dispel that ignorance and to display the immorality of that cupidity.

The last class consists of those who are politically opposed to the Church in the interest of religion. This class, which may be called that of the Dissenters, differs from the second, which may be called that of the Romanists, inasmuch as its belief is a matter of secondary opinion, and hence may be called political, whereas that of the Romanists is one of primary conscience. The question of whether the Church should be connected with the State or not is no part of the religion of Dissenters but belongs to what may be called, in respect to that religion, the realm of indifferent opinion, and this is also true of the adherents of the Church. Certain bodies of Dissenters may consist of those who generally oppose this connection, and others of those who generally support it, but in neither case is the religion of those bodies in any way affected. But opposition to State control is an essential part of the religion of Romanists, for Romanism cannot prevail except in the absence of such control. The old Catholicism could ally itself with the national principle but the modern Romanism which has usurped its place is necessarily an enemy to that principle.

There may be found in the Church itself numerous adherents of all these classes. There are those who care nothing about definite religion, and who are opposed to connection with the State because they fancy it hinders the realisation of their sentimental dreams of liberty; these must be put in the first class. Next, there are those who, whilst they are glad to enjoy the advantages of connection with the State, cry out against that connection whenever it interferes with their own personal caprices or priestly pretensions; these must be put in the second class. Next there are those, chiefly laymen, who although personally connected with the Church, would support its separation from the State for the sake of political partisanship or under the influence of that weakest of all motives, the conviction that the separation must be inevitable because it is somehow required by the spirit of the age; all these belong to the third class. And lastly, there are those in the Church, belonging to the fourth class, who, like the Dissenters, believe that religion should have nothing to do with the State, and that the Church would be much better if left alone.

It is to the last two classes especially, whether in the Church or out of it, that the following pages are chiefly addressed, for these are the two of convincing which there is the greatest need and the greatest chance. The Dissenters claim the most attention, as it is from them that the Church has most to fear, for it is the spirit of Puritanism which animates their opposition. And no candid reader can fail to acknowledge that this spirit has for the last two hundred years been as the salt of English history; it has reformed us religiously socially and politically; to it we are more indebted than to any other single cause for what has been manliest in our national achievements and for what is now sturdiest in our national character; it has brought us safe and hardy out of many dangers in the past and to it we must chiefly look for salvation in the future. This spirit takes many forms, and all of these ought to be treated at least with respect. Therefore it is improper as well as unwise to accuse those who wish to separate the Church from the State of unworthy motives. Undoubtedly many of the supporters of Disestablishment are influenced by feelings which merit strong condemnation, but the movement does not owe its force to such persons and will not be set at rest by their exposure. If ever the National Church is to be done away with in England it will have to be through the leadership and help of men who are conscientious and enthusiastic, although they may also be narrow-minded and mistaken; of men who are moved by the spirit of Puritanism taking a wrong form. In proportion as we admire the character of this spirit must we grieve to see it go wrong, and therefore our tone should be one of manly tenderness and not of angry recrimination. Whilst speaking with that bold plainness which is the truest evidence of respect, we should give these opponents, with whom we care to engage, the credit of being actuated by motives as good as our own; we should confine ourselves to proving that they are mistaken without asserting that they are bad. If there were no other reason for abstaining from accusation against the enemies of the Church that they are merely envious of its position or desirous of its wealth, at least this would be sufficient, that such conduct is plainly beneath the true dignity of those who are defending such an institution as a National Church. Some questions can never be properly settled except by fighting, and this may possibly be one, but at any rate the time for that has not come yet, and it is not for the Church to hasten it on, although fully ready to meet it when it does come. At present we must confine ourselves to trying to convince, and we should make it our highest object to show the opponents of the Church that the spirit by which they are moved and for which we have so much respect would be most truly and consistently obeyed by their becoming the friends of the national principle instead of its enemies.

Ignorant indifference is always a dangerous power, and especially in matters of this sort, for in these days many men have a vague feeling that anything to which the word Church is attached has nothing to do with them but should be left to those whom they call "the parsons." The bulk of the laity are now so much absorbed in the struggle for wealth and position, in the feverish efforts to get money and the foolish efforts to spend it, that they have little time or energy left for anything else, and least of all have they either the inclination or capacity to study such a question as that of the proper relationship between religion and politics. The danger is that a large portion—at least, a portion large enough to turn the scale—of such laity may, through the sentimentalism of ignorance and the weariness of effeminacy, be induced to support the proposal for Disestablishment, fancying that it is not a matter of much importance and therefore the easiest plan will be to get it out of the way. History shows that the probability of this danger is not great, and indeed there would be no such probability at all could we believe that the heart of England is still free from the fatty degeneration of riches. In spite of ominous symptoms we will believe this, and therefore we should try to stir up the indifferent and make them understand that this question of Disestablishment may not be carelessly settled, as it is one which most vitally affects the whole nation and every individual in it ; for even in political importance nearly all the movements about which, from time to time, there is so much excitement, sink, compared with this, into almost ridiculous insignificance We ought therefore to take care that the enemies of the Church shall know what they are about and that its friends shall have their weak hands upheld and their feeble knees strengthened.

Although the method here adopted, that of trying to answer objections, seems to be the best and most reasonable still it has itself plainly many grave drawbacks, if for no other reason than that it allows objections to be put up merely to be knocked down and others to be stated so as to make their refutation most easy. And even with every desire to be fair it is clearly impossible for any man so to put himself out of himself and into the position of his opponent as to state that opponent's case with full justice. It is not pretended that in the following chapters any such natural impossibility has been performed, or even that as much has been done in this direction as might have been under abler hands. The writer is too conscious of his own weakness not to know that the imperfections incidental to his method are amongst the smallest of those which may be found in his pages. Still he may venture to say for himself that he believes he has not been moved by any other motive than the desire to do his duty, and that he will be fully satisfied if he has helped in any degree to weaken the opposition of the enemies of the National Church and to strengthen the confidence of its friends.

CHAPTER II.

*SKETCH OF THE HISTORY OF THE CONNECTION BE-
TWEEN THE CHURCH AND THE STATE IN ENGLAND.*

IT must be borne in mind that in this our object is to consider merely the connection between the Church and the State in England. We have nothing to do with their separate histories except in so far as they bear upon this connection. We thus limit ourselves because it is the connection which is the real matter in dispute. It is not the Church, as a Church, which is attacked, nor is it the State, but merely the connection between the two. Therefore, in bringing history forward as a witness it is easy to see what are the leading questions we have to put to it. We must ask what has been the nature of this connection, and what have been its effects upon the State and upon the Church. From the answers to these questions we may infer the general influence of this connection upon the social and political condition of the nation and of the world at large.

But although our questions are plain it is not easy to understand what should be the answers nor what weight these should have. For catechising history is like questioning an echo; we generally get back the answer, whatever that may be, which we have already spoken to ourselves. When we think how difficult it is for the most impartial man to tell the truth about any simple incident of his own experience we can readily understand how unreliable are the statements of those who depend upon others for their information, especially when we consider that both they themselves, and those upon whom they depend, have often written history chiefly to justify some party theory or personal sentiment. Since this is the case, more or less, with all historians we must not rely too much upon what they say; not that the facts they give are themselves untrue but that necessarily there are far more facts bearing on the same points which they do not give us, and that out of the same facts very different effects may be produced accordingly as we bring some into prominence and shade down others.

The historical consideration of the connection between the Church and the State requires more care than that of any other subject, for it combines the two most fruitful sources of error, religion and politics. Over these reason and truth have very little influence compared with passion and imagination. Still history can help us a great deal in this matter, but we can only learn the great principles which underlie its teachings by taking a sufficiently broad view—just as if we wish to get a correct general idea of a landscape we must look at it from a spot too elevated for us to be distracted by its local details. If from such a standpoint we survey the expanse of history we shall through the mists of passion and uncertainty perceive, in reference to this matter, certain general features running through its whole extent, the knowledge of which will be very useful in teaching us what our future course should be. For the sake of simplicity we may take advantage of the old and convenient divisions.

PART I.—TO THE NORMAN CONQUEST.

We know so little of the nature of the religious institutions existing here for the first six centuries of the Christian era that we can form no idea sufficiently definite to be worth anything of their relations with the State. The little scraps of knowledge which we can gather on this subject give us the impression that the Druidical religion, whatever may have been its character, was thoroughly accepted by the people of the whole country and had a complete and efficient system, well organised for those rude times and in close connection with the State authorities in the different parts. In fact it is plain that an organisation which had exclusive control of the education of the people, as well as of their religion, must necessarily have been intimately connected with the ruling powers, and it is probable that there was such a union between them that while the State found the brute-force and final decisions the Church found the culture and guidance.

Of the first introduction of Christianity into Britain—under the Romans—we know scarcely anything except that by the third century this religion seems to have been widely adopted by the people. As Fuller says:—"The Light of the world shone here, but we do not know who kindled it." We are also in total ignorance of its official position. We hear rumours of British Bishops being at the Council of Arles, in A.D. 347, and of their having introduced the Gallican Liturgy into this country, but we know nothing of the organization of their Church, or whether it was connected with the State. The only thing certain is that the tender plant of the new religion had not had time to root itself firmly in the ground before it was trodden down under the rough feet of the invading pagan Saxons.

But Christianity has a unique power of resurrection; it often conquers the conquerors by the most unpretending and unexpected means. The account of the success of Augustine in introducing Christianity into Britain again at the end of the sixth century reads like some fairy tale to us, in these days when missionary enterprise, or at any rate missionary success, seems almost dead, and when the only hope of spreading our faith appears to lie in the fact that the physical vitality and mental energy of our race will enable us to displace those whom we cannot convert. But in considering the rapid spread of Christianity in Britain we must bear two things in mind. This religion had been widely adopted here before, and probably still possessed the allegiance of great numbers of the people, especially of those descended from the original inhabitants, who would cling to it with secret tenacity as a badge of patriotism and a protest against subjugation. Besides, Paganism, against which Christianity had to contend, had become completely worn-out and unreal; from this the religious sentiment of the people had already detached itself and was feeling about for some new and living faith to which to cling. Their conduct in this crisis plainly indicates one great difference of character between the Romans and the Anglo-Saxons. Both of them had lost all belief in their old religion, but the Anglo-Saxons did not lose their religious sentiment; they purified and intensified it, whilst the Romans, with far better opportunities, did not know the day of their visitation, and so fell into that corruption and decay which inevitably follow the loss of all religious faith.

The time of the second introduction of Christianity into Britain by Augustine marks a new epoch in the character of our knowledge of the relations between the Church and the State. We pass at once from disconnected rumours and vague speculations into the region of comparatively reliable facts, and two things are evident which we should bear distinctly in mind. One is, that the English kingdoms, after adopting Christianity not under fear but from deliberate conviction, did not accept, along with its doctrines, any foreign system of organisation, but developed their own system by adjusting the new religion to their ancient political constitutions. Their Church remained just as national as ever it was; indeed its nationality, as far as that depended upon its connection with the State, was greatly increased by the change. The conversion of England to Christianity was carried out by State influence and with State machinery. It was, in fact, as far as its outward system was concerned, completely effected by the State. The kings were first converted, as kings, and the people followed, as subjects. And the whole ecclesiastical system was built up on the political basis; dioceses were first commensurate with the kingdoms, archdeaconries with the shires, and parishes with the townships. The bishops sate as civil magistrates on the same bench as the ealdormen and sheriffs, the priests along with the reeves. The Church was not regarded either as the servant or master of the State; indeed we find no mention of the terms "Church" or "State," for these were but regarded as two functions of the same body. The bishops and superior clergy had seats in the Witenagemote, or Parliament, and were under the same obligations to the king as other earls, not as vassals to a lord but as citizens to a State. Land was granted to the Church, called bocland, in the same way as to the King's thegns, and under the same conditions; it was subject to the regular burdens of the State. Other parts of the ecclesiastical system grew out of the social habits of the people; lords having invited missionaries as chaplains, for the sake of themselves and their tenantry, built them churches, and so arose the custom of private patronage, which Theodore, Archbishop of Canterbury, encouraged by granting to them and their heirs the perpetual right of presentation. Thus the ecclesiastical system was created entirely in this country, or rather the previously existing political system was adapted so as to include religion as well. Augustine and his companions seem to have brought nothing into England but their missionary enthusiasm and doctrinal knowledge.

The second point to be observed, is that although the initiative in this conversion came from Rome, Rome had no authority over the Church of England, which merely looked to it for advice and not for commands. The papal system as we understand it was not yet formed, and the Popes did not then exercise in England any of the functions now supposed to belong to that system. They did not nominate to sees, nor exercise the power of veto, nor depose, nor command or forbid consecration, nor exact any fees, nor require any oath of allegiance. If ever they did interfere in these particulars, it was only occasionally, from domestic disunion and not as a recognised practice. The King in Council, from the very first, had the sole power of appointing bishops and fixing their sees; even Augustine was not named as a bishop by Gregory until he had been accepted by the State authorities. Not merely did the kings appoint and depose bishops at will, without reference to Rome, but they also refused to allow appeals of any sort to be made to the Pope, as we see in the case of Wilfrid, Bishop of York, who, having been deposed and expelled by the Archbishop of Canterbury and the King of Northumbria, appealed to the Pope, for which offence he was thrown into prison, the Pope's decision being disregarded. The archbishops were sometimes nominated by their predecessors but oftener by the king. From the Pope they received their pallium. Their chief duty was to travel about from kingdom to kingdom, exercising a general superintendence over the affairs of the Church and presiding at the meetings of the clergy. In considering the services of the Church to the nation we should not forget that by its means the people chiefly learnt that idea of national unity which led to the consolidation of the Heptarchy into one united kingdom. For the Church, although it was founded upon the political institutions of the country, only adopted those which were common to all the kingdoms, and thus, whilst the kingdoms themselves were chiefly occupied in exaggerating the little matters in which they differed the Church was embodying and teaching the great ones in which they agreed. Besides being the only organised society in the country the Church alone taught the whole people the desire of one object and the notion of one brotherhood. For this island was to those people their world, and they had no idea of national attachment beyond their separate little kingdoms. The Church quietly ignored these divisions, it treated the people as one nation and bound them together by one common faith. Thus by teaching a unity of organisation and a unity of feeling the Church prepared the way for that change by which, out of the separate kingdoms of the Heptarchy, was formed one united England.

In considering the character of the Church itself it is a noticeable fact that the kings and nobles attended the meetings of the clergy and took part in them. Thus there was complete reciprocity between the Church and the State, the separate affairs of each of them being managed by both in common.

It was to the Church also that the country was chiefly indebted for being able to rise again so comparatively compact after the grievous depressions of the Danish invasions. When we read how quickly the evils of these invasions seem to have been repaired we are apt to think that the extent of their ravages must have been exaggerated; but if we consider how plainly the marks of the Danes remain even now, and how large an influence we can still trace to them in our language and in the character and geographical distribution of our people we are forced to admit that the rapid recovery was due not to the weakness of the invasions but to the strength of the national sentiment and to the soundness of the national institutions. The Church had largely inspired that sentiment and reorganized those institutions.

In the case of King Alfred we see the reciprocal obligations of the Church and the State. Whilst the king was indebted to the Church for the dormant unity which sprang up again at his appeal the Church was indebted to the king for its reorganisation and reanimation. The lands of the Church had been seized and its system broken up; the clergy were poor and scattered, demoralised by ignorance and by the absence of all superintendence. Alfred set about to put all these things right; he restored the property and system of the Church and laid the foundations of those great institutions for the culture and the enlightenment of the nation some of which exist to this day. He made law again supreme over violence, and it is a sure indication of the nature of the relation between the Church and the State that all the laws of the period, those of Alfred Edward Athlestane and Edmund, all point to the king as the chief authority in spiritual as well as temporal matters; all ecclesiastical edicts are issued in his name with the consent of the Witan. In this connection it may be observed that it is due to the national character of the Church that the first written laws were in Saxon and not in Latin as elsewhere.

But Alfred, by endeavouring to restore the monastic institutions, helped to lay the foundations of that edifice against which the forces of the State had to be led so frequently and which did not fall until the Reformation. It is not sufficiently understood that those who are generally classed together as the clergy of the Church of England consisted until the Reformation of two distinct kinds called the secular and the monastic, who were always clearly separated from each other and between whom there was frequent and bitter antagonism. The seculars corresponded almost exactly with the clergy of the present day; they married and lived in their parishes with their families, whilst the others followed the usual monastic discipline. The great difference between them, as far as we are now concerned, was that the secular clergy were thoroughly loyal to the principle of a National Church; they refused, as citizens, to submit to any authority, even in spiritual matters, unless sanctioned by the State, whilst the monastic clergy regarded themselves as constituting a peculiar order, independent of the control of the State and subject only to the commands of their superiors, which meant those of the Pope. The struggle between these classes was carried on for centuries, the papal influence being always used to depress the secular clergy and so to make the whole Church conform to the monastic type. These attempts, however, had, in spite of favouring circumstances, such small success that it may be said that the great majority of the English clergy always refused to submit to papal control and remained throughout faithful to the State. Those who taunt the Church with so frequently changing its course, at one time following the king and at another the Pope, are only watching a few of the most erratic and presumptuous ships, forgetting to observe that the great body of the fleet is quietly following a steady and uniform track. We still see the struggle between the secular and monastic clergy frequently cropping up, or rather constantly regulating the cause of ecclesiastical affairs, for it was around these combatants that the forces always arranged themselves. At various epochs and under various uniforms we continually recognise the same antagonists, the State and the secular clergy on the one hand against the Pope and the monastic orders on the other. The kings were occasionally found going with the Pope, but the ruling influence of the nation, that which alone can be rightly called the State, kept always to the same side. The result was the continuous and complete defeat of the papal forces, of which defeat the so-called Reformation was only the formal and final declaration.

This struggle first made a decided appearance in history in the reign of King Edgar, who not only himself expelled many of the secular clergy and replaced them by monks but also, by raising Dunstan to the highest position, placed immense power in the hands of one of the ablest and boldest champions of the monastic cause. Dunstan's great object was to reform, as he called it, the Church on the foreign models, so as to make the clergy a more distinct body alienated from common social ties. His cause seemed to flourish after his death even up to the time of Edward the Confessor, who himself sided with the monks. But the heart of the nation remained sound, as was proved when the king attempted to set aside for a foreigner an Englishman who had been elected Abbot of Christ Church and so Archbishop of Canterbury. That foreigner and another foreign bishop were driven from their sees, and even expelled from the kingdom, by a sentence wrung by the Witan from the king by patriotic compulsion. Their places were filled by Englishmen without any canonical election; indeed, at this time the kings, though some of them had monastic sympathies, were just as resolute as the secular clergy in resisting papal dictation. Sometimes the bishops were chosen by assemblies over which the archbishop presided and which the king and Witan attended, and there are frequent instances in which the king nominated without regard to any other authority. Edward the Confessor himself simply notified appointments by royal charter. So strongly were the Popes impressed with the thoroughly national character of the English Church that they sometimes rejected aspirants merely because they brought no writ "from the king or folk." Indeed this disregard of even capitular election was one of the pretexts urged by William for his invasion of England. No doubt ecclesiastical dissensions were one cause of that weakness of the country which made it fall such an easy prey, especially since the monastic party was so anti-national as even if not to wish for, at any rate not to strenuously oppose, the success of the invaders.

Part II.—From the Conquest to the Reformation.

It is a true instinct which makes us stick to the year A.D. 1066, as the most important date in English history. For the Conquest was not merely the beginning of a new line of kings; it was not even chiefly this, for in comparison with the greatness of the other issues involved we lose sight of the kings, though they were strong-charactered as a race and the first of them had rare gifts of political genius and clear-headed courage. Still, much as we know of their characters and completely as their lives seem bound up with the history of the times, we feel that their personality was overcome by the strength of the new forces which were let loose by their accession. For the Norman Conquest of England stands alone in the records of the world. History can show many instances in which the conquerors, and some in which the conquered, have been victorious, but none in which both can fairly claim to have won. For whilst the Normans gained possession of the land and of political power they were themselves taken captive by the national genius and made to conform to the national character. The victory of the Normans is written on the pages of history and in the character of many of our institutions but the victory of the Anglo-Saxons may be read in the nature of our language and in the great constituents of our political constitution. Thus the Norman Conquest is no break in the continuity of our history. Looking back it seems like a marvellous interposition of Providence to introduce, in this unlikely way, those elements which were needed to make out of us that nation to which the world already owes so much and to which it will we hope yet owe far more. To use a homely figure, this Conquest was like the last stage in making a plum-pudding; there was already the Saxon flour with the Danish and British seasonings and it only needed the Norman currant to make a dish upon which, after being well boiled for centuries, the world might eventually feed.

The history of the Church during the Conquest illustrates most remarkably the strength, amounting to invincibility, of the national institutions, for just at this time, when the Church was most weakened by serious disorganization and internal dissensions it was simultaneously attacked by two enemies full of youthful vigour and strong with the confidence of growing success. One of these was the Pope, the other was the King.

The Pope now first begins to play a political part in English history. Up to the Conquest the Church of England had been thoroughly national, only looking up to the Pope for advice and general spiritual guidance. In fact the Pope had never seriously claimed any further authority, but with the Conquest he came out in a new character. It was not long before this period that the papal pretensions, as they are called, had properly developed themselves, for they had taken a long time to grow and were the outcome of a concurrence of many remarkable circumstances. By origin, as well as by nature, the Pope and the State are necessary enemies. The Pope arose on the ruins of the State. The Roman Empire had weakened the national unities by teaching all the States of which it was composed to look to Rome as their centre. When by natural decay, aided by the removal of the seat of empire to Constantinople, the civil power in Rome became weakened, the western world was at a loss for a ruler; its people had forgotten the faculty of guiding themselves and were as sheep without a shepherd. But a new power, that of the Church, was rapidly coming forward to take the vacant place. Circumstances were all in its favour; the civil power in the different countries, being weak and disorganised, counted on the influence of the Church to help it to rule the conquered people, whilst the people themselves, oppressed and helpless, begged the friendly intervention of the Church. Thus the Church, which had its centre at Rome, and was the only organised unity then possessing any vitality, was called to be the universal arbitrator just at the time when the States which had learnt to look to Rome for guidance were at a loss for a ruler. What was the natural consequence? That Church, through its Head, the Bishop of Rome, claimed to be that ruler. Not that this Church has ever so defended its position, for it professes to ask only a spiritual authority and to have for this a divine and special commission. But wherever the supreme power lies there is the ruler, and no unreal distinction can disguise the fact that the Roman Church has long asserted that power for itself, whilst the Popes, who claim divine infallibility, cannot unreasonably be considered the successors of those emperors whose statues were set up to receive god-like honours.

Nicholas I., in the middle of the ninth century, was the first vigorously to push forward the Papal Pretensions, but this position was not maintained, the bishops then having the greatest influence in the Church. As Hallam says, "The ninth " century is the age of the bishops; the eleventh and twelfth " that of the Popes." Gregory VII. (Hildebrand), with whom we first seem to hear the name Pope, was the first to claim for himself the disposal of all bishoprics, which has always been the real test of sovereignty. After the breaking up of the Roman Empire the Gothic Kings of France and Spain took a share in the choice of the bishops and Charlemagne restored their rights in this respect to the cities. But the Pope had gradually drawn to himself increased power in this matter over the Continent, and was at the height of his success and strength when William begged his help in the attempt for the conquest of England. This was just what the Pope wanted for he had for some time cast longing eyes at this country. England had acknowledged the spiritual primacy of the See of Rome but would not allow it any dominion or authority. The Pope's writs had never come here, nor his bulls, nor citations, nor appeals. As Mr. Freeman says (*Norman Conquest*, vol. iii. p. 284) :—" England's crime in the " eyes of Rome—the crime to punish which William's crusade " was approved and blessed—was the independence still re- " tained by the island Church and nation. A land where the " Church and nation were but different names for the same " community; a land where priests and prelates were subject

" to the law like other men ; a land where the king and his
" Witan gave away the staff of the bishop, was a land which,
" in the eyes of Rome, was more dangerous than a land of
" Jews and Saracens." Therefore the Pope eagerly jumped at
the long looked-for opportunity for he expected that William
would break the spiritual as well as the civil independence of
the Saxons. And the times were exceptionally favourable to
this hope for not only did William beg his favour but the
bishops also sought the help of the rising spiritual authority of
the Pope to protect themselves against the king. The Pope
also had a system of allies ready prepared in the monasteries,
which were spread over the land and, being exempted from
episcopal authority, were immediately dependent upon the
Pope.

Thus everything smiled upon this great attempt to establish
the papal system in England. The national character of the
Church of England seemed certainly doomed for the native
clergy had bitterly resisted William from the first ; they had
roused the people to resistance and after he got possession of
the throne they refused to be reconciled to his rule. Therefore he gladly availed himself of every opportunity to depress
them ; he excluded native priests and monks from all dignities in the Church so completely that by the next generation there was not a native bishop ; he replaced Stigand,
the primate, by Lanfranc, an Italian.

But in this hour of hopeless helplessness, when it seemed
as if the national Church must soon eventually perish,
friendship and preservation came from a direction in which
they could least be looked for. The king himself came out
as the champion of the English Church against the Pope.
For William no sooner found himself King of England
than he began to look at things from an Englishman's point
of view. That which, being another's, it was his object to
weaken because he wanted to conquer, it was now his
object to strengthen because it was his own. He had from

the first made up his mind that he would himself be the sole master of the country which he had conquered and throughout his reign he steadily followed up this resolution with so much far-sighted wisdom and prudent decisiveness as fully prove that he possessed a great political genius. He had two most powerful enemies to guard against—his barons, who wished to set up for themselves that independent authority which, on the Continent, so often rendered the monarch almost impotent, and the Pope, who wished to detach the Church from the nation and subject it to his own control. William skilfully played off one against the other, gaining the alliance of the Pope against the barons and relying upon the barons to help him in resisting the aggressions of the Pope. Having cautiously so distributed his grants of land to the barons that none of them were concentrated enough to form a centre of rebellion and having so modified the feudal system as to make all the sub-tenants immediately dependent upon himself, he further weakened the power of the barons by dividing the national and local assemblies into two separate bodies—the one spiritual, and the other temporal. Thus the Witenagemot was divided into a Council of kings and nobles and a Convocation of clergy, whilst the local courts were divided into provincial at which the elderman and sheriff sat, and diocesan presided over by the bishop and archdeacon. These ecclesiastical courts attracted most of the business because they were more mercifully disposed towards the people, and thus the jurisdiction of the barons was lessened.

But the Pope, as well as the king, was enamoured of the feudal system and wished to extend it to his own case. As the tenants held from the barons, and the barons from the king, so he wished that the king should hold from the Pope. Therefore when, under his alliance, William had conquered England he claimed for his share of the spoil two things; that the king should see that the money hitherto allowed to Rome was more carefully paid, and that he should do fealty to the Pope for the crown of England. William readily granted the first, though he made it distinctly understood that the payment of Peter's pence was merely a benefaction, but he distinctly refused the second request, declaring that such fealty had never been done by the kings of England before him. He thus bore testimony to the slight hold which the Pope had up to this time possessed over the Church of England. The king not only refused for himself to submit to papal authority but he also adopted strict measures to prevent any papal influence extending amongst his people. He forbade any Pope to be acknowledged whom he had not first recognised, or any papal briefs to be received unless first shown to him, or any censure to be passed by the Church without his approval. He would not allow any of the clergy to leave the kingdom without his permission and no bishop could punish any baron or servant with ecclesiastical rigour unless by his command. He certainly allowed a papal legate to reside here, but under his own control, and he made use of the feudal system to strengthen his hold over the bishops and abbots by compelling them, as barons under his vassalage, to do homage for the Church's temporalities. Thus the Pope, instead of having his authority established over the Church of England found that, small as it had been before, even that was diminished by the Conquest. But, although grievously disappointed, he was not foolish enough openly to quarrel for he knew how weak was his own influence over the nation and how hopeless it would be to struggle with such a king. Therefore there was a tacit truce during the life of the Conqueror, under whom the Church remained, as far as the Pope was concerned, thoroughly free and national.

But it was merely a truce and not a peace, hostilities only being suspended until the death of the Conqueror. For it was not likely that the papal power, which was increasing everywhere else, would long leave England alone. The violent and profligate conduct of William Rufus precipitated affairs, for by keeping so many livings open in order to get the income himself and then selling them or bestowing them on worthless favourites he alienated from himself the popular sympathy and forced the Church to look elsewhere for protection against his lawless oppression. But the cautious and able Lanfranc, until his death, managed the rough king who, in penitential terror, appointed as his successor Anselm, who was soon to inflict upon him the first real loss which the State had yet suffered in its contest with the Pope. For Anselm violated the Conqueror's laws by acknowledging a Pope without the king's authority. Rufus called the bishops together to depose Anselm but they refused saying that they could not do so without the authority of Rome. The king was obliged to submit, and so the State suffered in two ways, the law was broken and another court of appeal acknowledged. The king's vices are apt to blind us to the justness of his cause whilst in contemplating Anselm's virtues we forget that his conduct was illegal and unpatriotic.

The cause of the State suffered another defeat in the hands of Henry I., to whom the fact of his not being the proper heir was the cause of much weakness. In this reign, in spite of the king's high qualities of talent and courage, the papal power gained a decided advantage. Probably this must be chiefly attributed to the fact that at this time there existed that friendship between the Church and the people which continued for so long and which afterwards found such a striking expression in Magna Charta. The body of the people thoroughly sympathized with the Church in a very indiscriminating sort of way; they did not care about the papal pretensions, for their attention was not then directed to them, but they looked to the Church for protection against the rapacity of the nobles and the oppressions of the State. Besides, the Conquest had greatly fostered this tendency, for whilst the people still regarded the kings as intruding foreigners they clung to the Church as a native institution with that increased tenacity which is one of the natural results of such a condition. It is to the kings alone that England is indebted for the early struggle against papal encroachment, and we should bear this in mind in considering our obligations to them even if we credit them with no higher motive than jealousy of a rival. In guarding their own independence they guarded that of the nation, for the two must ultimately become identical.

Henry I. was anxious to make up for his brother's misdeeds and the Pope took advantage of his weakness and good disposition. Anselm, who in his brother's reign had received his pallium from the Pope without the king's consent, was still the great leader for the Pope and it is remarkable how often this cause has found in this country men of genius and daring to champion it and how generally the great interest of the struggle has centred round some individual. Anselm imported the latest foreign innovations for he had taken an approving part in an Italian Council which declared that the clergy had the sole right to nominate for Church appointments and that they ought not to yield any homage to laymen. Anselm had himself been invested by Rufus with the ring and crozier, the symbols of spiritual authority, and had also done temporal homage to the king, but he now demanded that the State should give up its claim to both of these. It cannot be too clearly understood that the real object of the Pope from the commencement of the struggle up to the Reformation was to get the power of appointing the Church dignitaries entirely into his own hands; his desire was to nominate the bishops and invest them; they were to be subject only to his authority so that the State should be totally powerless over those who from the nature of their office necessarily exercised the strongest influence upon the nation. We must not allow ourselves to be deceived by the fact that often the professed object of long and fierce struggles has been some symbol or ceremony which seems to us to be fruitless and meaningless. Our forefathers were not fools, and we may be quite sure that they did not fight and suffer without believing that the principle involved in their struggle, whatever might be its outward expression, was one which was worth all the trouble they were taking. In these days when the active positiveness of earnest conviction is cried down as bigotry and when people generally know just little enough about everything to escape caring much about anything, it is not uncommon for those who ought to know better to laugh at the folly or pity the ignorance of our ancestors because they sacrificed everything for the sake of a cause which seems to us of absurdly little importance only because we are now too ignorant to understand its meaning. If the conduct of our ancestors in the things we do understand was manly and sensible we ought to suppose that it had the same qualities in matters now out of our reach. At any rate laughing at the apparently trivial character of the avowed objects of their struggles ill becomes this generation which is enjoying the blessings of the establishment of the great principles of which these objects were merely the symbols.

Thus it may seem strange to some that the chief interest of the history of England should centre for a long time round the question of the investiture of bishops, but the mystery is cleared up when we understand that the real matter to be decided was whether the king or the Pope should choose the heads of the Church. The greatest wars of history have generally had an apparently trivial cause but everyone has known that the real cause, though often never openly expressed, was something far more important.

At this time three distinct conditions had to be fulfilled before any new bishop could enter upon his duties : firstly, he must be nominated ; secondly, he must receive spiritual investiture, which conferred upon him the right to exercise the religious functions of his office; and thirdly, he must receive temporal investiture, which being expressed in the ceremony of his doing homage, recognised his power over the temporalities of his office and established his social and political position. Now up to the time of Henry I. as a general rule, the king had controlled all the three conditions; the new bishops were first named by him and then received from his hands the symbols, the ring and the staff, of their spiritual power, after which they did homage to him for their temporalities and took the oath of fealty. This last was the natural consequence of the extension by William I. of the feudal system to the Church. The Pope had hitherto possessed no recognised power in the election of bishops; often, no doubt, his wishes were consulted but often also disregarded, and the only official channel by which his influence could be brought to bear was when the archbishop was friendly to his pretensions, for as the new bishops had to be consecrated by him great difficulties could be put in the way by this ceremony being refused. This was the course adopted by Anselm towards Henry I. Instead of the king having everything to do with the election of bishops he declared that he ought to have no voice whatever in it, that it was a matter which purely concerned the Church and that religion was degraded by the interference of the State. We shall see, all through the history of this struggle, how exactly the arguments urged on behalf of the Pope against the State correspond in principle with those which we now so frequently hear in vindication of Liberationism.

But Henry did not take such a limited view of the proper duties of the State and refused to be barred out of what he considered one of the most important exercises of his influence and preservatives of his freedom and power. So he resisted when Anselm refused to consecrate any bishops who had been nominated by the king or had done homage to him. But in spite of his best efforts the Church profited by the weakness of the king's personal position and the extent to which previous abuses had alienated the sympathy of the people from the crown. So Henry was obliged to compromise by giving up half his power over the election of bishops, that is he admitted the Pope as partner in what had previously belonged to the State alone. Thus the king abandoned his right to nominate and to confer spiritual investiture, but retained his claim to receive from all newly-appointed bishops the oath of fealty and full homage for their temporalities, these to be given before consecration could be performed. Thus the State lost the initiation and retained only the right of veto. This was a great victory for the papal power and the ease with which it was won can only be understood when we remember how widely the nation was then alienated from the State.

The papal power as a political institution has always had the unamiable characteristic of owing most of its success to other people's misfortunes; it grows chiefly out of decay. It sprang into life on the ruins of the Roman Empire and its spread has, in every country, been in proportion to the decline of national unity and vitality. It could make no way here until the embarrassments of Henry I., and the disturbances of Stephen's reign were most favourable to its development. When everybody is upset and confused those are at a great advantage who know what they want and have no scruples about getting what they can. It is pitiable to see how helplessly Stephen struggled against that enemy whom he felt to be stealthily stealing upon the treasures he was too weak to guard. He forbade the people to read the "Decretals," the decrees of the Popes and Church Councils, which were published in England for the first time during his reign, for the Pope, in imitation of imperial Cæsar whose power he wished to emulate, called his decisions "Rescripts" and "Decrees." Stephen's reign, when lawlessness was so widespread that the castles of the nobles had become mere dens of robbers and the people were so wretched that, as we read, "they openly said that Christ and His saints were asleep," is an epoch in our history, for it marks the close of the unsettled period of the Conquest. Many of the old usages and laws had been swept away by the stream of anarchy and so a comparatively clear space was left upon which to build up a new constitution. The accession of Henry II. marks the end of the period of destruction and the beginning of that constructive process which has gone on ever since. During the time of the Plantagenets, confused and chequered as it was, were laid those foundations upon which our present constitution is chiefly built. The twelfth century is the age of those charters which fixed the position of the Church as an integral part of the nation whilst the thirteenth century is the age in which the rights and liberties of the people and their political relationship with their sovereign were defined and the system of Parliamentary Government inaugurated. With the reviving prosperity and confidence of Henry II. there sprang up again that spirit of resistance to Papal aggression which has always been proportionate to the increase of national vitality. And this spirit was not confined to the people as distinct from the clergy but it animated both alike, proving that the Church was still in sympathy thoroughly national and not papal. For when Henry II. made a stand concerning the election of Archbishop Baldwin the bishops and clergy sided with him against the Pope, whose only allies however, the monks, had great power for they had the initiative in the choice of Archbishops of Canterbury, who had first to be appointed Abbots of Christchurch. The parochial clergy did not merely give the king their silent acquiescence but they also actively preached against the notion that the sentence of the Pope ought to have any force, by itself, in this country. Stephen was the first King of England who had allowed appeals to be made to Rome. Henry II. could not thoroughly undo this but he prevented any clergyman from making such an appeal unless he had first given securities that he would attempt nothing contrary to the rights of the crown, which might be made to mean anything. The king saw that it was necessary, for the sake of the State's proper independence, that its relationship with the Church should be defined more distinctly. He felt that now was the time to resist the growing claims of the Pope, whose influence was increasing everywhere, and he promoted A'Becket to the archbishopric believing that he would help him in this task. The Pope, having got from the State much of its initiatory authority, resolved to go further and free the Church from the civil control of the State. Therefore he claimed that the clergy should not be amenable to the law of the State even for civil offences but should in such cases be tried and punished by the Church Courts only. A'Becket, as is well known, heartily took the Pope's side, but the easiness of the victory proves how thoroughly the nation and the Church were with the king in this matter. The king replied by the famous Constitutions of Clarendon, passed 1164, which for ever set at rest this claim. These Constitutions were passed in the National Council and subscribed by clergy and laity alike, and very reasonably so, for their object was the establishment of the equality of all men before the law; they asserted that the Church is part and parcel of the nation and that clergymen are not an independent order but simply citizens with special religious duties. They decreed that disputes about presentations and Church property should be decided in the King's Court; that clergy should be tried by Civil Courts for civil offences; that archbishops and bishops were not to leave the kingdom without the king's leave; that elections were to take place in the king's chapel with his consent, and that those elected were to do homage for their temporalities; and that in all cases the final appeal was to be to the king. Thus Henry II. clearly laid down the conditions of what may be called a truly national Church, and it is evident that he did this with the approval of the great body of the clergy, for although Becket obtained a papal dispensation from obedience to the Constitutions of Clarendon this was considered of little value even in the Church itself. Some of the good effects of what the king had done were spoiled for a time by the evil consequences of his rash words about A'Becket which conferred upon the cause of unpatriotic obstinacy the delusively sentimental attractiveness of martyrdom. The cause of the Pope was helped throughout the world by the Crusades, which weakened the idea of national individuality and developed that of a common object, increasing necessarily at the same time the influence of him who was the recognized chief champion and representative of that object.

The papal power, as opposed to that of the State, was developed still further, so far as England was concerned, by the remarkable events of King John's reign, two of which, as being amongst the most important of history, should be carefully considered. These are the king's submission to the Pope and the enactment of Magna Charta. Still it is remarkable how little either of these events ultimately helped the cause to which they seemed at first so favourable; indeed, both of them, when looked at fully, prove most unmistakably that the Church and also the people remained sound in their national allegiance. One fact which the miserable history of King John most clearly brings out is that thorough opposition to papal advances was one of the strongest sentiments then ruling the body of the people. This explains the mystery of that strange changing of sides which otherwise seems so inexplicable. Up to this time we have seen the people allied with the sovereign and the Church against the barons, who were the natural enemies of freedom and law, but now we see the people together with the Church deserting the sovereign and uniting with the barons. What had the king done to be left so friendless? He must surely have been guilty of extraordinary oppression and wrong-doing. But we search in vain for proofs; nay, his own weak and vacillating character assures us that he could not have been strong enough for anything of the kind. The worst that history has to tell of him is trifling compared with many of the misdeeds of his predecessors, and yet these retained the people's allegiance. The fact is the people had willingly forgiven much in kings who they knew maintained the national honour and independence, but they completely turned against John as soon as he had tarnished that honour by yielding up that independence. As long as the national property was kept intact the different claimants were content patiently to wait but as soon as some of it was handed over to the foreigner they all rushed in determined to secure their own rights. Thus we must not regard King John's submission to the Pope and Magna Charta as two isolated facts of history but we must consider one as the prelude to the other. The degradation at Dover led to the lonely capitulation at Runnymede.

The king's first mistake was in not preventing the appeal which the monks and bishops made to Rome respecting the primacy, but the people approved his conduct when he refused to submit to the decision, and they backed him up when the Pope placed him under an interdict. In spite of the pictorial accounts of the effect of that act, and though undoubtedly the Pope's influence in England was then proved to be great, it is clear that the Church, as a whole, remained faithful to the king. In some dioceses the bishops would not even admit the interdict and it is plain that the great body of the clergy acted in the same spirit, for few left the country although all who remained did so on condition of not acknowledging it. King John had then a great opportunity and had he been as stanch as the people were he might have immortalised himself by anticipating the Reformation. But John, with the blundering common to cowards, chose the wrong side; he flung himself into the arms of the Pope, and begged

Rome to help him against his own people; his own people replied by demanding Magna Charta.

Two facts connected with Magna Charta throw considerable light upon the character of the Church at this time and prove that it was still unmistakably national. One is that although the Pope sided with the king in refusing to grant Magna Charta the Church thoroughly sided with the people in their efforts to obtain it, indeed it took the lead throughout the whole struggle. Archbishop Langton was the prime mover and chief adviser, and of the three sureties to whom the king bound himself when he found that he must succumb two were bishops. The archbishop himself approved of the conduct of the barons in refusing the king's offer to submit the dispute to the decision of the Pope, and the first nine names which appear on the Charter are those of dignitaries of the Church.

The other fact to be observed is that the first article in the Charter, which is the only one concerning the Church, and is very short, makes no mention in any way of the papal power, but is just such a one as would be exacted by a thoroughly national Church from an oppressive monarch. "That the Church of England" (observe the national title) "shall be free and have her whole rights and her liberties inviolable," does not mean that the Church shall be free to put itself in subjection to the Pope but that it shall not have its rights discarded by the king and its property despoiled. The only matter particularly specified, namely freedom of election, was merely the confirmation of an agreement resulting from the king's attempt, which had failed, to detach the Church from the side of the people. By this it was ordained that when a bishop had been elected and presented to the king the king's consent should not be refused unless lawful reasons were assigned. The object of this was not to increase the influence of the Pope in the choice of bishops, in fact there is no recognition of this at all, but to preserve the Church to the nation by securing it from the domination of a king who was at war with the nation. This is a necessary safeguard for the national character of a Church during those unnatural periods when the State and the nation have become separated from each other.

When we consider the great influence of the Church, and the leading part which it took in obtaining Magna Charta, we cannot but admire its moderation and charity. Instead of grasping for itself, as it might so easily have done, increased power and privileges it was contented with the declaration of a long accepted principle and of a previously granted condition. But it not merely sought little for itself, it also strove to obtain much for those who were poor and otherwise friendless. When we consider the helplessness of the great mass of the people at that time we may well wonder at the extent to which Magna Charta was favourable to them. It was not to the barons, their hereditary enemies, that they were indebted for this but to the Church, and it would be well if those who are so fond of turning over the injuries which they suppose the Church has inflicted upon the nation would also call to mind the benefits it has conferred. Whenever the Church of England comes up to receive final judgment, and its book of life is read properly over, it will be seen that in all the great crises of our national history it has steadily stood true and has taken a leading part in those achievements which have built up our national strength and are now our national glory.

The startling control which the Pope gained over King John, and the great influence which he exercised in English history at this time, forcibly compel us to observe the development to which the papal power had obtained. It is considered to have reached its height in the thirteenth century, and this fact should be borne in mind when we are criticising John's conduct. Without wishing to deny his vacillation and cowardice we in these days, who are so much controlled by the impulses and thoughts which prevail at the moment, though these constantly change, have no right to expect that the King of England would at that time keep himself above the reach of that power which had been steadily growing for centuries and had then become by far the strongest influence of the civilised world. Instead of being surprised because one or two kings of exceptional weakness and timidity yielded to this influence we should rather be filled with wonder and pride that the English nation from the first offered to it a united resistance and was the only one which won over it an early and complete victory. In these facts are to be found some of the plainest promises of that authority which our nation was afterwards to exercise over the world.

The Court of Rome had for a long time past been zealously developing its power on the feudal ideal and since Charlemagne there had been no monarch on the Continent strong enough, either in character or position, to offer any valid resistance to its steadily growing pretensions. Hence by the thirteenth century there was no feudal claim of consequence to which the Church had not something corresponding. As there was a lay so there was a clerical investiture ; as lands without a legal tenant escheated to the lords so benefices (the same word *beneficie* was used for grants of land) went to the Church if there was no proper presentation by the patron ; as there was an oath of fealty so there was an oath of canonical obedience; as there was the tax of feudal render so the Church claimed its tenths; for primer seisins we have annates and first-fruits ; for aids and talliages, Peter's pence ; indeed in that age, when love of money was a ruling passion, it may well be believed that the Church was an apt pupil in learning all the methods of exaction. But the Pope, emboldened by success, through a variety of pleas, as when the officials were attending at Rome on certain occasions or had been presented to a bishopric or abbey, gradually claimed for himself the right to present to all livings, and made money out of this claim either by what were called commendams, putting a clerk in charge and taking the income, or by provisions, that is by making previous nominations before a vacancy had occurred. Finally Rome claimed for itself universal and unlimited empire by the celebrated bull "Unam Sanctam" of Boniface VIII., which said that the Church had two swords, spiritual and temporal, of which the spiritual is used by the supreme pontiff himself and the temporal by kings, for the supreme pontiff. By another bull, soon after, it was declared that all persons, of whatever rank, were bound to appear, when personally cited, before the Pope's tribunal at Rome.

It is evident that in any country the acknowledgment of such claims was totally inconsistent with the State's independence. These claims were never thoroughly brought forward here until the thirteenth century, for England was the last country which it was attempted to subdue as it was well known that here would be offered the stoutest resistance; therefore the attacking power fully developed its strength before properly beginning the conflict. This then is the crucial period of our history as far as the papal power is concerned. If these claims were continuously and successfully resisted, if the State preserved throughout its own supreme authority, then it must be acknowledged that our Church has continued uninterruptedly national and has never been Roman Catholic in the sense in which that expression is now understood. Of course the English Church all along looked to Rome for religious guidance, but there is a vital difference between deference and obedience, and the history of England during the next three centuries plainly proves that what is called the Reformation was the rejection of spiritual influence and not of political authority. Rome never gained over the Church of England anything which can truly be called political authority or real control.

The three combatants now come plainly forward; the State and the Pope are contending for the mastery whilst the

Church, using the term in the narrow sense of a religious organisation, is divided between the two, some portions of it befriending the Pope but the great body sympathising with the State and generally standing by it. Still the Pope had sufficient friends in the Church to hope that he would win by their help added to the still stronger influence of the spirit of the age, which then ran so decidedly in his favour. The Church was the acknowledged bone of contention for both the State and the Pope well understood that mastery of the Church meant mastery of the nation, or at any rate was essential to it. What then were the chief points attacked, and how were those attacks resisted?

The great objects aimed at by the Court of Rome may roughly be divided into four:—

1.—To get control of the land by bringing it into possession of the monasteries, which were favourable to the Pope's claims and subject to his immediate authority. These attempts were resisted by the different Statutes of Mortmain, which rendered void all bequests of land to religious corporations.

2.—To get control of the appointments in the Church. Resisted by the various Statutes of Provisors.

3.—To weaken the civil courts by extending the area of ecclesiastical jurisdiction. Resisted by the Acts of Prohibitions.

4.—To foster in the country a power independent of the State and a rival to it. Resisted by the different Statutes against Præmunire (which word, derived from the opening sentence of the writs summoning to appear, came to denote this offence generally).

In all these attempts the Court of Rome ultimately and decidedly failed for whilst its own influence steadily decreased the Statutes by which it was resisted continually increased in number in strictness and in general acceptation.

Henry III. followed in his father's footsteps and reaped his father's reward, for he leaned to the alliance of the Pope and received in consequence the antagonism of his people, proving again how soundly national the feeling of the country remained. Here is another instance of how frequently bad kings are better than good ones for as the disloyalty of John was followed by Magna Charta so that of Henry III. led to the great Charter which established English liberty, and to the Barons' War which developed the organization of Parliamentary government and the recognition of the political equality of different classes of the people.

The first Charter after Henry's accession dealt with the question of Mortmain and decreed that all such attempts to transfer land into the hands of the Church should be void and that the land should be forfeited to the lord. When at the Parliament of Merton, in 1236, the ecclesiastics wished to legitimate, in marriage, illegitimate children the earls and barons refused declaring that they would not change the laws of England which had hitherto been used and approved.

Henry III's. reign has the unenviable notoriety of including the only instance in which the Roman canon law was officially recognized by the bishops and clergy of the Church of England. In 1237, chiefly by the king's help, the first papal legate promulgated his constitutions in England, and this was done still more officially in 1268, one solace being that this second time the legate was an Englishman, and the only one who has ever become Pope. Since this date no canons or constitutions have ever been made in England by any legate, and the strong dislike which was felt to anything of the sort was well expressed by the nobility in the next century when they declared that, " This realm of Eng-
" land hath never been until this hour, neither by the consent
" of our lord the king and the lords of Parliament shall it ever
" be, ruled or governed by the civil or canon law."

Besides this usurpation there were many other serious grievances to be complained of at this time, most of which were very practical and painful. The king, partly on account of his own foreign sympathies, willingly connived at the Pope's attempts to reward his own followers and to break down the spirit of the English Church by placing foreigners in its best positions. This had been carried so far that now nearly half the livings in England were held by foreigners and the sum sent out of the country as their income exceeded the royal revenue. It speaks well for the national clergy that when it was seriously attempted to destroy the national character of the Church it was thought that they could not be trusted to do this work and that foreigners must be put in their places. But the clergy were not disposed to quietly see themselves dispossessed, and their spirit of resistance found expression in the famous Robert Grostête, Bishop of Lincoln, who being ordered by Innocent IV. to confer a benefice on a Genoese flatly refused.

It was not merely the Church which suffered but also the general body of the nation, for not merely did the patrons of livings object to their rights being disregarded but both laity and clergy suffered grievously from the heavy burdens inflicted upon them to pay the subsidies promised to the Pope by King John. This spirit of disaffection found vent at last in two letters, addressed in 1247 by the general body of the clergy, one to the Pope, the other to the Cardinals. They both complained strongly of the papal exactions and of the infringement of their national rights.

There was continued under the able and patriotic Edward I. that constructive process which had been carried on so vigorously during the reigns of John and Henry III. It should however rather be called a process of active development than of construction, for it cannot be too distinctly understood that all the great steps in the growth of the English constitution have followed the ancient footprints, and none of them have struck out entirely into new paths. The old dress brought over by our Teutonic forefathers has often needed letting-out and altering but the material and cut still remain as the national costume; at no time have we tried to make anything like a totally new start, for all the great measures on which we pride ourselves and the effects of which still remain have merely professed to revive something which had fallen into neglect. Magna Charta was demanded as the old charter of Edward the Confessor, and Parliament itself was but the enlargement of the Council which had existed from time immemorial. The fact that the chief object of our legislators has been to revive ancient customs is not more true of any portion of our history than of that long series of enactments in the thirteenth and fourteenth centuries by which the national character of the English Church was preserved. What was new was papal usurpation, and what was required was to throw this off and to return to the primitive type of national independence.

Hales styles Edward I. the Justinian of England and says that more was accomplished in the first thirteen years of his reign than in all the time since. Certainly, in this respect, this is the most glorious period of English history and especially so in regard to the Church. The king at once took a bold stand against the papal usurpations. He would not suffer the bishops to attend any General Council unless they previously took an oath not to receive the papal benediction or do anything contrary to the State's supremacy. The fact that no English bishop had ever been summoned to such Councils until the preceding century shows how recent was the pretension of papal control. Edward I. cared nothing for the Pope's bulls and invaded Scotland in opposition to one, nor did he pay any heed to his processes. Archbishop Winchelsea, who seemed wishful to play the part of a second A'Becket, having produced a bull in 1296, to an assembly summoned without the king's writ, forbidding the clergy to grant any aid to the State without the license of the Apostolic See, the clergy, who were led away by surprise, agreed to a reply which talked about there being two heads over them, one spiritual and the other temporal, and about sending to Rome for permission to make a grant to the king. The answer from the King's Bench that they had thus outlawed themselves was soon practically impressed upon their minds when they were robbed without redress on their journey back and found their homes ransacked and their property confiscated. This proved a very successful, if rather rough, method of teaching the clergy that they must look elsewhere than to the Pope for their supreme governor, and the lesson was made still more impressive when they found themselves not summoned as usual to the next meeting of Parliament, for the plan of representation, as it came from the hands of Edward I., included the lower clergy by virtue of their payment of taxes as well as the bishops and abbots by virtue of their baronage. For about a century the clergy continued an estate of Parliament, but from the end of the fourteenth century they deserted and preferred to meet separately and tax themselves. By another century they found out that this step had been a mistake, and so tried to fall back on the old writs, but unsuccessfully.

Edward I. carried out his principle unflinchingly, and executed one of his subjects who had got a bull of excommunication against another. He also passed various statutes to increase the control of the State over the Church. By the Statute of Westminster First in 1275, the privileges of clerkships were considerably lessened, and by that of *Circumspecte Agatis*, in 1284, the jurisdictions of the courts were more clearly defined, many causes being removed from the spiritual to the temporal. He also greatly strengthened the Statutes of Mortmain. He was led to this no doubt as much by his interest as his principle, for land transferred to an ecclesiastical body avoided the payment of the usual services to the supreme lord, so that the State found itself deprived both of military strength and money revenue. It is a noteworthy fact that although the money exactions of Edward I.

exceeded those of Henry III., which had called forth such bitter opposition. The people bore them with comparative patience because they knew that they were chiefly for patriotic purposes and not for papal subsidies.

The reign of Edward I. is also remarkable because in its thirty-fifth year was passed the first definite statute against Papal Provisions. Throughout this reign there were no less than five distinct statutes passed in different years against Mortmain.

Edward II. had pretty much the same fate as John and Henry III., for he leaned to the Pope and found that in consequence the people first estranged themselves from him and finally broke out into open opposition. It is a fact to remember and be proud of that even at this early time we can distinctly perceive that the State and the nation were not necessarily identical. As long as the king, representing the State, was patriotic and honest he might rely upon the sympathy and support of the people, in spite of excessive taxes and despotic deeds, but no sooner did they lose confidence in him than they separated from him and developed a national sentiment to which he was eventually obliged to yield. This sentiment, with the conservative instinct of English history, has always first tried constitutional methods to get its way, but when these have failed, and the object has been great enough, it has not shrunk from resorting to mere force. The fact most to be noted is that such a sentiment, whenever it has reached this pitch, has always eventually prevailed. Therefore in reading the history of this question we must not always take the attitude of the State towards the Church as representing the feeling of the nation, for there has been frequently a relation between the Church and the nation quite different from that existing between the Church and the State. The State has sometimes coquetted with the Pope but the nation has been towards him throughout either suspiciously alienated or obstinately opposing.

Under Edward III. we find the king and the nation again pulling well together, as is plainly shown by Edward's valiant reply to the Pope, which would not have rung out as it did had he not known how thoroughly the people were at his back. For when he and his nobles had expostulated with the Pope about his growing exactions and pretensions they received a very menacing reply, being curtly told that the Emperor, who had in the Diet in 1323 established a law against Provisions, had given this up and yielded to the Pope. The Pope evidently considered it absurd to suppose that the King of England would stand out after such a potentate, and others with him, had surrendered, but Edward took quite a different view of the matter and replied that even if the Emperor, and the French king into the bargain, took the Pope's part he was ready to do battle with both in defence of the liberties of the State. This was no empty boast, and was soon followed up by more sharp and penal laws being passed against Provisions, which enacted—

1. That the Court of Rome should not present or collate to any bishopric or living in England.

2. That whosoever, by virtue of a Papal Provision, disturbed any patron should pay a fine and ransom to the king at will, and be imprisoned until he renounced such a Provision.

3. That the same punishment should be inflicted upon such as cited the king or any of his subjects before the Court of Rome.

By the Statute of Provisions in 1350 it was declared that " the king or other lords shall present unto benefices of their " own or their ancestors' foundation, and not the Bishop of " Rome." Also if any Provision or reservation was made by Rome the king for the time was to have the patronage. This was to prevent the connivance or timidity of chapters and spiritual patrons.

When Urban V. attempted to revive the idea of vassalage and annual rent it was unanimously agreed by all the estates in the Parliament of 40 Edward III. that King John's donation to the Pope was null and void, being without the concurrence of Parliament and contrary to his coronation oath, and all engaged together that if the Pope endeavoured to maintain these usurpations they would unitedly resist him to the utmost.

The substitution of the foolish and weak Richard II. for the clear-headed and bold Edward III. did not check the current of national resistance to papal aggression. The name of Richard II., otherwise connected with misfortune and shame, is attached to some of the most outspoken Acts of Parliament which vindicated national supremacy. By the Acts 3 Ric. II. and 7 Ric. II. it was enacted that no alien should be capable of letting his benefice to farm or of being presented to any ecclesiastical benefice in future. This was to prevent the evil, then grown to such disastrous proportions, of foreigners receiving the incomes of livings who never attended to the work but lived constantly abroad, most of them never even seeing their churches. By the 12 Ric. II. all liegemen of the king who accepted any foreign Provision were put out of the king's protection and their benefices were declared void; and in the following year there were added for this offence the punishments of banishment and forfeiture of goods and lands. Also it was then enacted that any person bringing any citation or excommunication from beyond the sea should be imprisoned, forfeit his goods and lands, and suffer pain of life and member.

But the chief measure of Richard II.'s reign was that passed in the sixteenth year, which is specially called the Statute of Præmunire, although it was merely a more explicit and emphatic repetition of previous statutes. The offence of Præmunire came to include all cases of maintaining papal power contrary to the State's supremacy. The nation was now considerably alarmed at the growth of this power, and the Parliament of Richard II., like that of

Edward III., repeatedly complained of the way in which the various statutes to control it were disregarded. That this alarm was not unreasonable is shown by this one fact, amongst many, that at this period the Church had got into its possession nearly half the soil of the country. If the Pope could have made himself uncontrolled ruler of such a Church he would, with this material power added to the spiritual influence of religion, soon have necessarily become the real ruler of the nation. It seems a pity that we have not now such plain and forcible circumstances to help to enlighten the nation on this subject, for although many things are greatly changed since then the real issue involved is precisely the same now as it was when Richard II. reigned.

This Statute of Præmunire enacted that whoever procured at Rome or elsewhere any translations, processes, excommunication, bulls, instruments, or any other things which touched the king, against him, his crown and realm, and also that whoever assisted therein, should be put out of the king's protection, his lands and goods should be forfeited, and he himself should be attached by his body to answer to the king and his Council.

This statute was again repeated in the reign of Henry IV., in the second year of which it was also enacted that any person who accepted papal Provision exempting from canonical obedience to the proper ordinary should be subject to the penalties of Præmunire. There was evidently during this reign a resolute determination to resist all papal usurpations upon the civil power.

The reign of Henry IV. is unenviably remarkable for the persecution of the Lollards, who were the Dissenters of those days, and, like the Dissenters of these, were in reality more political than religious. This is proved by the petition presented in 1402 by Prince Henry, afterwards Henry V., together with the Lords, to the King expressing alarm at the communistic principles attributed to the Lollards. It is often convenient to glorify as martyrdom for religious principle the punishment incurred merely for political restiveness.

The two chief points insisted upon by Wickliffe are two of the fundamental articles of a National Church; one, that the Papal Supremacy should not be allowed, and the other, that the clergy ought not to refuse to pay taxes to the State. Although Henry IV. and Henry V. persecuted the Lollards they both held their ground firmly against the Pope and refused to repeal any of the statutes by which he was held in check. Henry IV. threatened to deprive the Church of its land, and the Pope was very conciliatory in his bearing both to him and his son.

Henry V. suppressed the abbeys for foreign monks and took their lands to the crown; and when Cardinal Beaufort was admitted, by consent of Parliament, to the King's Council, it was stipulated that he should absent himself whenever any question between the king and the Pope was being discussed.

During the reign of Henry VI. a Papal Nuncio was imprisoned for delivering letters from the Pope in England without the consent of the State. In the reign of Henry VI. the Archbishop of Canterbury refused to consecrate a Bishop of Ely who had been nominated by the Pope, and also he would not obey the Pope's command to try to get repealed the Statute of Præmunire, "execrabile illud statutum" as the Pope called it.

From this time to the Reformation the power of the Pope gradually declined, not only in England but throughout Europe. This was greatly helped by the schism which resulted in the setting up of a rival Pope at Avignon, thus breaking the illusion of that unity which had constituted one of the strongest attractions of the papacy. That the State had maintained, and even increased, its supremacy is shown by the concordat with Pope Martin V. Not merely were the terms of this concordat entirely in favour of the rights of the National Church, but the mere fact of such a concordat being made is a strong argument in the same direction.

Whilst the power of the Pope was declining that of the kings, all over Europe, was increasing. History is not the statement of a series of chance circumstances, but each period is governed by its own special prevailing influence by which these circumstances themselves have been mastered. Thus the ninth and tenth centuries were the time of bishops, the thirteenth and fourteenth that of popes, whilst the fifteenth and sixteenth may be considered especially that of kings. Two circumstances were especially favourable in England to the kingly power, namely the victories of Henry V., which increased the glory and prestige of the throne, and the War of the Roses, which almost annihilated the power, as it decimated the number and wasted the means, of the nobility and thus took away the chief check upon the despotism of the crown.

Two things prove that the papal power was very weak in England about the time of the accession of Henry VII. For the opportunity when the country was weakened by civil war, and the attention of the State was distracted and its energy absorbed was just such a one as the Court of Rome would have eagerly taken advantage of had there been any hope of success. Also during this struggle neither party thought it worth while to treat for the Pope's help, as they would certainly have been eager to do had they believed it would have been good for much.

These two circumstances, the increase of the royal power and the decrease of the papal power, coming together at the same time, were in England the chief causes of the Reformation.

PART III.—DURING THE REFORMATION.

IN each great period of history there are generally one or two subjects which seem, like deep places in a field, to drain into themselves all the waters of sentiment. Often we see in one part plants, which we think most precious, parched and dying for lack of just a little of that moisture which, in another part, is forcing others, apparently far less worth growing, into huge and unnatural proportions. We may be sorry, but we cannot do anything, for when once the channels are formed their courses must be followed. Historical sentiment obeys the inexorable law of gravitation, and the water will keep flowing on in the same direction to the end of the epoch. Then comes a great geological crisis, when either by some volcanic overflow of burning passion or by the glacier action of icy indifference the character of the surface becomes changed.

National attention is always very partial and capricious. It is so now just as much as ever for although we boast so loudly of our improved civilisation and extended information it is evident to the most cursory observer of contemporary politics that the English nation is yet incapable of carrying in its head much more than one idea at a time. Not merely the mass of the people, but also many leading politicians, often allow their minds to be absorbed for long periods by a single secondary object. This is hardly becoming conduct for those who are called upon to govern a vast and diversified empire.

This tendency of the national mind to exaggerate some subjects and neglect others has been very strikingly illustrated by the Reformation, which has been so much dwelt upon and talked about, has pointed so many morals and adorned so many tales, that from having a very true meaning at first it has now come to have quite a false one and promises soon to have no meaning at all. It is not difficult to see how this confusion has arisen for in reality the word Reformation, with that vagueness so common in the English language, has had from the first two totally distinct meanings. Sometimes it signifies that general resuscitation of Western Europe which occurred in the sixteenth century, and at other times its meaning is confined to the change in the relations between the Church and the Pope which was made in several countries at that time. If asked to define, people generally give the second meaning, but the bulk of what is said about the Reformation is inapplicable unless the word is supposed to have the first meaning.

One of the worst consequences of this word being used to describe two changes, one very great and the other comparatively small, has been that the great change has been lost sight of and its greatness has been transferred to the small one.

Scarcely any language can be too strong to speak of the greatness of that revival which at the beginning of the sixteenth century altered the whole face of civilisation. A number of new and stray beams were then gathered together in a focus, to flood the world again with light. The discovery of the art of printing gave an immense development to that revival of learning which had already made such progress. The Copernican system of astronomy suddenly opened out the heavens to men's comprehension, whilst at the same time the vast and startling discoveries of new lands revolutionised their ideas of the earth. As the curtains of ignorance were raised with such marvellous rapidity it was impossible for those whose horizon of mental vision was being so vastly extended to see the old things in the same proportions as before. All things seem great until we have seen greater; the little hill in our neighbourhood is a mountain as long as we know no other, but it sinks into an undulation as soon as we have caught a glimpse of the Alpine peaks. Who could listen to the old story of papal glory whilst the whole universe was breaking out into a new song, whilst the very heavens could be heard declaring the glory of God? The papal power was one of the old things which must pass away from those to whom all things were becoming new; its only chance of preservation was to prevent men seeing these new things. The Court of Rome was wise in its generation when it declared itself the enemy of the new knowledge; a sure instinct made it know that henceforth it could only hope to keep its rein over those who could be made to wear blinkers.

England would not have her eyes darkened but boldly looked abroad on the whole of the newly disclosed landscape, therefore in England the Reformation, as referring to the papal power, was inevitable.

One of the necessary consequences of the awakening of men's minds here, but not by any means the most important, was the change which was then made in the definite relationship between the Pope and the Church. This was a very much smaller affair than it is generally represented. The prevailing idea is that up to this time the Church of England had been Roman Catholic and that by the Reformation it was suddenly made Protestant. This mistaken idea leads two classes of the people, amongst others, into serious error. Enthusiastic Protestants greatly exaggerate the importance of this ecclesiastical change and attribute to it all the benefits which have followed from those greater causes of which it was itself but one effect, whilst equally enthusiastic Roman Catholics think that by the Reformation the National Church finally seized the position and property which their Church had previously possessed and which many of them fancy it will yet eventually regain as by right.

It should be clearly borne in mind that there were two distinct Reformations in England, the one civil, under Henry VIII. and the other spiritual, begun under Edward VI. and completed by Elizabeth. The civil Reformation was not the dethronement of the Pope from the government of the Church and the establishment of the State in his place but it was merely the completion of a process, already nearly completed, which had long been going on, and the explicit definition of that supremacy of the State which had always existed. It is a parody of history to talk as if the Reformation took away the headship of the Church from the Pope and gave it to the State; the Pope could not be deprived of what he had never possessed, and the Church of England had continued uninterruptedly from the earliest times a State Church. The State had never lost its mastership of the citadel of supremacy although so long, and often fiercely, attacked by the Papal forces. The siege had been at times hot and threatening; more than once dangerous breaches had been made in the walls, but the enemy had always been finally driven back. Ever since the fourteenth century the attacks had been growing rapidly weaker, and the Reformation was merely the formal declaration of the termination of a siege which everybody had seen for some time was quite hopeless. If by the Reformation is meant the establishment of the supremacy of the State over the Church, its real date, as an important epoch, should be fixed when the tide of the siege was turned and not when the last remnant of the forces was driven from the field.

It is not an uncommon taunt to hear from those who dislike the Reformation that the less we say about its cause the better, for it was merely the result of the thwarted caprice of a sensual monarch. It is represented that the Pope was the champion of law and morality, and because he would not consent to be the tool of the king's faithless fancies Henry cut his connection and made himself his own Pope. This is an instance of that hasty habit of mind which leads men to hold up as the real cause of great events the circumstances, generally trifling in themselves, which seem to have immediately brought them about, just as if a match could be the real cause of an explosion for which a gunpowder train had previously been laid. The divorce of Henry VIII. was the igniting spark, but this would have been totally harmless had it not fallen upon a heap of fuel which was gathered ready for the conflagration and was certain soon to catch fire in one way or other. Henry's desire for a divorce had no more to do with the English Reformation than Luther's disgust at indulgences had to do with the German. Both of these were merely like the trifling incidents which often bring to a head those quarrels which mutual bad feeling has long rendered inevitable. But it is the bad feeling which is the cause of the quarrel and not the incident.

The fact that the king applied to the Pope at all about his divorce might seem to indicate that the previous alienation from Rome could not have been as great as is represented, but it must be remembered that questions of divorce have always, even almost up to our own times, been supposed to belong peculiarly to the Church as a religious institution, and do so yet in most countries. Henry wished to obtain the advice and approval of the chief authority of his religion but he would not recognize that the Pope had any right to command. Therefore as soon as the Pope by summoning the king and queen to appear at Rome assumed a power of jurisdiction inconsistent with the State's supremacy, Henry at once turned his back upon him and sought the advice he required from the Licensed Societies. The fact that he did thus turn from the Pope to these Societies proves how real the Reformation had already become and how widely the power of the Pope was considered to be one merely of moral influence and not of authoritative command.

Although Henry possessed remarkable strength both of intellect and will, for he was one of the ablest as well as most despotic and obstinate monarchs in European history, still he was most manifestly the plastic and obedient instrument of Providence, or fate, or whatever we choose to call that power which, however it acts generally, seems at certain epochs to take the world entirely into its own hands. At such times we find the men and their work fitted for each other with an accuracy never perceptible in the ordinary course of affairs. Thus in the last war between France and Prussia any thoughtful Frenchman might have anticipated the fate of his country if he had observed that his enemies possessed a ruler, a statesman, and a soldier, each of them remarkable enough to stand alone in history, and who would not have been thus brought together with such admirable adaptability had there not been a great work laid out for them to do. So in the same way Henry, with all his virtues and all his faults, was exactly the man to carry out the Reformation in England. It is the strongest men who are most the servants of fate, for Providence seems to leave the common sort pretty much to themselves but picks out the ablest workmen to do the best work. Had Henry been less unscrupulous he would have been more incomplete, had he been less despotic he would have been more timid, had he been less extravagant he would have been more dangerous. Henry was also just the man to define his work for he made it abundantly evident that the Reformation, as far as he was concerned, was exclusively a political matter and had nothing to do with religion. It is significant that the abolition of the papal power was conducted by the only sovereign who had obtained from the Pope the title of "Defender of the Faith."

The Reformation was carried out in that steady, orderly, determined manner which has so honourably distinguished the course of political history in England. The Reformation was not an act of revolution but a change of law, worked out systematically and continuously through a series of years. The first step was taken by the king, who fearing that the Pope might issue a Bull in the queen's favour, sent forth a proclamation in 1530, declaring severe penalties against publishing anything emanating from Rome. This was not the assumption of a new principle but simply embodied the terms of a statute of Richard II. In 1531 the king attacked the legatine authority, and declared that all who had submitted to it had rendered themselves liable to the penalties of Præmunire, which he threatened to enforce. This frightened the clergy who sent up a Petition from the Convocation of

Canterbury, in which the king was styled "The Protector and Supreme Head of the Church and Clergy of England." Besides this they agreed to pay large sums of money and promised not to offend in this way again. The quickness and completeness with which the clergy acknowledged the State's supremacy proves what a slight hold the Pope had previously had over them. Besides the reforming spirit, the spirit of Wickliffe and Erasmus was abroad amongst the people undermining all superstitious reverence and leading them to question the rights of the clergy and to be indignant at their corruptions. Thus the clergy, finding enemies on two sides and feeling that the Pope could give them no help, eagerly purchased the protection of the State as a shelter from the attacks of the people.

In 1531 a Bill, beginning in the House of Lords, was passed for the abolition of the payment of annates to the Pope, in which it was stipulated that if the Pope refused to consecrate any bishop the ceremony should be performed by an archbishop or bishop, "in like manner as divers other archbishops "and bishops have been heretofore in ancient times by "sundry the king's most noble progenitors made, consecrated, "and invested within this realm." It was also named that the divine services and sacraments were not to be interrupted.

In 1532 Parliament complained of the clergy, and the clergy presented an address called "The Submission of the Clergy" in which they acknowledged that the Convocation could only be assembled by royal authority, and that no canons could be enforced which had not received the royal assent. At the end of the year Henry wrote a letter to the Pope, in which he stated that "he intended not to impugn the Pope's authority "further except he compelled him, and that what he did was "only to bring it within its first and ancient limits, to which it "was better to reduce it than to let it always run on headlong "and do amiss." A priest was cast into prison for preaching in favour of the Pope's authority, whilst another priest, who had been imprisoned by the Archbishop of Canterbury for heresy, was liberated by the King's Court.

In 1533 Parliament passed an Act forbidding appeals to Rome, the preamble of which says that "The Crown of Eng-"land is imperial and the nation is a complete body within "itself, with a full power to give justice in all cases, spiritual as "well as temporal." It also refers to Edward I., Edward III., Richard II., and Henry IV. as having preserved the liberties of the realm, both spiritual and temporal, from the annoyances of the see of Rome and other foreign potentates. This Act decreed that all causes should be determined within the kingdom, and that all persons appealing to Rome or obtaining Bulls from Rome should be subject to the penalties laid down in the Law of Provisors 16 R. ii.

The Pope did not realise the fact that the time for threatening had gone by, for the England of Henry VIII. was not the England of John. Therefore his sentence against the king instead of arresting the process of alienation quickened it, for it led to the grounds of his power being questioned, and thus to the general conviction that they had no foundation in Scripture and were contrary to the laws of England, as these had existed even so far back as the time of Henry II.

In 1534 a Bill was passed for discharging the subjects of the realm from all dependence on the Court of Rome, in which it was declared that there was no intention to vary from Christ's Church about the Articles of the Catholic faith of Christendom. This Bill was completed in eleven days, proving that both Houses of Parliament readily assented to it. An Act was also passed at the same time repealing one of Henry IV. which enabled bishops to punish for heresy. In this year was also passed the Act called "The Act of the Submission of the Clergy," which embodied the legal recognition of the State's Supremacy over the Church which the clergy had themselves acknowledged. In this Act, which is in fact the legal declaration of the Reformation, the king is styled "Supreme Head" of the

Church of England. By this it is declared that Convocation shall be assembled only by the king's writ; that no canons shall be made without the royal assent, a committee half of Parliament and half of clergy nominated by the king being appointed to consider them; that the power of granting dispensations shall be transferred from the Pope to the Archbishop of Canterbury, and that appeals from the Archbishop's Court shall be made to the king in the Court of Chancery. It was declared that the title of Supreme Head on earth of the Church of England should be added to the king's other titles, and that whoever denied this supremacy should be considered guilty of treason. First-fruits and tenths were transferred to the crown.

The next Act provided for the election of bishops. Up to this time this had been done, since the reign of King John, by the process of *Congé d'Elire* (king's license to elect) which was substituted for the old invesiture of the ring and staff. Up to the sixteenth century Rome and the crown were almost partners in filling English bishoprics; still, although the Pope had much indirect power, the State influence predominated. The chapter nominally elected by *Congé d'Elire*, but although the crown did not, since Magna Charta, name the person to be elected, still the royal will was in some way or other intimated and generally prevailed. The person chosen had, before entering on his office, to receive the pallium from Rome and to take an oath to the Pope. The evil of this oath was abated by the subsequent oath of fealty to the king, by which the elected bishop renounced all engagements to the Holy See which might be prejudicial to the realm. This continued to the Reformation. It was now decreed that no bishop should be presented to the See of Rome but to the archbishop. When any see became vacant the king was to grant a license for a new election, along with a letter-missive bearing the name of the person to be chosen. The dean and chapter were then to return an election, and the person elected was to swear fealty to the king and then to be invested by him.

In 1535 the bishops swore to the king's supremacy, following the advice of the University of Oxford, which decided that the Pope had no more authority than any other foreign bishop. Only the monasteries refused to take the oath of supremacy, hence the king decided upon that visitation which ended in their destruction. The monks had always been the allies of the Pope in his struggles against the State and consequently throughout the course of history all the kings who had upheld the State's rights had felt it necessary to curb the power of the monks. In deciding to destroy the monasteries altogether Henry did not adopt a new line of conduct as a consequence of the Reformation, but merely completed a process which several of his predecessors had vigorously carried on. No doubt this measure, both in its nature and in the summary method in which it was carried out, seems to us harsh and arbitrary; judged in the light of our present ideas it was undoubtedly illegal and a most dangerous violation of the rights of property, but we ought to remember that this was a time of war and must not be judged by the rules of peace. The monks and friars had done a good deal to bring on the war and Henry had just as much right to turn them out as a general has to expel traitors from his camp. This step helped the Reformation in more ways than one for by exposing to the public gaze the state of corruption existing in many of the monasteries it helped to strengthen the feeling of opposition to the Roman system itself.

The Protestant spirit was still more developed by the publication of the English translation of the Bible, ordered by the king. Henry was no doubt sincere in his devotion to the Roman Catholic system of religion but by giving the Bible to the public he was unconsciously acting as the greatest enemy to that system, for priestism depended upon secrecy and mediation and was checked by anything which laid open the Book of religion and brought the people into more immediate intercourse with their Maker.

Thus, although Henry's Reformation was not in itself concerned with religion it led directly to that religious Reformation which took place in the reign of his son. Henry showed that he was by no means disposed to repent of the course he had adopted or to be afraid of carrying it out still further, for when the Pope, after the execution of Anne Boleyn, tried to bring about a reconciliation between himself and the king, Henry rejected the offer and answered it by enacting still more stringent punishments against all who in any way tried to restore the Pope's power. He also published the Articles of Religion solely by royal authority.

Thus was the Reformation under Henry completed, and it is remarkable how willingly the people seemed to have acquiesced in what he did. There were several local risings, but these were principally on account of the temporary distress caused by the suppression of the monasteries, upon which the poor had hitherto chiefly depended for relief. It was inevitable that there must be a great deal of disturbance and suffering after the old system had been destroyed and before a new one had grown up.

In summarising what the Reformation had done we cannot too distinctly impress upon ourselves that it did not establish any new principle or create any new institution. It is a remarkable feature of English history that in all our great steps we have gone forwards by going backwards—the English nation has never attempted to make a new constitution or professed to build up political institutions according to new theories. We have always reformed by being conservative, we have never set about building ourselves a new house but have only cleaned up the old one, after clearing away the rubbish and creepers which untended time had got about it. So the Reformation was not the creation of a National Church but only the process of clearing away from that

Church the corruptions which had grown about it; it was not the marking out of a new field but only the pulling up of the tares which an enemy had planted in the old one. The Act of Supremacy, like the Petition of Right and the Declaration of Rights, did not affirm anything new but merely placed old principles in a new light ; it did not establish the State supremacy but only reasserted it. Papal supremacy was always illegal in England; whatever influence it obtained was due to its hold upon popular sentiment and was always contrary to well-defined laws. The Reformation merely reasserted these laws and carried them out. It left the same bishops priests and deacons, the same ecclesiastical courts, the same seats for bishops in the House of Lords, the same dioceses, the same cathedrals and parish churches frequented by the same worshippers, the same worship Sacrament and Liturgy, and the same recognised tie between the guardians of the Church and governors of the State. From the time of William I. it had always rested with the State to determine to what extent the Canon Law should prevail in England, and this is all that Henry VIII. did by the Reformation.

Under Edward VI. the process of separation from Rome was carried a stage further. Henry VIII. had confined himself to destroying the Pope's civil authority ; he left the Church of England thoroughly national in its polity but it remained thoroughly Roman Catholic in its religion. The sacramentarian doctrine of transubstantiation was a fundamental part of Henry's religion, and was the leading principle inculcated in his Articles of Faith. Edward VI., and those who acted for him, attacked the Pope's spiritual authority and endeavoured to replace the doctrines which were especially Roman Catholic by those which are considered to belong peculiarly to Protestantism. No period of English history is judged more variously or more violently than this—and naturally so, for this was purely a religious reformation, and religion is always treated with less reason and more prejudice than any other subject. Some people confer upon Edward a sort of Protestant canonisation, because they believe that under him the pure religion of the Bible was first inculcated in this country, whilst others cannot find words strong enough to condemn the conduct of the king and his associates not merely in despoiling the Church's property but also in demoralising its ancient faith. In judging of such matters our opinions are only our likings in another form, but there is no doubt that under Edward VI. Protestantism, as a system of religious doctrine, was first set going in England, and there is no doubt also that in thus pushing forward these doctrines the government of Edward was going contrary to the expressed wishes of Henry VIII., and was acting in decided opposition to the feelings of the great body of the people. The Reformation of Henry left the nation Anglo-Catholic in doctrine, but that was no reason why it was always to remain so; indeed this was not possible in the presence of those causes which were now actively at work undermining the chief tenets of the Roman Catholic religion. The German Reformation had, up to this time, been little connected with the English one, for Henry would not accept the Confession of Augsburg and Luther would not have Henry's Six Articles; but now the Protestantism of Germany was beginning to make its influence felt here. Besides, the spirit of doubt and destruction roused by the Reformation was sure to lead to unbelief in the old doctrines, especially since Henry enforced these doctrines with such exacting cruelty, for amongst a high-spirited people persecution is one of the most effective means of making heretics. Thus the government of Edward VI., whatever may have been its motives, was by its doctrinal changes rather anticipating the feeling of the nation than opposing it. There was nothing inconsistent in such conduct in those days, for although now we consider that the State should be merely a mirror reflecting the nation as it is, it was then expected to be rather a painting showing the nation what it ought to be.

The best argument in favour of the line of conduct adopted by the State under Edward VI. is that it has always been severely condemned by the extreme people on both sides, some calling it too Protestant and others not Protestant enough. To temperate and loyal friends of the Church of England the conduct of the State at this time appears both wise and dignified. It assumed the spiritual authority of the Church, in so far as that which has to do merely with the outward expression of religion can be called spiritual, and proceeded to organize for the Church a statement of doctrine and a form of service, but in doing this it did not, as weak-minded people always do in such cases, rush into the opposite extreme from that which it had left; it did not, to show its independence, set about creating a new system of its own. Instead of this it stuck to the old faith and the old service as far as it possibly could, only altering with great reluctance when it believed corruption and error had crept in. Thus the spiritual Reformation of England, like the civil, was carried forward by going backwards. In the civil Reformation there was no idea of erecting anything new; nobody dreamt of establishing a new Church, and those who talk as if at this time a sort of compact was first made between the Church and the State see these events in a totally different light from that in which they appeared to those who carried them out. So those who conducted the spiritual Reformation merely intended to reform the old faith of the Church of England, and had no idea of setting up a new one.

Cranmer, by whom this second Reformation was chiefly carried out and to whom it is chiefly indebted for its character, has yet but received scant justice from his countrymen; nor does he seem likely at present to be better appreciated, for the popular mind, which keeps gaining greater influence, is always disposed to overrate what it calls thorough-going, which means extreme, men and to underrate those who are moderate, and who choose that middle course in which the truth generally lies. People have yet to learn that it is the easiest thing in the world to be all on one side or all on the other; it requires no continued exercise of mind and saves a man from troublesome doubts besides securing to him plenty of enthusiastic friends, whilst he who resolves to seek only for truth and stick to that must be always on the alert and after all his pains must expect misunderstandings and mistakes, besides being certain of the abuse of all extreme men, which generally means nearly everybody who says anything, for those moderate men who admire him rarely give themselves the trouble of saying so. This last has been the fate of Cranmer, but surely the time will eventually come when the English nation will properly appreciate him to whom it chiefly owes those Articles of Faith, so simple and complete, and that Book of Prayer, so sublime and broad and human. Cranmer's greatness will be understood if we realise his position, and then remember that after three hundred years of progress none of us dare think that his work can be mended.

In considering the effect of the reign of Edward VI. we have nothing to do with those little acts of injustice and corruption which no doubt were plentiful enough. We must not be led off the scent into inquiries about the private lives of the chief men or into speculations about their motives; we have only to observe the great outlines of the picture which they painted upon their piece of the canvas of time and have not to spot out every broken line and pore over every faulty tint. Whether or not the government of Edward had the approval of the nation in what it did at the time it is certain that it received it eventually, for in spite of the reactionary reign of Queen Mary the legislation of Edward was revived and the doctrine and worship of the Church of England have remained ever since almost exactly as he laid them down.

The events of Mary's reign clearly proved that the nation as a body did not go with Edward's doctrinal reforms in the same way as it had done with Henry's civil measures. The part played by the English nation at this time seems at first very difficult to explain, for we appear to be driven to one of three suppositions, none of which are very creditable, namely that the people must either have been insincere with Henry and Edward in their Protestantism, or with Mary in her Catholicism, or else they cared nothing either for Protestantism or Catholicism and so acted with a fickleness very much out of harmony with their general conduct in history. Probably not one of these suppositions is correct, as is generally the case with attempts to account by a simple principle for the actions of complex human nature. The truth seems to be that the people as a body knew very little about the matter but generally sympathised, as Englishmen, with Henry's efforts to uphold the national dignity by restricting the power of the Pope; they did not, however, want their religion changing and therefore welcomed the accession of Mary because they believed that she would preserve to them that old faith of which they fancied Edward meant to deprive them. They cared much more about their religion than they did about the Pope, and therefore they were not unwilling to follow Mary in returning to the old obedience to the Pope provided she returned to the old form of religion. They actively desired the reversal of the spiritual Reformation and passively allowed that of the civil, or barely so, for this could not be done legally without a packed Parliament and much oppression. Still, had Mary acted wisely, she might undoubtedly have delayed much longer the final victory of Protestantism, but she made herself the strongest helper of the cause to which she was bitterly opposed, for the fires of Smithfield burnt the brand of Protestantism indelibly into the heart of the English nation. The haughty tyranny and grim cruelty of the friends of Roman Catholicism sealed its doom.

Still the apparent return of the English nation, under Mary, to the papal bosom is much misrepresented and its extent greatly exaggerated. It was not a surrender of the national character of the Church, but merely of some of the ground taken up by Henry VIII.; it did not repeal the laws of Provisors or Præmunire or any of the great statutes by which the papal power was curbed; it did not even attempt to upset the practical legislation of the Reformation, for the reconciliation with Rome took place on the express condition that the alienated lands and possessions should remain in their present hands.

We shall find ourselves totally at a loss to understand the history of this period unless we disabuse our minds of most of our modern notions about the State and the nation being the same thing. In these days the supreme power rests with the people themselves and the State does what they dictate, but in the time of the Tudors the State ruled the people, it exercised the guiding influence and moulded the course of history. Henry VIII. and Edward VI. were ahead of their people, Mary was behind hers. Had it depended upon the popular decision neither the civil nor the spiritual Reformation would have taken place when they did, if they had ever taken place at all, and those who pin their faith to the immaculate supremacy of the people should remember that many of the wisest deeds of English history have been done against their wish, whilst those who talk about the evil influence of the State on religion may reflect that the Church of England is indebted to the State for the lasting vindication of its independence and the sober purification of its doctrine.

The reign of Elizabeth may be divided, as far as the Church is concerned, into two distinct periods, the first marked by the restoration of Protestantism and the second by the development of Puritanism. In no part of her conduct was Elizabeth's wisdom and moderation more remarkably displayed than in her ecclesiastical policy, especially in the early part of her reign, justifying the name of "Lady Temperance" which her brother playfully conferred upon her. The queen's attachment to Protestantism, and her strength of character, were too well known to allow the Roman Catholics to expect anything else but the reversal of Mary's policy, and they even anticipated that this would be violently done, whilst the extreme Protestants believed that now their own favourite ideas would be carried out. Both of these parties found themselves wrong, for the queen did indeed carry out her Protestant opinions, but so moderately and gently that during the first ten years of her reign the Catholic population, which still comprised two-thirds of the nation, continued to worship at the parish churches along with the rest; there was then no distinction in this respect.

Elizabeth followed her father rather than her brother, and personally leaned to several of the doctrines and practices which her brother had condemned as Roman Catholic. With reference to the Church she aimed at two main objects; one to vindicate the supremacy of the State over the Church, effected by the Act of Supremacy, and the other to establish a regular discipline and worship in the Church, effected by the Act of Uniformity. The Act of Supremacy scarcely differed from that of Henry VIII., except that the queen declined the title of Supreme Head and substituted that of Supreme Governor. By this Act the supremacy was declared to be restored to the Crown, all the Acts of Mary concerning ecclesiastical jurisdiction were repealed, and an oath of supremacy was also ordered to be taken by all official persons, lay and clerical. There was also a clause empowering the Crown to put the supremacy into commission, and thus arose that famous and unhappy Court of High Commission which was afterwards the cause of so much mischief. From this again came the present delegation of power to the Judicial Committee of the Privy Council.

By the Act of Supremacy, which finally asserted the supreme jurisdiction of the State over the Church, Elizabeth had no idea of erecting a new Church any more than

Henry VIII. had. Her object was distinctly stated to be "the reducing of the Church of England to its former purity." Elizabeth did not establish a new Church, but only re-established the old principle that the sovereign ought to be the fountain of law in his own realm. The Reformation, now formally consummated, was merely a matter of law, and neither this statute, nor any other before it, recognised any such distinction as that between spiritual and ecclesiastical jurisdiction. The Act of Uniformity, which authorized the Prayer Book, at the beginning of which it may still be read, was passed by the same Parliament which had passed the Act of Supremacy, and which also had granted to the Crown the first year's revenue of livings and one-tenth of the annual revenue, such as the Pope had previously received. The Prayer Book was well received, so that the Catholic laity did not object to resorting to the churches where it was used, whilst out of nearly ten thousand beneficed clergy not more than two hundred left their livings on account of religion, showing how gently the transition from Mary's policy to Elizabeth's had been effected. Even these defections were chiefly amongst the bishops and superior clergy who refused the oath of supremacy, proving that the nation, with which the lower clergy were chiefly in sympathy, did not disapprove of the changes which had been made. This conduct of the bishops exercised a strong influence upon the history both of the Church and of the country. For partly in consequence of the disturbance caused by the Reformation, and of so much of the property hitherto devoted to education having been squandered, besides the organisations being broken up, the education of the clergy had been so lamentably neglected that Elizabeth was driven to fill up the places of the bishops who had withdrawn by men who had been exiles during the Marian persecution, and whom suffering had made narrow-minded and fanatical. These men into whose hands the queen so unaccountably committed so much of her authority used that authority so unsparingly and exactingly that they alienated Catholicism and developed Puritanism.

Along with the famous Parliament of Elizabeth which completed the ecclesiastical Reformation of England there sat the Convocation (1562-3) which, with so much moderation and liberality, shaped the completion of the doctrinal Reformation. This Convocation drew up the Thirty-Nine Articles by eliminating from the Forty-Two of Edward VI. their rancour and intolerance, and also the Second Book of Homilies, which restored much of the Catholicity wanting in the first.

We may now consider the Reformation completed, for the second part of Elizabeth's reign marks a distinct epoch and begins quite a new period of history. The Church had now fully developed into that National Church of England such as it has continued ever since. We have next to follow the fortunes of this Church.

Part III.—From the Reformation to the Present Time.

It is a fact much to be regretted, and one which gives the sting to many a taunt from the enemies of Protestantism, that no sooner was the Church of England cut off from connection with the Pope and established as a completely independent National Church than it began to split itself up into pieces which have never yet been joined together again. The end of the first portion of Queen Elizabeth's reign marks the beginning of a decidedly new epoch in the ecclesiastical history of England. The Roman Catholics, as a distinct party, drop into comparative insignificance, becoming eventually one of the bodies of Dissenters, though completely isolated from the rest. The Protestant Dissenters, developing out of the Puritans, now come forward and claim great and constantly-increasing consideration. We have thus three distinct bodies to observe—the State, the Church, and the Dissenters. The State is to be considered in its connection with both of these, and therefore it will be better to separate, as far as possible, the history of its dealings with the Church from that of its dealings with Dissent. Therefore we will first continue the sketch of the history of the connection between the Church and the State, confining the Church to what may strictly so be called, and we will afterwards attempt separately a sketch of the history of Dissent. This will necessitate numerous repetitions and some apparently arbitrary divisions, but it seems that these evils will be more than counterbalanced, as far as our specific purpose is concerned, by increased plainness and clearness. It is especially necessary just now to get a correct idea of the history of Dissent, which cannot be readily done when that is mixed up with the history of the relations between the Church and the State.

No stronger proof of the weakness of the Roman Catholic, as distinct from the religious Catholic, sentiment in England can be given than the smallness and feebleness of the party which, after the completion of the Reformation, was constituted on behalf of this sentiment. Elizabeth's reign left the bulk of the nation Protestants in politics and Catholics in religion. This combination was principally the cause of that strictness with which the State regulations for the Church were enforced, and which led to the development of Dissent. For since the majority of the people were attached to the Catholic doctrine and ceremonies, and also believed strongly in the authority of the State over the Church, it was absurd to expect that they would either relax this authority, then so newly acquired in completeness, or would use it to enforce that Puritanism to which they were so strongly opposed.

Many theories are propounded to account for the different characteristics of the two parts of Elizabeth's reign. All Protestants glow over the first part, in which the Reformation was completed with such moderation and wisdom, but those who sympathise with Puritanic Dissent, and those also, often the most religiously opposed to Puritanism, who are jealous of the State authority over the Church, both of these assert that the queen afterwards quite lost her head and handed over the management of religion to a number of bigoted and unscrupulous bishops. The general course of Elizabeth's conduct contradicts this theory, for it shows that she never did lose her head and never was the woman to abdicate her control over anything, especially over ecclesiastical affairs, in which she was so strongly interested. The fact seems to be that instead of deputing her State authority to the bishops, the queen merely used the bishops as the instruments for exercising that authority in a stricter way than it has ever been exercised since; it sounds oddly to speak of authority being abdicated by her who talked so readily about "unfrocking" the bishops and who held over them continually such an exacting rod. Elizabeth is not to be excused in this way; she must be held thoroughly responsible for what was done in her reign—a responsibility which would be readily accepted, and even claimed, by her who, being a Tudor of the Tudors, would have resented any suspicion that she had not always been the mistress of her own affairs.

The fact seems to be that in her ecclesiastical policy Elizabeth was resolved to maintain two things—one, the State supremacy, and the other, the Catholic system of ceremonial and doctrine, though she did not insist so much upon doctrine, for we hear little of prosecutions for belief, Elizabeth's reign comparing very favourably with her father's in this respect. There is no doubt that in these two resolves the queen had the majority of the nation at her back, and had she carried them out with more gentleness and less irritating fickleness she would have been more successful, and would have left the Church a compact unity, instead of fostering the growth and embittering the alienation of what was at first a small and well-disposed minority.

The queen was inclined to be very forbearing with the Roman Catholics, and it seems likely that she hoped eventually to draw them into the National Church. She did not put the penal laws which had been passed against them into operation until her temper was roused by the excommunication issued against her by Pius V. in 1569. Many circumstances came together at that time all tending to stir up a strong feeling against the Roman Catholics, not merely in the sovereign but also amongst the people. Protestants everywhere were stricken with horror and fear by the massacre of St. Bartholomew, and Protestantism was confirmed into an intense national sentiment amongst the English people when they saw that on its account they were threatened with invasion and subjugation. When we consider the consequences which generally follow the sudden transition from foreboding fearfulness to masterful victory, instead of complaining of the increased strictness we may well point with pride, as a proof of a manly national character, to the way in which the Roman Catholics of England were treated after the defeat of the Armada. Those also who object to the treatment of the Puritans should reflect how natural it was for Elizabeth to be annoyed with those whom she believed to be breaking to pieces that national Protestantism for the sake of which the country had encountered so much danger and expended so much effort.

Whether wise or not, the policy of Elizabeth was certainly consistent when, at the same time, she began to be more strict both with Papists and Puritans, for both of these must be classed together as enemies of the established order of things. To her, who meant to walk upon the narrow ledge of Protestantism, those were alike enemies who wished to pull her over either into Puritanism on the one side or Popism on the other.

Having got the Church independent Elizabeth was determined to make it orderly, for she had no idea that separation from Rome was to mean anything like chaos. We can see now that she was too exacting, but it must be remembered that her strictness applied to the whole Church and not merely to that particular section which afterwards openly dissented; all parties in the Church felt the pressure of her grip, and for each one who broke away in rebellion there were dozens who in patient endurance remained loyal to the Church. It must also be remembered that the queen's strictness was undoubtedly intensified by the obstinacy of that Puritanism which brought upon itself and upon the Church much of the suffering of which it so bitterly complained.

The queen used the bishops as her instruments for regulating the Church and they, like frightened and too-willing servants, often mistook her wishes. She wanted Liberal Conformity, which seems a thing very difficult indeed for the clerical mind to comprehend, and so they went in for Strict Uniformity, which the clerical mind is always eager to enforce The Thirty-Nine Articles, themselves so simple and moderate, were insisted upon with such strictness as to become a weapon of oppression, and in 1571 subscription to these Articles was made a statutory requirement. The bishops then proceeded to make additional Articles of their own. In dress and ceremonial the same strictness was exercised as in belief, and a number of the bishops, including Parker, drew up the noted " Advertisements " which minutely described the dress to be worn and required exact uniformity. The queen's severity was consummated and ended by the famous " Act to retain the Queen's subjects in their due obedience," passed in 1593. By this Act imprisonment, without bail, was declared against all who obstinately refused to come to church, or who denied the queen's supremacy, or who frequented any unlawful conventicle. " Prophesyings of the clergy," which were assemblies in the different dioceses to enable the clergy to consult with each other, or with the laity, were forbidden, whilst Convocation, after 1562, sank into insignificance.

Not merely was the Church thus dealt with so strictly, but it was also robbed. By means of Commissions several of the cathedrals and colleges were deprived of a large part of their possessions, whilst sees and livings remained vacant for years because their revenues were gone. All this was done in order to prevent the queen applying to Parliament for money, for she was as despotic over Parliament as over the Church. She often imperiously stopped debates and sent members to prison for raising questions of which she did not approve. Parliament learnt that it must not during her reign attempt to meddle with ecclesiastical questions. Those who now object to the government of the Church by the State should bear in mind that the meaning of the word State has been completely changed since the time when Dissent began, for now it means that Parliament which was then forbidden to have anything to do with such matters.

The connection formed between Elizabeth and the bishops was destined to exercise an immense influence over the subsequent history of England, for it soon developed into that alliance between the Crown and the Church which led to the Revolution. It would be more correct to say between the Crown and the heads of the Church, for during Elizabeth's reign the exactions of the bishops brought on that alienation between the superior clergy and the rest of the body which was one cause why the Church lived so well through the shock of the Revolution. For when the combat arose the clergy did not as a whole vigorously espouse the king's side; many of them, indeed, sympathised with Parliament, and therefore Parliament, when it became master, treated them with much more gentleness than would otherwise have been the case.

With James I., as with Elizabeth, the chief interest centred in the royal authority. Coming from the poverty and bondage of Scotland it was not unnatural for him to exaggerate the importance of his newly-acquired position and to stickle for its utmost privileges, especially when he followed a sovereign who had stretched those privileges to such an extreme. Besides objecting to their spirit of refractoriness against his royal authority James had this additional cause for unfriendliness to the Puritans that their sympathisers in Scotland, the Presbyterians, had held him for some years to a very unwilling acquiescence in their religion which he so much disliked. Thus for both these reasons he was quite ready to join with the bishops in keeping down the spirit of Puritanism. James resembled Elizabeth in this also that although he liked to be a despot he was not a bigot. He was willing to allow considerable latitude in religious opinions, and his reign ought to be remembered with gratitude if for no other reason than that during it was made that admirable translation of the Bible which we still use, and which by its simplicity and dignity has done more than anything else to recommend the pure faith of our religion. Then also the Church received an authorised body of canons, and a law was passed which prevented the conveyance of ecclesiastical estates to the crown. James himself was personally inclined to Arminianism, and the representatives of the Church of England at the Calvinistic Synod of Dort showed their liberality when the followers of Arminius were condemned for heresy. They also were alone in recommending episcopacy. The cause of Calvinism, unhappily for the Church of England, was greatly helped by the Gunpowder Plot, which inflamed the animosity against the Roman Catholics and turned the current of sympathy in opposition to all the doctrines with which they were especially associated. This Plot also fed the enmity to the Crown, which was thought to lean towards the Roman Catholics.

In order to understand the course of events during the great Revolution we must first try to get some clear idea of who were the real combatants. These seem to have been—

1. The king, striving for despotic political power and insisting upon the divine right of the Crown.
2. The High Church party, striving for despotic religious power and insisting upon the divine right of the Church.
3. The Puritans, striving for religious changes.
4. The Parliament, striving for political changes.

To these were afterwards added the Scotch, striving for the supremacy of Presbyterianism, for whilst in England affairs, although beginning in religion, soon began to turn upon politics, in Scotland they continued throughout religious. In principle the Scotch most resembled the High Church party, for they claimed divine right for the Church, only it was to be the right of the General Assembly, in place of that of the bishops, to rule Parliament. The Scotch cared little for political freedom, and would, even at the last, have turned round to Charles if he would have agreed to the claims of the Presbyterians. The tendency of the Reformation in Scotland had been to ally the Church with the Crown, for whilst in England the king had opposed the Church, partly out of desire for its riches, in Scotland the king had sided with the Church, partly out of opposition to the nobles. We have not named in this list the Church as a body, for as such it took no distinctive part in this contest. It is a mistake to talk, as is so often done, about the Church having sided strongly with the king in his arbitrary attempts upon the liberties of the nation. This is an instance of that common tendency to judge a great institution by the conduct of a few of its most conspicuous members. Those who accept the conduct of the High Church party about the Court as representing that of the whole Church forget that history only brings upon its canvas the few who were remarkable, omitting the great body of the clergy, who went on quietly doing their duty, knowing little and thinking little about what was going on in the busy centres.

It was only fellowship in danger which threw the king and the High Church party into each others' arms, for Anglo-Catholicism did not like the Royal Prerogative then any more than it does now. Had the Revolution not bound them together, Charles might have played the part of a second Henry VIII., or Laud might have been a second Langton. As it was both the king and the High Church party felt themselves drawn together in opposition to Parliament, the king because he wished to set the Royal Prerogative above Parliament, and the High Church bishops because Parliament was the friend of the Puritans. Had Parliament been beaten, the fighting would not have been done with, for the king and the High Church bishops would then have had to struggle for the mastery, and it does not seem certain that the king would have been the winner. Thus the Revolution saved Protestantism, for the High Church party was lapsing into Romanism, Parker, Whitgift, and Laud, marking the declining stages.

The Church did not lean to the alliance with the Crown because it was itself in favour of political despotism, but because it looked to its own preservation. It knew that the Parliament was mainly under the influence of its enemies, and therefore when it found itself attacked it sought the help of the Crown which was inclined to be its friend. It is not on this account to be held responsible for the mistakes of the Crown, any more than a man caught in a storm is accountable for the faults of the wall behind which he shelters himself. It is true that the Church did in some degree help the schemes of Charles, by preaching in favour of forced loans and divine right and passive obedience. Still this was not carried out to anything like such a great extent as is often represented ; the sycophancy of Sibthorpe and Mainwaring was exceptional, or we should not have heard so much about it. The Church, too, is widely blamed on account of the oppressions of the Star Chamber and the Court of High Commission. The Star Chamber consisted of nobles as well as bishops, and was political in its object, which was to set the royal will above the statute law, and the Court of High Commission was created by an Act of Parliament according to which no Churchman need have sat upon it.

The Church could not have conducted itself with very excessive one-sidedness during the struggle or it would not have been spared after it was ended, for it must not be forgotten that the National Church continued its unbroken existence through the Revolution, the Commonwealth, and the Protectorate. To talk, as is so often done, as if the Church had died with Charles I., and was revived with Charles II., is to mistake altering a National Church for destroying it. Instead of giving up the national principle the victors of the Revolution held to it more tenaciously even than their predecessors, which they would not have done had they found it any hindrance to solid freedom, for they were not the men to stick at anything which stood in the way of carrying out their thorough policy. It is true that bishops were abolished, but episcopacy is no essential part of a National Church; and the Presbyterianism which took its place was based on the old parochial system, and was still more closely allied with the State. Cromwell, who never liked changes unless he believed them absolutely necessary, thoroughly recognised the rights of patrons, and issued a commission in 1654, to inquire into the subject, and unite parishes where small, allowing the patrons to present in turns. He even carried the State control over the Church so far, further indeed than it has ever been carried either before or since, that he chose a number of learned men, called "Triers," who went about the country testing the fitness of clergymen. In many other ways Cromwell proved that he had no belief in allowing the Church to liberate itself from the government of the State. After Cromwell's death many benefices were filled by the election of the inhabitants, but nothing was done to weaken the national character of the Church, indeed it is in connection with Presbyterianism that we first hear of the term "established" being applied to the Church. It ought never to be forgotten that Cromwell adopted those principles of toleration which were then new both to his friends and his enemies, and would have carried them out much further had he been allowed, for a ruler, however powerful, cannot go too far in advance of his people. He re-admitted the Jews, banished since Edward I., and protected the Quakers.

That the changes of the Revolution, both political and religious, were opposed to the feelings of the bulk of the nation was amply proved by the strength of the back-flood of the Restoration. No friend of the Church, no lover of his country, can help regretting that the helm of the nation was not then held by a hand worthy of the time. This was such an opportunity, especially for the Church, as seldom occurs once, and never twice. The Independents, and other extreme sections, were dejected, and would soon have disbanded had not fresh recruits been driven into their ranks, whilst the Presbyterians, who composed the largest and most respectable part of the malcontents, were burning with loyalty and eager to come back to the Church on very easy terms. Had there been even one wise and able man to guide the Church the subsequent religious history of England would not have been the pitiful thing we must confess it is. But such wisdom and ability were not then to be found in the land; Sodom did not contain a single saviour; the nation had exhausted itself with the Revolution, and lay helpless. The field was in splendid condition for the good seed, but stupidity, infinitely the most mischief-making of all the evil spirits, sowed it freely with tares, which to this day keep bearing fruit plentifully.

Instead of throwing open the gates of the National Church to their widest swing Charles II., under the guidance of those bishops in whose hands he left such matters, closed them still more, and ordered all who passed through to be so strictly examined that the multitude which was waiting outside refused to come in, and went away. We may form some idea of the mental destitution of the land when we reflect that Parliament did not merely acquiesce in this policy but was even more eager for it than the king himself. Indeed we should think Charles II. liberal if we could believe him honest, but we know that in as far as he had any religion at all he was a Roman Catholic, and cared nothing for the Church of England except as a political ally. His Declaration of Indulgence, which embodied from policy that great principle of toleration which Cromwell had adopted from enlightened conviction, had no chance with a nation the majority of which hated the Puritans, and nearly the whole of which hated the Roman Catholics. Instead of meeting the king's advances Parliament passed that series of acts which forced both Puritanism and Roman Catholicism into open and confirmed dissent.

It is not uncommon to hear the Restoration spoken of as if it brought back despotism and swept away the work of the Revolution, but the legislation of Charles II.'s reign tells a different tale. Charles II. was not disposed to be despotic, but that he could not have been so had he wished is proved by the fact that in reference to religion, which was the only thing he cared about besides his pleasure, Parliament passed a series of acts in direct opposition to his strongest wishes. From this time the word State has a different meaning; it has ceased to be the Crown as it was with Henry and Elizabeth, and henceforth it is the Parliament.

The common infatuation of the time took full possession of the Church itself, which thoughtlessly allowed its Convocation to fall to pieces, merely from short-sighted parsimony. For hitherto the clergy had contributed a certain lump sum to the national exchequer, apportioning the assessment amongst themselves in Convocation, but, thinking that they paid too much, they begged to be taxed along with the rest of the people. This was agreed to, and henceforth Convocation was rarely summoned by the State, which now got no money from it and never wanted anything else. Convocation was not clever enough to follow the example of Parliament, and extort power in return for money.

The enactments passed during Charles II.'s reign which pressed so heavily upon the Puritans were not passed so much against them as against the Roman Catholics, for dread of Roman Catholicism was the governing impulse of the time. And this impulse must not be judged according to the common rules of ordinary sentiment, for it passed quite beyond them and became a mere frenzy. The story of Titus Oates reads like a fable to us, but the panic-stricken conduct of an age whose nerves had been unstrung by the Great Plague and the Great Fire is not to be measured by the regular standard of cold common-sense. James II., with the usual luck of the Stuarts, took at the flood that tide which leads on to misfortune. Personally he did little to deserve his unhappy fate; indeed he could have done very little, but he certainly did what he could. Instead of allaying the terror of the people by keeping quiet his own liking for that Roman Catholicism which he knew they so hated and feared, he gratuitously published it from the housetops; instead of keeping his red flag in his pocket he would persist in poking it under the nose of the already infuriated bull. To have expressed his own attachment for Popery even constitutionally would have been foolish enough, but the folly was infinitely increased when, by his "Declaration of Liberty of Conscience," James II. violated the most cherished political rights of Parliament in doing this. Such a usurpation for any purpose would have been resented, much more so was this certain when its object was to help a cause against which the nation was resolutely set. The English people knew that the king cared nothing for general liberty of conscience; he only wanted such a liberty for the Papists as should give them a chance of eventually destroying the liberty of everybody else. No one could believe in the honest attachment to liberty of a monarch who at this very time was congratulating Louis XIV. on his suppression by force of the Huguenots.

The conduct of the National Church at this crisis was both very creditable to itself and very beneficial to the nation; it may indeed be fairly said that the Church saved the nation from the evils of an appeal to force. For Roman Catholicism was then making far greater advances than people now generally suppose; politically it had the power of the Crown at its back, whilst theologically many weak-minded persons, always a large proportion of every population, were glad to seek refuge, in those doubtful times, in a system which at any rate claimed certainty for itself; besides not a few were eager to turn to what they believed the rising sun. The Church boldly took up the combat in both directions; whilst Tillotson, Atterbury, Tenison, Stillingfleet, and others exposed the weakness of Rome's theological claims, the famous Seven Bishops resisted the king's illegal attempt to help Rome politically. It was from the Church, and not from Puritanism, that those works came forth which are still a glory to Protestantism; it was the Church, and not Parliament nor the Puritans, which successfully opposed the king's usurpations and finally compelled him to retreat. It is not true to say that Sancroft and his comrades cared nothing for political rights and were merely actuated by opposition to increased liberty being given to Catholics and Dissenters. As the Bishops expressly declared "they did not object to publish " the Declaration from disloyalty to the king or from a want " of due tenderness to Dissenters, in relation to whom they " were willing to come to such a relation as should be thought " fit, after discussion and settlement in Parliament and Con- " vocation, but such a dispensing power as was exercised had " by Parliament been thought illegal." Others were not so tender on this point, for not only the Catholics, but also many Dissenters, welcomed the Declaration, including the Anabaptists, the Quakers led by Penn, and many Congregationalists; but the Presbyterian party, under Baxter and Howe, like the Church, objected to it as unconstitutional and refused to thank the king for it.

Not unfrequently it is said that the National Church is merely the minion of the State, ready to do whatever it orders. The history of the Church of England contradicts this theory, for although the Church stuck by the State, which then meant the Crown, as long as it was opposing Popery, as soon as it became the friend of Popery the Church stood out in opposition to it. Nor did the Church welcome William III. as it would have done had it been guided by the time-serving spirit with which it is often credited, for eight bishops and four hundred clergy refused to take the oaths to the new sovereign and therefore were deprived of their livings. These, who were called the non-juring clergy, included Sancroft, the leader of the Seven Bishops who had resisted James II.

There is no doubt that the clergy as a whole remained chiefly Jacobite; hence William III. believed it to be to his interest to keep the Church down. Convocation was summoned about 1698, but disputes between the Low Church bishops, appointed by the Crown, and the High Church Jacobite clergy rendered it useless, so that from 1717 up to quite recently though summoned with Parliament it was always immediately prorogued.

Apart from political considerations William III. was in favour of thorough religious toleration, and this was the spirit which continued through the succeeding reigns. By the Act of Toleration, 1 William III., exemption was granted from Elizabeth's Act for Obedience and from Charles II.'s Act of Uniformity to all such as took the oath of allegiance and subscribed the declaration against Popery, for disloyalty and

Popery were the only heresies William cared about. During Queen Anne's reign the Schism Act and Occasional Conformity Act were repealed, and the Test Act was mollified by the Act of Indemnity. The reign of George II. was the first reign since the Reformation in which no new law was enacted against the Catholics; but, as Hallam says, "such "a genuine toleration as Christianity and philosophy alike "demand had no place in our Statute Book before the reign "of George III." Acts were passed for protecting the congregations of Dissenting chapels and for extending toleration to Unitarians. In William IV. Dissenting chapels were exempted from church and poor-rates, and the Test and Corporation Acts were repealed, besides Catholic Emancipation being passed. The work of religious liberty was completed by the Acts 9 and 10 Victoria, in the year 1846, which abolished all statutes and parts of statutes imposing any penalties for religious belief. Compulsory church-rates have also been abolished, the Universities have been thrown open to Dissenters, and by the Conscience Clause sectarian propagandism in schools is prevented.

It is undoubtedly true that most of this religious toleration has not come so much from enlightened liberality as from religious indifference. This is also largely true of our own age, for it is easy to be tolerant of what we do not care about. Many causes conduced to bring about that general indifference which held possession of England through the eighteenth century. A wave of scepticism and infidelity then passed over Europe whose force was indeed somewhat spent when it reached us but still we felt it severely, for whilst in France it caused the Revolution, with its deification of Reason, here it strewed the land with indifferentism and immorality. Philosophy, or what claimed to be such, was then undermining both reverence and conduct. Descartes and Spinoza, Voltaire and Rousseau, were the divinities of the hour. The French Revolution had also a bad effect upon England at first though a good one eventually, for its excesses provoked a reaction in this land of common-sense and moderation. The eighteenth century most strikingly illustrates the truth that a nation's religion—not so much its system of doctrine as its tone of faith—is the key to its whole condition. No sooner does the harlequin-wand of infidelity take sway than a sad and wonderful transformation goes on: instead of realms of beauty and purity we have haunts of ugliness and crime; instead of noble heroes with virtue triumphant we have petty buffoons who make vice carry away the laugh. Religion is like the peg of a stringed-instrument—the quality of all the tones depends upon where it is screwed.

So in England the time of religious indifference was also that of indolence and immorality. We can hardly form an idea now of the state into which the nation sank during the eighteenth century. Even in 1694, in *A Proposal for the Reformation of Manners*, it was stated that "Atheism and profaneness never got such a high ascendant as at this day;" and Swift said that Christianity had ceased to be a subject of inquiry because every one knew it to be fictitious. The same dry-rot had got into everything: under Walpole politics was only another name for corruption, and such was the social condition of the people that even the not too virtuous Earl of Chesterfield said "I fear we have reason to complain of the general decay of virtue and morality amongst the people." It was said that the word "not" ought to be taken out of the Commandments and put into the Creeds. The people generally had got into that most unhealthy condition when earnestness is considered vulgar and poverty a crime.

We cannot reasonably expect that the Church could escape the infection of the spirit for a national Church necessarily shares the failings as well as the virtues of the nation. And besides the general causes it had special causes of its own acting in the same direction. It had been deprived of meeting in Convocation and yet was not allowed a voice in the House of Commons; it was ruled by bishops appointed merely for political partisanship, and who were expected rather to render political services than to perform episcopal duties. The Act of Toleration itself at first did injury for the people felt themselves relieved from compulsory attendance at Church and had not yet learned to like going there voluntarily, whilst the reaction from Puritanism had caused a widespread dislike to clerical pretensions in general. The Church, too, like every institution, was demoralised by the prevailing uncertainty about the Crown, as a very large number believed for a long time that the Stuarts were certain to come back, and it was only after the battle of Culloden that the country began to get settled. George III. was the first Hanoverian who felt himself safe enough to be tolerant. But undoubtedly the strongest cause affecting both the people and the Church was the reaction from the excessive strain of the exciting times from Henry VIII. to William III. The nation had in that period done enough for several centuries, and had earned the right to rest; indeed it was obliged to rest, for nations, like fields, must lie fallow, or at any rate have their crops changed.

The nation rested, and the Church rested with it; and so did the Dissenters. We may wish that the Church had done more, but it is unnatural to expect it, especially when we reflect that just at this time, when the work to be done was so unusually severe, the Church was degraded to such a low position that the clergy, even at the houses of people of small consequence, were not expected to stay at table for the second course.

Still undoubtedly the Church went on quietly doing a good work, and probably we are indebted to it that England did not during that period run into the excesses committed in other countries. Painters caricatured the Church and poets satirised it; still, although during this period it made no heroic figure in history we know that it won the enthusiastic affection of many of the best of Englishmen; and that it kept its heart sound and vigorous was proved by the marvellous revival of its vitality in the early part of this century. We can forgive it for having slept a little when we see the healthiness of its energetic awakening, for the Church of England of our time has the glorious but almost solitary honour of teaching the world that there can be faith without bigotry and zeal without intolerance; that a Church can be at the same time both enthusiastic and elastic. The enthusiasm of the Church of England arises no doubt chiefly from the religious character of the people, but its liberality is due almost entirely to its national connection with the State. It is this connection which enables it to contain within itself so many varied and yet necessary elements, for the Gorham Judgment has secured the position of the Evangelical party, the Bennett Judgment that of the High Church, and the Judgment on *Essays and Reviews* that of the Broad Church.

CHAPTER III.

SKETCH OF THE HISTORY OF DISSENT.

WE have seen how the Church of England has grown up from the earliest times as an integral part of that complex and inexplicable entity called the Constitution. Hence it is as misleading and incorrect to speak of the *Established* Church as it would be to apply that adjective to the House of Commons or the Monarchy; indeed the Church has less claim to it than one of these, at any rate, for it is much older than the House of Commons, its origin is much more obscure, and the epochs in its history to which this term could be imagined applicable are both fewer and less distinctly marked. Looking back over the whole extent of English history we can only find three points when it can be supposed that the Church of England was in any sense established; these are the time of the introduction of Christianity, the Reformation, and the Restoration. As to the first, it is plainly unreasonable to connect such an idea as that of establishment with a change so remote, and one about whose legal details, with which the word established is alone concerned, we have so little, if any, reliable knowledge. And as to the last, the use of the word Restoration correctly indicates that then the Church could only have been re-established had it ever been previously established; but as it had not we can only say that it was restored. This Restoration also had a much narrower application to the Church than to other leading parts of the Constitution, as the Crown and the

House of Lords, for whilst these had been wholly suspended during the Revolution the Church in its essential elements had continued intact; the same incumbents had held the same livings, done the same duties, and obeyed an authority of the same character; only the bishops, with their offices and emoluments, had been suspended, and these are no necessary part of a National Church.

As to the Reformation, we have seen that this was not a sudden but a gradual change, whose object was not to create a new Church but to clear away the corruptions which had grown up about the old one; not to establish a new relationship between the Church and the State but to restore the purity of that which had existed from the earliest times, and to protect it from the threatening usurpations of the Papacy. Henry and Edward and Elizabeth never dreamt that in what they did for the Reformation they were establishing anything new for they repeatedly protested that they were merely asserting the rights which had always belonged to the State. The Reformation was, at most, what is implied by the word, a reforming and was not in any sense a creating; the Church was the Church of England before it occurred and it remained so afterwards; there was established neither a new Church nor a new connection between the Church and the State.

To those who think that the theological changes made at the Reformation were sufficient to constitute a new Church it need only be said that the question of the connection between a Church and the State has nothing whatever to do with the theology of that Church. A Church may change its theology any number of times and yet remain the same Church in that legal and historical sense with which alone we, in this inquiry, are concerned.

But although the Reformation did not create a new Church or a new connection with the State it effected a complete revolution in the way in which the relationship between the Church and the State was generally regarded by the nation. This fact is too little remarked and insisted upon although it explains much in preceding history which otherwise seems inexplicable and has had an immense influence upon all the subsequent religious history of England.

When we consider the nature and extent of the theological changes of the Reformation, and with what variableness and vicissitudes they were made, we are apt to be amazed when we learn that the ministers and congregations remained the same, that is, went on in the same way through them all, and that the number was quite insignificant of those who, even at the most startling periods, ever thought of abandoning their connection with the Church. Judged by our own feelings about such matters this conduct looks very suspicious, and those—the majority of the nation it is to be feared—who assume that the ideas of the nineteenth century ought to be the standard of all ages are very ready to see in this a proof that the clergy, at any rate, cared very little about the religion they professed and very much about the livings they possessed. The "Vicar of Bray," whose selfish laxity is immortalised in the famous song, is spoken of as a fair representative of the class, but the general character and conduct of the clergy of the Reformation show the absurdity of such an accusation. The mystery is cleared away when we reflect that until the Reformation, with the exception of the Lollards, who had too little influence up to this time to be taken into account, nobody ever thought of regarding the Church as a separate religious body, or as in any way distinct from the nation; it was merely the nation in its religious aspect; the clergy were national officers to look after its religious duties, as the soldiers were to look after its military and the judges after its judicial. It was believed to be not merely the right, but also the duty, of the State to prescribe the religion of its subjects, and those subjects, whether ministers or laymen, no more thought of disobeying the laws about religion than they did those about politics. They might not agree with them, and might probably have done their utmost to make them different, but when once those laws were passed they felt bound to submit to them, just as much as in these days opponents of Reform Bills or Ballot Acts, or any other political measures, are expected to acquiesce in the decision of the majority. The Church was the nation, and people no more believed that there ought to be several distinct Churches than that there ought to be several different forms of government, as monarchy and republicanism, existing side by side in the same nation. Just as now we call it sedition if a man defies the State because he does not like some political law, so then a heretic was punished not because he held peculiar opinions but because he was a rebel. Whilst we now often point with pride to the fact that even those who have most opposed the passing of any new law always submit to it when passed, as a proof of the manliness and wisdom of the English people, it certainly seems very unfair to talk of the same conduct in our ancestors as indicating cowardice and indifference, merely because the laws related to a different subject. Everybody then believed that the State had just as good a right to pass laws about religion as we think it has to pass them about schools, and railways, and public-houses. This belief in the identity of the Church and the nation continued unbroken for sixteen hundred years, and worked very well on the whole, which is quite as much as can be said of the opinion which has succeeded it. It was the Reformation which ultimately effected the change, which, however, was very gradual, for during a long time at first no one thought of separating from the Church and setting up a separate religious organization, although many differed widely about the changes which were made, some thinking that they went too far, and others not far enough; some regretting to see any alteration in the old prayers and ceremonies, and others wanting everything to be newly modelled. Whilst these differences were growing stronger the power of the State was growing weaker, and so at last the nation split itself up into several distinct bodies, those who thought that the changes of the Reformation went too far becoming Popish Dissenters and those who thought that they did not go far enough becoming Protestant Dissenters, whilst those who abided by the decision of the State were said to belong to the Established Church. These last were compelled by the Revolution to become separatists in their turn, and the political animosities which turned upon religion were so long and fierce that they separated the various parties still more widely, and made their differences irreconcilable. So the long struggle which began with the Reformation and ended with the Restoration demolished the national ideal, and left in its place three distinct religious communions, with their branches, existing side by side. But it was a long time before the nation reconciled itself to this state of things; each party when it had the power persecuted the others, not so much because of differences of belief but because they all still hankered after a National Church, only each wanted it to be after its own pattern. Gradually they felt obliged to abandon this object, and to acknowledge that henceforth the people must be allowed to organise themselves into as many separate religious bodies as they liked. This is that plan of toleration which has been followed ever since, and from this period the word established, as applied to the Church, began to have its present narrow signification, signifying a religious body having certain relations with the State, instead of the ecclesiastical constitution ordained by the law. The divisions which then began have continued ever since, for the religious bodies existing in England at the present time may all be classed either as adherents of the Church, or as Protestant or Popish Dissenters.

It now remains only to take a slight historical survey of

these two kinds of Dissent, although strictly this does not come within the scope of our subject, which merely concerns the connection between the Church and the State, but it is impossible to realise the nature and force of the objections to that connection unless we have first understood the history of those who have broken away from that connection, and who now furnish its principal opponents. For Dissenters, like every other class of men, are governed much more by the history of their ancestors, and much less by their own reason, than they are willing to acknowledge. We find that the ideas about which we pride ourselves as the products of our own faculties are generally the results, for the most part, of past causes; each generation can add but little to that sum of forces which forms the opinions of men and determines their conduct. If we subtract from what we consider our most original opinions those parts which are the results of tradition or training, we shall have but little left to claim as our own. The present is chiefly the result of the past, and cannot be understood unless that past is also understood.

Of the Popish Dissenters little need be said here, partly because there is little to say, and partly because they have never taken up any decided position, either as enemies or friends of the connection between the Church and the State. Between the Restoration and the Revolution of 1688 they took an active part in politics with the hope of gaining power, or at any rate toleration, for themselves, but at the accession of William III. they retired into that position of an isolated religious communion constantly receiving more toleration which they have since continued to occupy. This sectarian seclusion has gradually developed in them all the evils which necessarily follow from such a condition, aggravated by the additional evils inherent in the larger system to which they belong. When we add to these two causes, sectarianism and Papalism, the fact that their numbers chiefly consist of recruits from the neighbouring island who are aliens in sympathies and objects, we can easily understand why the Roman Catholics, although they live in the land, are not of it and act rather like a band of emigrants in a foreign country, who take little broad interest in the general affairs of the nation but are guided chiefly by consideration for their own welfare. Thus the English Catholic of Queen Elizabeth's time has developed into the Roman Catholic of our own time, if the word development can fitly be applied to a process which contains in it all that is implied by the change of the adjectives. The Roman Catholics of the present day have no right to claim to be the descendants of the English Catholics before the Reformation, for they differ more from them than do the present adherents of the Church. Ultramontanism, as it now moulds Roman Catholicism, was then unknown, and had it been known would have been rejected. The Roman Catholicism of which we have experience is a modern exotic, and threatens to become a very troublesome one, since it is dangerous for a country to possess a large body of men who obey a foreign authority and who possess great political power which they use, not for the national good, but merely for the advancement of their own religion. The Roman Catholics may ultimately prove more dangerous to the Church even than the Dissenters because it is safer to have those who are opponents from honest conviction than those who may any time become opponents from selfish interest. Judging from recent political history it does not seem too much to say that the present absence of antagonism amongst the Roman Catholics to the connection between the Church and the State chiefly arises from their wish not to injure a power which they hope they may yet gain for themselves, and that if they thought that this hope must be abandoned, and that this connection stood in the way of their own advancement, they would not hesitate to become its enemies.

The history of Protestant Dissent is a more interesting, as well as a more agreeable, subject for although it is marked by much narrow-mindedness and mischief-making, much that irritates our understanding and moves our sorrow, although we know that this Dissent has done incalculable injury to the cause of Protestantism and, which is far more important, to that of Christianity itself, still there is a refreshing feeling of manliness about it which makes us regret that we are obliged to differ from men whom we must so much respect. For looking at him from this mean distance of veracity, far enough away for his general proportions to stand out plainly and not so far that their outlines are becoming dim, the Puritan cuts a noble figure on the canvas of English history. His dress may be fantastic, his gestures often grotesque, and his professions so extravagant as to savour of hypocrisy, still we feel that at the back of all this there is a real man, who wants to do what is right and is moved by a high purpose. Puritanism is a great factor in history and is, on the whole, a factor for good. If we owe to it much of the jealous animosity which still perpetuates and embitters sectarian divisions, we also owe to it much of the manly thoroughness and religious earnestness which so honourably characterise the tone of English politics. It has also done good service in the struggle for political freedom, and we cannot but do homage to a flag emblazoned with the names of so many glorious fights through which it has been valiantly borne. Therefore because those who have to confine themselves to the subject of the connection between the Church and the State are compelled sometimes to speak strongly about Protestant Dissenters it must not be supposed that they fail to appreciate their virtues or are ignorant of their services.

The Reformation seems to have created the demand for definition in religion; it may be said, indeed, to have given birth to theology, as we understand it. For before this time religion was rather a general sentiment than a body of creeds. It is remarkable how rarely, through all those centuries, any questions of doctrine were raised, and how little interest they attracted. Conscious of a solid agreement in thought and feeling, the people did not care about analysing or explaining the grounds of it. But the Reformation brought in a new feeling, for having applied reason and criticism to one of the articles of their faith men were not willing to stop there but wished to put all the rest through the same process. The spirit of inquiry, like many other newly-roused spirits, went rampant through the exuberance of youthful energy, and led many of those whom it possessed to run into all sorts of excesses, and some even, like the swine, into the sea of destruction.

When Henry VIII. published his Six Articles as a statement of the chief doctrines of the Reformed faith he discovered that the teachings of Wickliffe and the Lollards, although they had yet brought forth no perceptible fruit, had all along been exercising a growing influence upon the minds of the people, and that many of his subjects were not only willing to go along with him in setting aside the decrees of Popes and the traditions of Councils but also wished to abolish that doctrine of transubstantiation to which the king clung so much. These were called Sacramentaries, and were strongly persecuted; they were the first Dissenters, in that earlier sense of disagreeing with the Church although not openly separating from it. The slumbering spirit of Dissent, called into being by Wickliffe, remained both limited in extent and feeble in strength until the Reformation, when the substitution of dogma for faith roused it into activity. Not that there was no dogma before the Reformation, or no faith after it, for the flesh of faith must always depend upon a skeleton of dogma for form and strength, but the tendency of the Reformation was to direct attention almost exclusively towards this skeleton; to bring the bony structure outside, so to speak, and to give religion the character of a crab instead of that of a human being. When the spirit of trustful faith is exchanged for that of analytical criticism there is no limit to the extent of the differences of opinion which may arise. Not that therefore this critical spirit is an evil; on the contrary, its awakening was necessary to that religious fulness which mankind can only attain through centuries of varied development. The Reformation was a necessity, and did infinite good but, like all other great blessings, it carried evils in its train, and Dissent was one of them.

Dissent has remained true to the traditions of its origin, for as now it receives its chief support from the middle class, so it sprang from this class, and not from the poor, who stuck to the old doctrines and ceremonies. Indeed the mass of the people, as well as the majority of the bishops and inferior clergy, did not see why the Reformation should involve any change in these points; they regarded it as a national and not as a theological event, as merely a gentle reform whereas the others expected it to be a radical revolution. This difference of expectation led to the divisions which have continued ever since. Those who were for going so far complained that the Prayer Book was too rigidly enforced, and that it contained doctrines, as that of transubstantiation, to which they could not agree; they also objected to the retention of the vestments, on the ground that they had no countenance in Scripture and promoted superstition and idolatry. The opposition of the bishops also led them to question their claims, and so they began to declare that there are only two orders warranted by Scripture viz., bishops and deacons, and that therefore bishops are only priests.

The persecutions of Queen Mary drove many of those who held these opinions abroad when, associating exclusively amongst themselves and isolated from the current of national unity, they developed their peculiar doctrines still further and gradually attributed to them an exaggerated importance, as was natural to men who were suffering expatriation on account of them. The doctrine of justification by faith alone rapidly came into prominence, as also did that controversy about predestination and free-will which has ever since occupied so much attention but which never gets any nearer a settlement, though it is probably now as near as ever it ever will be; it is a mental dragon which is kept alive by a continuous supply of the best blood. The exiles were most numerous at Frankfort and there the evils of their system soon began to show themselves with significant propheticalness for differences of opinion, ending in permanent dissensions, arose about the form of service, some wishing to stick to the whole Prayer Book whilst others, amongst whom was John Knox, persisted in picking and choosing, refusing to retain what Calvin called "Popish dregs."

Those who were left in England, many of whom developed into what were called "Gospellers," began to hold secret meetings for worship. These were especially numerous in Suffolk and Essex.

Most of the exiles returned at the accession of Elizabeth, full of hope that now their time was come. Thus the queen was placed in a difficult position, for there were now three parties contending for the mastery viz., the bishops who held that the Catholic Church was so true a Church that they could not recognise the changes made by the State and therefore refused the oath of supremacy; the queen, who also believed that it was a true Church but insisted that the State had the right to control its usurpations and clear away its corruptions; and the Puritans, who held that it was no true Church at all but that the Scriptures were the sole standard of discipline and doctrine and that the State had no right to exercise any authority in such matters. Thus the High Church party, as they may now be called, and the Puritans agreed in denying the authority of the State, and for fundamentally the same reason, namely that the Church should be supreme, only the Church meant to one party the decrees of Councils and the commands of the Pope whilst to the other party it meant the decisions of Synods and the dictates of each man's understanding. The queen resolved to maintain the supremacy of the State, so she removed those bishops who would not take the Oath of Supremacy and punished those Puritans who would not conform to the requirements of the Act of Uniformity. Now the objections of the Puritans began to come out more distinctly; they wished to abolish copes and surplices, and particularly objected to the cross in baptism and to kneeling at communion. Those who would not conform were not allowed to preach, their licenses being taken away. In London alone thirty-seven out of three hundred refused and were suspended. Many of these still remained in the Church as lecturers and chaplains whilst others definitely separated from it, throwing aside the Liturgy in favour of the Geneva Service Book. These held secret assemblies for worship, and in 1567 they agreed to have a sermon and communion at Plumber's Hall. Afterwards a presbytery was established at Wandsworth, and in 1571 what were called "Prophesyings" began to be frequent. In London the punishment for the first offence was deprivation of the freedom of the city, and for the second what further punishment the queen might direct.

As Puritanism had now developed so distinctly it is well to consider carefully what were the chief grounds upon which it set itself in opposition to the Church. These may be divided into those which relate to ceremonial and those which relate to Church government, for the Puritans did not differ from the Church about any of the principal doctrines of belief.

Ceremonial.

1. They objected to the surplice and other habits.
2. They objected to singing prayers and chanting psalms and to musical instruments.
3. They disliked the Liturgy because of
    a. The repetition of the Lord's Prayer.

β. The responses of the people.

γ. The passage in the Marriage Service: "With my body I thee worship," and that in the Burial Service: "In sure and certain hope of the resurrection to eternal life."

4. They disliked the reading of Apocryphal Books.
5. They objected to sundry Church festivals.
6. They objected to certain rites and ceremonies, as
    a. The cross in baptism.
    β. Godfathers and Godmothers.
    γ. Children being confirmed too young, merely when they could repeat the Lord's Prayer and Catechism.
    δ. The laying-on of hands.
    ε. Kneeling at the Sacrament.
    ζ. Bowing at the name of Jesus.
    η. The ring in marriage.
7. They wanted liberty for extempore prayers.
8. They demanded that none should be ordained ministers who could not preach.

Government.

1. They said that bishops were not a superior order to presbyters, and had no right to the sole use of the keys or to ordination. They disliked the temporal dignities of the bishops and their engaging in secular affairs.

2. They objected to archbishops, deans, chapters, and other officials of cathedrals as having no foundation in Scripture and being contrary to the rights of presbyters.

3. They complained of the jurisdiction of the Spiritual Courts as being derived from the Canon Law of the Popes and not from Scripture.

4. They objected that the highest censures, as absolution and excommunication, were exercised by laymen instead of by the spiritual officers of the Church.

5. They objected to promiscuous and general access to the

Lord's Table. The State considered that the religious offices of the National Church should be open to all who chose to claim them and that the responsibility of using them unworthily should rest with the people themselves, whereas the Puritans claimed that there ought somewhere to be lodged the power of investigating the qualifications of such as desired to belong to the Church. The State considered that the Church ought to be an open instrument of religion whilst the Puritans wanted it to be a private society.

Looking back after the lapse of three centuries, with all charity and calmness, at these reasons which the Puritans gave for separating from the Church there are surely few people in these days, even amongst the Dissenters themselves, who will not acknowledge that most of them are narrow and trivial, and that those which are true are not of sufficient importance to justify the introduction of the evils of schism. It is not pretended that schism is in all cases unjustifiable, but simply that it is only justifiable when the good to be derived from it exceeds the evil it must necessarily cause. No doubt the Puritans, when they decided to secede from the Church instead of trying to make it more conformable to their views by remaining in it, believed that they were acting rightly. Still their conduct must be judged not by the purity of their motives but by the wisdom of their actions, and we cannot allow our judgment to be blinded either by respect for their courage or sympathy for their sufferings. It is no defence to say that they believed these points to be of sufficient importance to justify their schism, for if they gave them an exaggerated importance that was a mistake, and consequently the conduct based upon it was a mistake also. Looking back over the whole controversy we cannot help declaring that the Puritans made two great mistakes; they greatly overestimated the importance of their own particular opinions, and they greatly under-estimated the importance of that separation which they made on account of those opinions. The results of these two mistakes have been so great and grievous that could the Puritans have foreseen them it cannot be believed but that they would have acted differently. And as far as appealing to our sympathy for freedom is concerned the verdict of history must be that, in spite of political services, the cause of Puritanism was on the whole that of religious intolerance, whilst, in spite of political blunders, the cause of the Church was that of religious freedom and Christian liberality.

It was for the reasons enumerated that the Puritans separated from the Church and not on account of any particular opinions respecting the proper relationship of the Church to the State. On this point they were much divided amongst themselves, the majority being quite willing to accept the authority of the State provided it was used for the enforcement of their own opinions. But a few, of whom Cartwright was the leader, were beginning to enunciate those views which afterwards were adopted by the Independents. In *An Admonition to Parliament* Cartwright says: "The " Christian sovereign ought not to be called head under Christ " of the particular and visible Churches within his dominions ; " it is a title not fit for any mortal man ; for when the apostle " says Christ is κεφαλή, the head, it is as much as if he " had said Christ and no other is head of the Church. No " civil magistrate in councils or assemblies for Church matters " can either be chief-moderator, over-ruler, judge, or deter- " miner; nor has he such authority as that, without his consent, " it should not be lawful for ecclesiastical persons to make " any Church orders or ceremonies. Church matters ough: " ordinarily to be handled by Church officers. The principal " direction of them is, by God's ordinance, committed to the " ministers of the Church, and to the ecclesiastical governors : " as these meddle not with the making civil laws, so the " civil magistrates ought not to ordain ceremonies, or deter- " mine controversies in the Church, as long as they do not "intrench upon his temporal authority. Nevertheless our "meaning is not to exclude the magistrate from our Church "assemblies; he may call a council of his clergy, and "appoint both time and place; he may be there by himself "or his deputy, but not as moderator, determiner, or judge; "he may have his voice in the assembly, but the orders and "decrees of councils are not made by his authority, for in "ancient times the canons of the councils were not called the "decrees of the emperors but of the bishops. It is the "prince's province to protect and defend the councils of his "clergy, to keep the peace, to see their decrees executed, "and to punish the contemners of them, but to exercise no "spiritual jurisdiction."

These words seem to mean that in religious matters the State ought to be merely a humble policeman under the command of the clergy. This has always been the opinion of the Roman Catholics and High Churchmen, and thus we see how these Puritans must on this question be classed with those from whom they apparently differ so widely, just as two men when they walk in a circle, although starting from each other in opposite directions, are sure to meet on the other side.

Cartwright's opinions on this matter were shared by the Brownists, who went further and insisted that every Church ought to be confined within the limits of each congregation, and that the government ought to be democratic. This sect fled to Holland, and sent out from there the first batch of pilgrims, as they were called, to America.

The opposition of the Puritans began now to be greatly increased by the spread of Arminianism amongst many of the bishops of the Church. The subsequent animosities intensified this feeling and had a great influence in bringing about that close alliance between Puritanism and Calvinism which has continued ever since.

The Puritans now began to publish pamphlets secretly, like

those of *Mar-Prelate* and others. They also besought the help of Parliament, which would have yielded had not the queen and the bishops been so strongly opposed. The Parliament agreed with the people in wishing to carry the Reformation still further, but as it could not do anything in this way it revenged itself by attacking the bishops. It insisted upon a reformation of the bishops' courts, and in 1561 Bills were brought in to examine bishops' leases, to put down plurality and non-residence, and to abolish archdeacons' courts.

The rigour of the State against the Puritans was considerably relaxed towards the end of Elizabeth's reign, probably partly because the heir to the throne was then a Presbyterian and believed to be friendly to the Puritans.

James I. had scarcely got seated on the throne before the Puritans found out how grievously they had been mistaken in setting their hopes upon him. It is hard to see what solid reason they could ever have had for entertaining such hopes, for kings are no more apt than other men to acquire a liking for a religion merely because they have been forced hypocritically to conform to it. The Puritans did not display this tendency in regard to the Church, and it can only be supposed that they fancied King James must act differently because no one could witness, even unwillingly, the superior virtues of Presbyterianism without becoming converted. If he had not learned to like Presbyterianism he had learned to dislike schism, and therefore he at once set about to try to get rid of it in England as soon as he came to the throne. He tried two methods, first persuasion and afterwards compulsion. By way of persuasion he called the Hampton Court Conference, in the hope that, their objections having been formally stated and openly discussed, some means might be found of reconciling the Puritans to the Church. He was the more hopeful of succeeding in this because the Puritans, in what was called the "Millenary Petition," which they presented to him in 1603, stated that "they were not schismatics "aiming at the dissolution of the State ecclesiastical," but merely wanted redress for their grievances, which chiefly consisted of the three often-repeated objections against the cross in baptism, wearing the surplice, and kneeling at communion. They also wanted the communion to be restricted to those who had previously passed a doctrinal examination, and also that the established statement of doctrines might be so altered as to include predestination. To this the king demurred, saying that he objected to increasing the number of articles and to "stuffing them with theological niceties, "because were they never so explicit there will be no pre- "venting contrary opinions." Those who can free their minds from associations of antipathy must allow that in taking this attitude the king had sense on his side and was, whether intentionally or not, really standing up for religious freedom. It must be allowed also that the Puritans were on their side animated by a very temperate spirit, for they professed themselves willing to subscribe to "the doctrinal article, the king's "supremacy, and the statutes of the realm," but they would not yield on any of the three points to which they principally objected. Whatever blame must be attached to them ought to be attributed not to any perversity of disposition but to their mistake in exaggerating the importance of matters which have come to be considered, even by their own descendants, as comparatively insignificant. That is an admirable quality which leads men to stick to their principles regardless of consequences, but it is also a dangerous one unless we are very careful about the principles to which we apply it. The business of the world cannot be carried on if we are to consider all our opinions as of so much importance that we must not yield about them. It is very unfortunate for bodies of men, as well as for individuals, to have too many principles, that is, too many beliefs to which they think conscience obliges them rigidly to adhere. This is only another form of that old idea of divine right which has always been, and is now, both in religion and politics, such a great obstacle to unity and progress.

Finding that he could not persuade the Puritans to come back into the Church, except on terms to which he could not agree, he next tried to force them in. Accordingly—and here he began that course of illegality which led to the destruction of his son—he published the Prayer Book by proclamation merely, which was contrary to the Constitution. He declared that all must conform or suffer the extremities of the law. This severity led to a division amongst the Puritans themselves some, as the Brownists, who ultimately became the Independents, maintaining that the State ought to have nothing to do with religion, that the National Church was a limb of Antichrist, and that each congregation should be in itself a self-governed Church, whilst the others, who afterwards constituted the Presbyterian party, were for remaining in the Church because they believed that it was wrong to separate from it since it was a true Church. The Brownists mostly fled to Holland where those who had settled at Amsterdam soon began freely to excommunicate each other on account of small doctrinal differences. Here also the dispute between Calvinism and Arminianism rose to a great height.

Political circumstances greatly favoured the Puritans at this time, for the Parliament and nation generally not merely resented the king's hard-handed illegality but they were also offended with him because he did not give more help to his son-in-law Frederick, who had been chosen king of Bohemia and was considered a great champion of Protestantism. The Commons at last remonstrated with the king, and met his denial of their right to meddle by asserting "their ancient " and undoubted rights and inheritance." Already the coming storm might be foretold; the first cloud, no bigger than a man's hand, was above the horizon.

Meanwhile opposition to the Government had the necessary consequence of greatly increasing the spread of Puritanism amongst the people, and also of bringing about that alliance of Puritanism with political freedom which the succeeding reign so thoroughly confirmed.

In reading the history of the reign of Charles I. we are apt to feel an exaggerated gratitude to the religious Puritans unless we remember that their great services to political liberty arose as much from an accidental concurrence of circumstances and from the blunders of their enemies as from any inherent principles of their own. For although the party which opposed the king's usurpations was chiefly directed by the Puritans, and became characterised by their peculiarities, it was largely composed of those moderate men who did not sympathise with their religious views but were driven into their alliance by political circumstances, and without whom the Puritans themselves would have been incapable of success. These men had to choose between friendship for the Church on the one hand and political bondage on the other; they must be ruled either by their religious or their political sympathies so they chose the political, and rightly, especially since the Church was itself trying to throw off that national character which to them was its chief recommendation. For in 1640 Convocation sat after Parliament was dissolved and drew up a body of canons and constitutions in which the doctrine of the king's Divine Right was promulgated, and which were issued by the king's license without the consent of Parliament. Thus the Church was set up against Parliament and was trying to throw off the character of a National Church, for the Crown was not then, nor has it ever been in English history, the same thing as the nation. Clarendon, speaking of the Long Parliament, says they were all members of the Established Church, "and almost to a man were for " episcopal government;" indeed no one could sit in it who had not received the communion according to the rites of the Church of England. Even after the battle of Edgehill the Lords and Commons had no designs against the Church but were in perfect conformity with it. The Book of Common Prayer remained an object of common veneration.

But these moderate men, who composed the chief part of the nation, were driven into alliance with the Puritans chiefly by the following circumstances amongst others. Firstly, the king tried to do without Parliament and set up pretensions opposed to the fundamental principles of the constitution; secondly, the Church tried to do without Parliament and used its influence to support these pretensions; and lastly, both the king and the Church directed their zeal chiefly against the Puritans, and connived at the Papists, to whom the mass of the people were so strongly opposed. Indeed the Church itself began to preach many doctrines identified with Roman Catholicism, as auricular confession, priestly absolution, penance, purgatory, and the worship of images. Those who point to this as indicating how little a National Church is to be relied upon, and how readily it will lend itself to the service of despotism, must remember that the Church did not adopt this line of conduct until it had ceased to be national by denying the authority of Parliament and even that of the king, for the bishops, contrary to the Act of Submission, framed and published new Articles of Visitation without the king's consent. The Church, as it figured in the reign of Charles I., had no idea of submitting to any authority but its own, and wished to form itself into what would have really been a free sect. Whatever injury such a Church was able to do to political liberty must be attributed not to its national but to its sectarian character.

But whatever may have been its political attitude, there is no doubt that the general tendency of the conduct of the Church was in favour of religious liberality, whilst that of its opponents was the reverse, and thus we have the combatants

I

so curiously intermixed that whilst the Puritans were fighting for religious liberty with the weapons of intellectual bondage the Church was fighting for political bondage with the weapons of intellectual liberty.

That the Church was endeavouring to denationalise itself is proved by the attitude which the Parliament was soon obliged to adopt towards it. For it was passed unanimously that "The clergy of England convened in any convocation, or "synod, or otherwise, have no power to make any constitu-"tion, canons, or acts whatever in matters of doctrine or "discipline, or otherwise to bind the clergy or laity of the "land without the consent of Parliament." This evidently meant both that the Church was to remain national and that the Parliament was to remain an essential part of the national government.

It may seem difficult to understand how it was that if the Puritans composed only a comparatively small portion of the great party which arrayed itself against the king, they were able to exercise such a preponderating influence over that party that they directed its conduct, moulded its character, and used its influence for their own purposes. The wonder ceases when we remember that in certain conditions parties are generally ruled by their extremest number. That law of nature by which a dog wags its tail on account of superior strength is often reversed in times of excitement, for the history of political parties shows how frequently the tail has managed to wag the dog.

The history of Presbyterianism in England is another instance of this, for we cannot otherwise understand how a system which obtained such a mastery that it became generally accepted by the nation, collapsed so suddenly and was so soon practically extinct. The fact is that Presbyterianism was a thorough exotic in England and never gained either the understanding or sympathy of the people, but political circumstances, especially the necessity of securing the help of the Scotch, enabled it to secure for itself a very disproportionate, although a very temporary, influence.

We may reasonably regret that the Parliamentary party abandoned itself so completely to the Puritans and that it did not follow the advice of the Bishop of Lincoln, who was one of its friends, when he exhorted the people not "to go after tub preachers and conventicles," and said " Look back " from the beginning of Queen Elizabeth. Can the gospel " stand better against the Church of Rome than it has done " under the bishops, liturgy, and canons? Therefore don't " abandon the good old way for another which you do not " know how much evil may be in it." But it is the common failing of moderate men to be weak and timid, and so, although they alone know the right way, they allow themselves to be led by the extreme men into the wrong one. This is how the moderate men behaved during the Revolution, which was therefore carried, apparently by the consent of the nation, far beyond the point of which the majority of the nation actually approved. Moderation and vacillation seem generally to go together, and a single resolute man can easily lead away a crowd of excited and vacillating ones, even though each individual of that crowd may be his intellectual superior.

The king had no sooner abandoned his power over the government by raising the standard of war, than his opponents began to differ as to where the Power of the Keys should now be lodged, one part, of which the Parliament was the champion, maintaining that the State ought to retain the control of religion, whilst the other part, consisting of the Presbyterians and Independents, believed that the Church was above Parliament and had the right to manage its own affairs.

The Parliament consisted chiefly of those who were in favour of episcopacy but who desired to secure the constitution and check the extravagances of the bishops. Most of them were

Erastians, who held that the pastoral office is only persuasive, that the Church should be open to all, and that no form of Church government is commanded by the Scriptures, but this should be decided in each country by the State. This was the opinion of Whitgift as it had been of Cranmer. The Parliament acted consistently when it abolished the temporal power of the bishops and restricted their spiritual power, for both of these measures were intended to increase the authority of the State. On the strength of the same principle the Parliament claimed the right to reform the Church government and liturgy. As to Communion, the Erastians, headed by Lightfoot, Selden, Colman, and others, maintained that it should be left open. The Parliament inclined to this view, and would only yield to the cry for exclusiveness so far as to consent that a warning should be given. The Lords and Commons at once asserted their claim for the State control of the Church by declaring that "they would use their best endeavours to establish "learned and preaching ministers, with a good and sufficient "maintenance, throughout the whole kingdom." The Parliament wished to carry this principle so far that it would not allow any divergence from it; especially was it disposed to press hard upon the Papists, for very early it petitioned the king that the votes should be taken from popish lords, and that "an oath should be established by act of parliament "wherein the Papists should abjure and renounce the pope's "supremacy, transubstantiation, purgatory, and the worship-"ping of images." Also a Bill was passed for taking away the children of Papists and educating them as Protestants.

The Presbyterians, on the other hand, began to urge more strongly that their own particular form of Church government possessed divine right, and therefore ought to be above the control of Parliament. The Independents took the same ground, and we thus see that the Puritans were on this subject quite at one with the High Church bishops whom they had helped to turn away. For Laud's great doctrine was that "Parliament might not meddle with religion without the assent of the clergy in Convocation." This is just the same opinion, although put in less violent language, as that of Cartwright, the great leader of the Independents, when he said that "the civil magistrate is but the servant to lick the dust off the feet of the Church." We thus see that Parliament had now to go through the same struggle as Henry II. fought five hundred years ago, for A'Becket justified his disobedience on the ground that "it is not for kings to judge bishops but to bow before them."

Unhappily the Parliament was not so successful as the Plantagenet king had been, although at first it stood out bravely. For it rejected the petition of the Independents presented in 1643, which begged that—

1. Each separate congregation should be a Church in itself, but offending Churches should be examined by the neighbouring Churches, and if found wrong, be cut off from Christian communion until they repented.

2. The service should not be by fixed form, but left to the ministers themselves.

3. The ordination should not be performed until after election by some Church.

The Parliament was disposed to stick out thoroughly for its rights, but the necessity of gaining the help of the Scots introduced a new element into the conflict.

It often happens that those who are conquered in war ultimately subjugate their conquerors by the arts of peace, and so it was with the Scots, for nothing is more remarkable in the history of the Revolution than the immense influence they were able to exercise. It is one of the anomalies of history how a nation which was small, and weak, and suspected, should have been able to interfere in the affairs of the greater nation so far as to hold the balance and to force upon that nation an alien and disliked form of Church government and discipline.

There is no need to go back to Bannockburn for a victory; it is sufficient to emblazon upon the national banner the title of "The Solemn League and Covenant," for that tells not merely of successful resistance, but of astounding and, for the time, complete conquest. Here was a profession of faith drawn up in Scotland, which the English people were not merely induced to adopt far more widely than they have ever adopted anything else of the sort but also to persuade themselves that they liked, yet how little they really cared for it is proved by the readiness with which they gave it up and forgot it. The Scots played a characteristic and congenial part, for they held the balance between the two evenly divided parties, and so were able to insist upon very exacting terms.

They demanded that there should be uniformity of doctrine and discipline between the two nations. They were also able really by their influence, although without their ostensible intervention, to bring about in 1643 the Westminster Assembly of Divines, which consisted of thirty Lay Assessors and one hundred and twenty-one Divines. In spite of its own opinion to the contrary, this was one of the most intolerant and presumptuous religious assemblies which has ever been gathered together in England. Not only did it draw up a Confession of Faith which still stands unrivalled in the annals of Protestantism for its hardness and bigotry but it put forward pretensions which, unless strenuously resisted, must soon have ended in its gaining the control not only of the Church but also of Parliament and the country generally. All ministers were ejected who would not take the Covenant, and no new ones could be appointed unless they had first received a certificate of approval from the committee of the Westminster Assembly. It is worth remembering that there were ejected by this means a number as large as that of the Puritans who were turned out at the Restoration. Although the Presbyterians never, except in London and Lancashire, obtained footing sufficient to get their own Church system properly grounded, still they managed to force the Parliament not merely to accept itself the Solemn League and Covenant but also to compel all the public officers of the State to swear to it. The bishops alone refused to take it, and those of them who belonged to the Assembly left it when the Covenant was adopted. From this time the bishops had nothing further to do with the government of the Church until the Restoration.

Parliament went still further and replaced the Liturgy by the Directory, as they said—"Not out of any affectation of "novelty nor with an intention to disparage our first "reformers, but that we may answer in some measure the "gracious providence of God which now calls upon us "for a further reformation ; that we may satisfy our own "consciences, answer the expectations of the reformed "churches, ease the consciences of many godly persons "amongst ourselves, and give a public testimony of our "endeavours after a uniformity in divine worship, pursuant "to what we had promised in our solemn league and cove- "nant." Which, translated into plain language, means that Parliament took this step in obedience to external pressure and on account of a reluctantly given promise. This is not a pleasant fact for Englishmen to reflect upon.

Still there was a point beyond which Parliament would not yield, and in 1646 it determined that a committee of Lords and Commons should decide upon the unfitness of ministers. This greatly annoyed the Scots and Presbyterians who declared it insufferable for the Church to have to appeal to Parliament. What sort of religious freedom would have prevailed had the Church been allowed to govern itself may be inferred from the fact, stated by Neal (p. 250, vol. iii.), that "The Presbyterian hierarchy was as narrow as the "prelatical ; and as it did not allow a liberty of conscience, "claiming a civil as well as ecclesiastical authority over men's "persons and properties, it was equally, if not more, insuf-

"ferable." The Independents only wanted toleration and consideration for "tender consciences," but the Presbyterians wanted to use the power of Parliament to persecute the Independents and all others who differed from them. That is to say, there was to be introduced into England that which always ultimately follows the destruction of a State-governed Church, namely, a Church-governed State. But Parliament was not willing thus to abandon its rights, so instead of yielding it girt the law still closer about the Church and decreed that an appeal should be allowed from the Presbyterian "classes" to the parliamentary commission, and then to the Parliament itself. In reply to the request of the Scots and Presbyterians that the government and assemblies of the Church should be liberated from the control of Parliament, the Commons published an answer in which they say that "they cannot "consent to the granting an arbitrary and unlimited power "and jurisdiction to near ten thousand judicatories to be "erected within this kingdom, and this demanded in such a "way as is not consistent with the fundamental laws and "government of the same, and by necessary consequence "excluding the Parliament of England from the exercise of "all ecclesiastical jurisdiction. This has been the great cause "that Church government has not been settled long since; "and we have the more reason not to part with this power "out of the hands of the civil magistrate since the experience "of all ages will manifest, that the reformation and purity of "religion, and the preservation and protection of the people "of God in this kingdom have, under God, been owing to "the Parliament's exercise of this power." Here is a plain and bold declaration, by men who knew what they were talking about, of a great truth which, unhappily, it seems that the people of England have now to be taught again.

Parliament abolished the names and titles of bishops and archbishops, and alienated their revenues for the payment of the public debts, but it did not find itself particularly happy with those who had taken their place. The pulpits resounded with invectives against the Parliament and the chief men in power because they would not allow the Church to be independent of the State. Indeed, preaching now began to break out into all sorts of extravagant excesses. This was a natural consequence of the extraordinary causes which were then at work, for the whole atmosphere was charged with electricity; men's minds were thoroughly unsettled, and through having refused authority in one sort they were soon led to refuse it in all sorts. Besides, lay preaching had done a great deal of harm, especially in the army, for the recent changes having deprived most of the regiments of chaplains, the officers were led to set up for preachers, and soon this spread to the common soldiers, and so amongst the churches in the country.

Tired of these disorders and extravagances, the Parliament tried to make terms with the king, but they insisted upon the establishment of the Presbyterian form of Church government, to which the Scots added the extirpation of all sectaries and the uniform acceptance of the Covenant by both nations. The king was willing to confirm the Assembly of Deacons and the Presbyterian Church government for three years, but this was not considered enough, and so the Treaty of Newport fell through. It is a noticeable fact that religion was almost the only question which prevented the king and Parliament coming to terms.

This was the time in history when the national character of the Church was nearest destruction, for Parliament, which was its only champion, had kept getting feebler and feebler until now the sword of defence was falling from its nerveless grasp. But then, by the inscrutable order of that Providence whose ways are past finding out, a strong hand sprang forward to wield the sword; the sectaries, rushing on to consummate their victory, were driven back, and the National Church of England was saved. Its saviour was Oliver. Cromwell, the

Independent, and all those who value the national principle in religion should never forget to be deeply grateful to the man who saved that principle from a ruin from which, in all human probability, it could not again have been restored. In comparison with such a service it matters little that we differ from him about the form of the State or the discipline of the Church, for all history teaches that it is far easier to alter the State or the Church than it is to establish a proper connection between the two. Cromwell's State might be republican, but it was still the State; his Church might be Independent, but it was still the Church; the great thing was to keep that Church, whatever it might be, under the control of that State, whatever it might be. This Cromwell did, and so when the State and the Church were restored to their old forms they found themselves still joined by a connection which he had preserved.

And Cromwell, like all true State Churchmen, was liberal and tolerant; he had his own opinions, which he believed in and cherished with all the thoroughness of his strong nature, but he was too large-minded to wish to force them upon everybody else, or to split up the Church on account of them. When he set out for Ireland he recommended that all penal laws against religion should be removed. It is true that the "engagement" had to be sworn to by all ministers and heads of colleges, and that without it no minister could enjoy any preferment in the Church or sit in the Assembly of Divines, but this was merely a political precaution to protect the State. Under Cromwell the terms of conformity were more liberal than for a long time before; the Covenant was laid aside, and none were obliged to conform to the public religion by penalties, but all who differed were protected in the profession of their faith provided they did no injury to others or to the public peace. Ministers were not allowed to use the Liturgy in public, but they might make prayers as near it as they liked.

Cromwell had not merely to contend with his avowed enemies but also with his professed friends, for the Independent party comprised many Fifth Monarchists, who were opposed to ministers and tithes, and everything in the shape of a State Church, whilst the Presbyterians were also opposed to the control of the State, for they boldly enunciated at this time the doctrines that Church government is of divine authority, that the civil magistrate ought not to be at the head of the Church, and that government by synods and classes is the one appointed by Christ.

What might have been expected if the Church had been left to itself is indicated by the conduct of the thirty-eight "Triers," who were composed of Independents, Presbyterians, and Baptists; for although they were appointed by the State and supposed to be under its authority, the political exigencies of the time withdrew from them so much of its control that at first they were allowed to act pretty nearly as if they were independent. Godwin, himself an Independent, says of them that "they made their own narrow Calvinism the door of admission to Church preferment," and exercised greater power than the bishops had claimed. But this was checked, and the Commissioners who were appointed by Cromwell to examine ministers only ejected those who were convicted of malignancy, or negligence, or misconduct. Cromwell kept a tight hand upon the Papists, not on account of their religion, but because he considered them enemies to his government.

Even the Independents, in spite of their opinions to the contrary, began to appreciate the evils of that system which is now so much lauded in England, if the word system can fitly be applied to a disintegrated mass of isolated congregations. Those who make such fair promises of what Independency would do for us if we would only generally adopt it should be asked to explain the evils which its own friends acknowledged it produced when it prevailed in England far more widely than ever before or since. Listen to the petition for permission to hold a synod which the Independents presented to Cromwell shortly before his death. Hitherto, they say, "there have been no associations of our "churches, no meetings of our ministers to promote the "common interest; our churches are like so many ships "launched singly and sailing apart and alone in the vast "ocean of tumultuous times, exposed to every wind of "doctrine; under no other conduct than the word and "Spirit and their particular elders and principal brethren, "without associations among themselves, or so much as hold-"ing out a common light to others, whereby to know where "they were." (Neal, iv. 173.) Eventually in 1658 an Assembly was held at the Savoy, which drew up the Savoy Confession of Faith, founded on the Westminster Confession.

Cromwell did, indeed, preserve the life of the national principle, but owing to many causes, partly the unsettled temper of the times and partly the uncertain tenure of his own power, he could not prevent the intoxicated spirit of sectarianism from running into all sorts of rampant excesses. The reaction of the Restoration proved how thoroughly sick the nation was of this sectarianism; so sick that it was willing to sacrifice personal freedom and even the necessary safeguards of political existence to put it down. Much as we, in our philosophic calmness, may deplore the folly with which the Restoration was managed and the excesses to which it led, we must remember that we owe it greatly to Cromwell that that folly was not greater, and that those excesses did not bring down the whole constitution into such a heap of ruins that only the hands of another bloody revolution could have built it up again. For if the reaction was so great from the previous excesses, severely checked as they were, we can easily imagine what it would have been had Cromwell been the man to leave those excesses alone, much less to encourage them.

We are certain greatly to misread the religious history of the Restoration period unless we clearly understand the character of the different parties who were then most influential. It is very easy, but like most other easy things of the sort it is also very untrue, to talk about the Acts passed against the Dissenters during the reign of Charles II., as if they were merely the work of a tyrannical and revengeful State Church, whereas the truth is, they were the result of complicated causes. The character of these Acts was determined by the struggle between the king and the Parliament, which recovered much quicker than any of the other institutions from the epidemic of sickly subservience which had seized them all at the Restoration. The State Church had ceased to be a crucial principle, and its place had been taken by the Papists; there was no need to discuss about the Church, for that had again become an accepted fact, whereas the Papists were coming into such prominence as to threaten the existence of Protestantism itself. Not that they were numerically very powerful, but the Court was known to be with them, and both domestic and foreign affairs seemed to be running in their favour. The London Plague and Fire had shaken the national nerves, which were still further agitated by the success of the French arms on the Continent. Besides, the Papists were showing unwonted activity; the Jesuits and other fraternities were not only permitted, but even largely favoured; the magistrates were very remiss in carrying out the law, and this spirit extended so widely that many Popish recusants received presentations, whilst the future was rendered still more ominous by the fact that large numbers of the boys belonging to the better classes were sent abroad to receive that foreign Catholic training which has always been considered so antagonistic to the spirit of English liberty. But the language of calm judgment is out of place in speaking of that dread of the Papists which then took possession of the English nation, for when a feeling, even though originating in reason, has once developed into a scare, it becomes subject to quite a new set of laws, and must be judged by different rules.

It is absurd to complain of the Acts of Charles II.'s reign on the ground of their being contrary to the principle of toleration when we know that there was no party in England at that time which believed in toleration, much less cared to carry it out. The Roman Catholics wanted toleration for themselves as a matter of policy, but they had not then any more love for the principle in the abstract than they have usually manifested; and the Puritans also wanted toleration for themselves, but preferred to be without it rather than that the Papists should receive it too. The Parliament's chief care was the preservation of Protestantism, and for this purpose it resolved upon two objects: one, to build up a strong National Church, and the other to keep down the Papists. The king was about the only man in the country willing to be tolerant, and two causes led him to have this feeling; one was that he cared very little about religion, and the other that he wanted to favour the Papists. Thus we have the Papists, the Puritans, the Parliament, and the Prerogative, all sometimes pulling different ways, and sometimes some pulling together which at other times were opposed. The Puritans also were themselves divided, and at this time, according to Burnet, the name of Puritans was changed into that of Protestant Nonconformists, who consisted of Presbyterians, Independents, Anabaptists, and Quakers. The Presbyterians wanted their own objections complied with, but were against the toleration of the other Nonconformists, whilst the others were above all things wishful that there should be no toleration for Papists. The Presbyterians endeavoured to come to terms at the Conference of the Savoy, to which the Independents were not invited. This attempt, however, failed, for the bishops who took part in the Conference, being now in the ascendant, were in no mood to yield to the demands of those from whom they had recently suffered so long and so smartly. The State Church, as named before, did not take any distinctive part in the struggle; the bishops were willing to go with the king and Parliament in oppressing the Nonconformists, whilst both the bishops and the whole body of the clergy sympathised with Parliament in opposing the king's project for tolerating the Papists. The best of the clergy, as Tillotson, Stillingfleet, Whichcote, Wilkins, Cudworth, and others, were in favour of less oppressive measures both towards the Nonconformists and the Papists; these were, indeed, the only men who had then any idea of our modern doctrines of toleration. Considered generally, the adherents of the Church may be said to have been at this time roughly divided into two classes, namely, Low Churchmen, who were Whigs and in favour of the toleration of Nonconformists but opposed to the Papists and to the royal prerogative, and High Churchmen, who were in favour of the prerogative and opposed to the Nonconformists.

The course of ecclesiastical legislation during Charles II.'s reign was, however, chiefly the result of a contest between the Parliament and the king, not about the power of the Crown but about the toleration of the Papists. Parliament was quite willing, and indeed anxious, not merely duly to uphold the proper regal authority but also to carry it to extravagant lengths; hence it was disposed to be increasingly violent against the Nonconformists, because, besides being enemies to the Church, many of them were believed to be also disloyal to the State. The Act of Uniformity, passed in 1662, was the first fruit of this feeling. By it all clergymen were compelled to abandon their livings unless they gave complete assent and consent to the whole Book of Common Prayer, including all rites and ceremonies therein laid down, and, abjuring the Solemn League and Covenant, took the Oath of Canonical Obedience, and acknowledged the unlawfulness of taking up arms against the king on any pretence whatever, and submitted to reordination if they had not been episcopally ordained. Two thousand clergymen refused to agree to these conditions, and so cast themselves upon the world on the famous St. Bartholomew's Day, 1662. The practical effect of this single Act was far greater than that of all the Acts together which constituted the Reformation, for during the whole changes of Elizabeth's reign only about two hundred of the clergy abandoned their livings. If these two figures were more frequently considered together the nation would probably arrive at a truer conception than it now possesses of what was the real character of the Reformation.

It would be a mistake to suppose that the people generally were as oppressively disposed as the conditions of the Act of Uniformity seem to indicate, for the House of Lords tried hard to make those conditions less stringent, and this Act only passed the House of Commons by a majority of six.

It now became part of the policy of the Court to coincide with the extreme measures passed by Parliament, because it was hoped that the Nonconformists would thus be driven to seek the alliance of the Court, and so might be willing to help in gaining relief for the Papists as well as for themselves. Hence now were passed, in unresisted fanaticism, those Acts which are such blots on the pages of English history. First came the Corporation Act in 1663, by which every officer of a corporation was compelled to receive the sacrament according to the rites of the Church of England, and to take the oaths of supremacy and allegiance and passive obedience. In 1664 was passed the Conventicle Act, by which it was made a crime, punishable by a heavy fine or imprisonment, for any person above sixteen years of age to attend any conventicle, which word meant any house where five or more persons, besides the inhabitants, assembled for religious worship. This was followed in 1665 by the Five Mile Act, which subjected every nonconformist minister, or clergyman not duly qualified, who came within five miles of every corporate town wherein he had previously preached, to a penalty of forty pounds, or six months' imprisonment, unless he would take the oath against taking up arms against the king under any pretence whatever. Nor were these ministers, or any person not frequenting the Church of England, to teach in any public or private school.

This series of acts instead of stamping out dissent strengthened it with the obstinacy of religious conscientiousness and beautified it with the lustre of political martyrdom.

Finding that the Dissenters did not, as he expected, on account of fellowship in suffering grow more friendlily disposed towards the Papists, and that these Acts were chiefly meant for the Papists against whom they were much more strictly enforced than against the Dissenters, the king resolved to break with Parliament, and to do by usurpation that which he had failed to do by strategy. Accordingly in 1672 he published his Declaration of Indulgence, which, by royal authority alone, suspended all penal laws against religion, granted liberty of worship to Papists and promised to license places of worship for Protestants provided they met with open doors. The king expected that the Dissenters would be so glad to get liberty for themselves that they would not object to the Papists having it also, and it was so with some of the extreme sections including many Independents. But the large majority protested against the king's Declaration on two grounds—firstly, that it granted liberty to the Papists, and secondly, that it was a violation of the rights of Parliament and a breach of the Constitution. For these reasons they refused to accept the king's offer, protesting that they could not recognize his right to make it, and that even if he had that right, still they preferred to suffer themselves rather than that the restrictions against the Papists should be slackened.

This conduct of the Dissenters soon began to turn the popular feeling in their favour, for the majority of the nation hated the Papists and accordingly respected the Dissenters for being willing to suffer in order that they might be punished, while Parliament was glad to have such allies in defending its own rights. Several attempts were made by the Liberal leaders to bring back the Dissenters within the Church, and some of these would have been successful had not the Dissenters been so rigidly exacting. Parliament also began to relax towards the Dissenters, and had it not been prevented would have passed a measure for relieving them from some of the penalties which they suffered along with the Papists.

Parliament protested against the king's dispensing power and stopped the supplies. By way of rejoinder to his Declaration it also passed in 1678 the Test Act which enacted that no person should sit in either House of Parliament unless he had previously taken the oaths of allegiance and supremacy, and had declared without reservation against transubstantiation, invocation of saints and the mass. Thus again did the Stuarts, within the course of a single generation, succeed in arraying Parliament against the Crown, but this time Charles II. managed to avoid a more open conflict by dismissing Parliament and ruling for the rest of his reign without it. He was enabled to do this because the people had still left in them enough of aversion to the Revolution and of enthusiasm for the Restoration.

The Court was so enraged with the Dissenters for siding with Parliament that it got up the pretended conspiracy to assassinate the king and his brother called the Rye House Plot, in order to cast discredit upon them and turn the feeling of the nation against them.

James II. thoroughly agreed with his brother's political conduct, and differed from him as to religion only in being more honest, for he was openly a Papist whilst Charles was one secretly. James also possessed all the intolerance of sincerity, for whilst Charles had all along been quite willing for the Dissenters to have liberty if only the Papists might have it too, James was resolved that the Papists should have it and not the Dissenters, against whom all the enactments were put into full force which had recently been considerably relaxed. Their places of worship were closed, and they were forbidden to meet in private houses or even in the open fields. They were beset by spies in every direction and their personal liberty and domestic privacy were most ruthlessly interfered with. The rigour against them was greatly increased after the Monmouth Rebellion, because they were suspected of secretly favouring it as a body.

But soon a sudden change occurred, for the Church growing alarmed at the progress of the Papists, began to oppose the king's measures, whilst the king turned round and began to court the Dissenters, who were allowed to re-open their conventicles with full liberty to worship as they liked. From this date no penal laws have ever been enforced against them in England. Now when the Protestant Dissenters arose again as a body into public view it was seen that all their sufferings had not materially diminished their comparative number. They were less numerous than the adherents of the Church and even than the Papists, but they were able to exercise an influence quite out of proportion with their number and so to hold the balance between parties. This was probably owing to their general intellectual and moral superiority, for they were mostly well-educated and well-behaved, two qualities far from common in those days.

All this newly displayed liberality of the king towards the Dissenters was only intended to win their support for that next step which James in imitation of his brother had resolved upon. When he thought the way prepared, by the Dissenters being conciliated and the judges forced to acknowledge his right to do it, he published in 1687 his celebrated Declaration of Indulgence, "making no doubt of the con- "currence of his two Houses of Parliament when he should "think it convenient for them to meet." In this all restrictions were removed from the worship of both Protestant and Papist Dissenters and they were liberated from all tests and disabilities. Most of the Dissenters, deceived by the king's professions, gladly accepted his offer, and had it not been for the Church it is probable that at this crisis the political liberties of the whole people would have been sacrificed to the religious idiosyncrasies of a few.

This declaration was only read in about two hundred churches in England, and the bulk of the people, who have always largely followed the political lead of the Church, turned against the king, and so he thought it best to retreat. James II. did not consider that the intervening vicious rule had completely destroyed those sentiments which made the nation submit to the previous similar attempt of his brother.

That the bishops were not opposed to the principles of King James's Declaration, as far as the Protestant Dissenters was concerned, was proved by the readiness with which they, together with all the Protestants of the nation, accepted the Act of Toleration which was passed almost directly after the accession of William and Mary, and which merely carried out legally the doctrine which James II. had tried to enforce illegally. By this Act full liberty for religious worship was granted to all Protestant Dissenters, but this was not extended either to Roman Catholics or to those who denied the doctrines of the Trinity. All who did not conform to the Church of England were still left, however, under many disqualifications, most of which were sentimental rather than practical and all of which have been gradually removed.

The passing of the Act of Toleration in 1689 marks the beginning of our present epoch in religious history, for since then the distribution of parties and their relative attitudes towards each other have remained pretty much the same. The Church as a whole followed the lead of the State, although the rebellious Jacobite faction continued for a long time a cause of trouble and anxiety. The Roman Catholics subsided into the position of a small and neglected non-conforming sect, which is only now awakening from a slumber of nearly two hundred years, whilst the different bodies of Protestant Dissenters quietly settled down into pretty much the same positions which they have continued to occupy ever since. In looking round at this time there is one very striking fact, which has not been sufficiently remarked but which is full of significance, and that is, the sudden collapse of Presbyterianism. We have seen how powerful the Presbyterians had been during the preceding fifty years, how they had often directed the course of ecclesiastical, and even of national, affairs ; how for some years they had succeeded in forcing their system upon the acceptance of the majority of the people, and how, even after the Church was restored to its position, they were considered to be of so much importance that when an attempt was made to make terms with the Dissenters, they alone were treated with. Yet no sooner was the Act of Toleration passed than there was hardly one of them to be found ; Presbyterianism was like summer snow ; it only lasted during the abnormal chill of temporary oppression, and disappeared quickly before the natural warmth of toleration. A few isolated and languishing chapels, which have fallen into the hands of those who hold a creed against which their founders would have been the first to cry out, are all that is now left to tell the tale of that Presbyterianism which was once so proud and apparently triumphant. This result has certainly justified the wisdom of the Church in refusing to accept the Presbyterian discipline for itself and in resisting its general extension. We may also learn another lesson, which is that the prominence into which any set of opinions has pushed itself, and even the power which it has been able to gain, are no accurate measure of its real hold upon the people.

Another sect to be noticed here is that of the Quakers which sprang into existence during the Commonwealth, under the leadership of George Fox, whose peculiar opinions, to most of which they still adhere, are well known. It is a remarkable fact that the Quakers were much more harshly persecuted by the Puritans than ever the Puritans themselves had been by the State Church; when a printed account of them was presented to the Parliament which the Protector convened, it appeared that one hundred and forty of them were then in prison. By the year 1652 they had become very numerous in many of the central and southern parts of the country, for like other sects they flourished by persecution as they have decayed under toleration; as Hugh Peters remarked to Oliver Cromwell, "he could not give George Fox a better op-"portunity of spreading his principles in Cornwall, than by "imprisoning him there." The Quakers welcomed the restoration of Charles II. as a promise of better times, but they shared in the sufferings caused by the Acts which were directed against the Nonconformists. The Quakers, who did not rank with any political party, welcomed the Declaration of Indulgence, and they then enjoyed a short period of peace, but their sufferings were renewed when that Declaration was revoked. During this time the Society derived both honour and influence from the writings of Penn and Barclay, although these could not prevent the evils of separation which already began to weaken the body. When James II. ascended the throne the Quakers drew up a petition stating their grievous sufferings by no less than ten penal laws. The king appointed a commission to examine into their complaints, which resulted in the discomfiture of the Informers from whom they had suffered so long, and in the relaxation of the penal laws. Grateful for this, the Quakers presented an address to the king thanking him for his Declaration of Liberty of Conscience, as did those other Dissenters, who either did not observe, or did not care for, the political dangers involved. In 1688 they petitioned King James to be relieved from titles and oaths, but the king directly afterwards abandoned the throne. Under William III. they shared in the benefits, not merely of the Act of Toleration, but also of that tolerant spirit which then took possession of the nation and which has continued in an increasing degree. From this time the Quakers have occupied a position of dignified respectability, but of gradually diminishing numbers and influence, and although it would manifestly be very injurious for the national welfare if their opinions were largely acted upon, still we cannot help regretting the decay of a system which has done so much to purify the tone of private life, to exemplify the duty of suffering for the sake of principle, and to beautify the character of religion by developing the much neglected attributes of simplicity and manliness.

Taking then a geographical survey of the religious condition of England after the passing of the Act of Toleration, we find that the great majority of the nation adhered to the National Church, whilst the Nonconformists consisted, comparatively speaking, of a few Roman Catholics, a few Independents, fewer Baptists, and still fewer Quakers.

In the preceding chapter a few of the causes have been named of that lethargy which after the Revolution of 1688 settled both upon Church and Dissent alike. If the principle were true of that lazy and inglorious maxim that the nation is happy which has no history, we should expect that this was a joyful time for religion in England; but we know that it was quite the contrary. The people, unchecked by religion, abandoned themselves to the full swing of the reaction against Puritanic strictness and morality; those two companion thieves, unbelief and vice, plundered the house, whilst the watchman, religion, lay asleep on the hearth. It was the same all through, for Dissent was just as drowsy as the Church; and those who blame the Church for its inactivity at this period should remember that it was from the Church, and not from Dissent, that the first energetic awakening came. Religion was the last champion to enter the lists against vice ; and it was the only one which had any success. Literature had tried by talking it down, and had failed ; art, as in Hogarth, had tried by showing it up, and had failed also; the victory was left for religion, despised by philosophers, disbelieved in by the masses, and neglected by nearly everybody.

The two novel features of Wesleyanism—which at first were the sources of its strength, as they have since become through exaggeration the causes of its weakness—were its appeal to enthusiasm and its revival of the idea of Christian brotherhood. Religion was then cold, and formal, and inoperative ; it was regarded merely as a system of doctrine to be examined by the mind, and not as a body of faith to be felt by the soul ; many of those who languidly accepted it had a sort of corporate idea that it would benefit them collectively, but no one considered that it ought to constitute any bond of personal union. Whitfield and Wesley declared, on the contrary, that religion to be worth anything must get hold of the heart, and that no man could be a real Christian unless he felt a passionate and absorbing love for his Master ; they taught also that those who had this feeling ought to be united to each other by the closest ties of intimate fellowship, and were bound not only to be mutually helpful but also to watch over each other's spiritual welfare. It was this idea which led to the Methodist Class Meetings and other society combinations, and it was this which was also the principal cause of the bitterness and turbulence with which the masses at first opposed the Methodist movement. For they got the notion that Methodism was somehow akin to Roman Catholicism—and there were indeed some points of resemblance, for a strict religious body meeting in private houses and enjoining confession and fasting would remind the superficial observer of some of the most disliked practices of Romanism. And the people were then in no mood to allow anything of this·sort; for whilst the directing spirit of English history had from the Reformation to the Revolution of 1688 been intensely religious, it had now become intensely political. The natural effects of reaction, the state of foreign affairs, and the widening of the country's arena, all tended to develop the national sentiment, and with this sentiment Protestantism was most closely associated, for then as now the English hatred to Roman Catholicism was only in a very small degree religious. John Bull has always detested any foreign authority, and he considers the Roman Catholic as an alien who is under the control of a foreigner and belongs too little to his country and too much to his creed. And there was then in England a dread of Roman Catholicism far greater than anything which is felt now. "Popish bishops," we are told, "distin-"guished by mock titles, and invested by a solemn show of "authority, have, it is well known, methodically parcelled "out this kingdom into four districts, over which they exer-"cise a regular jurisdiction." (Charge by Archdeacon Sterne, 1737.) Bishop Sherlock, in a letter to the clergy of 1750, says: "There is a great and grievous evil amongst us; I "mean the great increase of Popery in this kingdom." The Press teemed with warnings and denunciations, and even Parliament was besought to adopt very violent measures to stop the spread of Popery. The public mind, then so alarmed and angry, was very ready to be suspicious of anything which looked like Roman Catholicism, and to meet it with violent opposition.

The clergy also were not friendlily disposed towards the Methodists, and for the following reasons, amongst others; they disliked preaching in the fields and unconsecrated places; they considered it dangerous to encourage the people to assemble together to expound the Scriptures in an irregular manner; they resented the pretensions of the Methodists to an extraordinary inspiration and an inward feeling of the Holy Spirit; and above all they objected to the enthusiasm which the Methodists so distinctly demanded and so widely excited. Still, in spite of these objections, there was no reason why Methodism should have separated from the Church, and it would have been better both for itself and for the Church if it had never done so. The Church is often blamed, and no doubt very justly, for its treatment of Methodism. The truth is that the Church had not then awakened out of its sleep, and was consequently crusty at being disturbed. Methodism would have got a very different answer had it not pressed its demands until time had been given for a breath of refreshing morning air. Then the Methodists would have become what they ought to have been, namely an order in the Church, for there is no more reason why in Protestantism those who choose to be more enthusiastic should separate from the rest than that monks and nuns should break away from Roman Catholicism.

The principal leaders of the Methodist movement were all strongly opposed to separation from the Church. Wesley himself was especially so; indeed to the last he continued to declare himself a member of the Church of England. He was displeased when any of his societies held their meetings during the hours of Church service, and the last important letter he wrote (June 26, 1790) was a remonstrance with a bishop who, by giving information against Methodists meeting in unlicensed houses, and by getting them fined, had forced them to apply for a license as Dissenters. Had John Wesley foreseen the position which would afterwards be taken by his followers, it is probable that he would have ordered his course differently.

The causes which led to the separation of Methodism from the Church were principally two. The first was that no one could claim the benefit of the Act of Toleration without first declaring himself a Dissenter. Thus the Methodists, though very unwillingly, were ultimately obliged to class themselves as Dissenters in order to gain that freedom which this Act alone allowed. The other cause was the difficulty of ordination. The Methodists were obliged to have a fresh supply of ministers, and as no bishop would ordain them, Wesley at last decided to ordain them himself. It was this act which constituted the real breach, and which so grieved his admirable brother Charles, who wrote, respecting this step of his brother, " How was he surprised into so rash an action ? " Lord Mansfield told me that ordination meant separation. " This my brother will not see, or that he has renounced the " principles and practices of his whole life." John replied, " I " firmly believe that I am a scriptural *episcopos* as much as " any man in England, for the uninterrupted succession I " know to be a fable which no man can prove. But this does " not interfere with my remaining in the Church of England " from which I have no more desire to separate now than fifty " years ago. I still attend all ordinances of the Church at all " opportunities and I earnestly advise all who are connected " with me to do so." That the Church after all was not so badly disposed towards the Methodists is proved by Charles Wesley's reply : " I do not understand what obedience to " bishops you dread ; they have let us alone to act just as we " pleased for fifty years. At present some of them are quite " friendly to us, particularly to you. The Churches are also " open to you, and there never could be less pretence for a " separation." Directly after this both the brothers died, and not long elapsed before their followers had formed an organization of their own and separated themselves entirely from the Church.

This development of Methodism is the last fact in the History of Dissent which claims notice here, except it may be stated that the course of legislation has continued increasingly favourable to religious liberty. In Queen Anne's reign the Schism Act and Occasional Conformity Act were repealed, and the Test Act was modified by the Act of Indemnity. That Dissenters suffered no real hardships on account of religion is proved by the fact that during the whole of the eighteenth century they made no earnest efforts to remove the disabilities still remaining in the Statute Book. Pitt, in opposing the repeal of the Test and Corporation Acts in 1787, said that practically the Dissenters had no grievances, for the spirit of the times was too liberal. In 1791 Parliament took off the social and fiscal disabilities of Roman Catholics.

One fact should not be forgotten, and that is that the Methodists have already split up into a number of isolated divisions. This has been the case with all the sectarian bodies, except the Independents, now called Congregationalists, who have no union to divide about. This disease of disintegration would soon take possession of the Church of England also if it was separated from the State.

CHAPTER IV.

WHAT IS A NATIONAL CHURCH?

BEFORE we are qualified to consider what are the objections to the existence of the National Church we must first clearly understand what we mean by this Church. This may sound a trite remark but it is not by any means a superfluous one, for we live in a period when such a warning is especially necessary. Those who are not gifted with any extraordinary acuteness, but are merely too sensible to be led away by the common talk of the hour, cannot help observing that the public mind is just now in a very weak and flabby condition. Undoubtedly many causes have helped to bring this about; amongst the most probable may be named the increased quickness, and consequently increased shallowness, of life generally; the lamentably excessive attention to newspapers and other transient literature which not only neither stores nor strengthens the mind but also does it great positive injury by rendering it averse to, and incapable of, sustained and concentrated thought; the undoubtedly materialistic tone of the age, which makes it grossly exaggerate the importance of those practical utilities which, though seen, are temporal, and very temporal, and blinds it to the greatness of those deep principles which, though unseen, are the only things which are real and eternal; and last, and probably the most effective cause of all, must be included the altered character of our political condition, which has placed our destinies largely in the hands of those who neither care for principles nor understand arguments but are chiefly led by impulses. The law of demand and supply operates as truly in politics as in trade, and we cannot expect painstaking logic and careful language so long as the majority of those whose votes have to be won cry out for plausible declamation and striking phrases. There is something painfully significant in the generally accepted belief that one of the two great political parties of the country cannot gain or hold power except on the strength of what is called "a popular cry," and so the control of a vast and diversified empire is largely determined, not by practical capacity or principles of government, but by the fate of some trivial institution or the whim of some interested class.

The present agitation, to use a common though often misleading word, against the existence of the National Church is strongly marked by both these characteristics, for its chief hopes depend upon excitement and its chief arguments depend upon vagueness. An organisation is now being developed in order to get up the steam of popular frenzy so that Disestablishment may become an election "cry." Numberless meteors of flashing phases are darting about the heavens, but few of them will run in the orbits of reason and truth; we hear much about the injustice and mischief of the connection between the Church and the State but there is no one to tell us what that connection really is. Definition and declamation are rarely companions.

Our first object then, in discussing this question of the National Church, must be to get to know what we are talking about, and if we proceed with reasonable justice and judgment we shall not improbably find that most of the arguments against the connection of Church and State are founded upon false ideas of the nature of that connection.

This question has been so much misunderstood and obscured that the very phrase "connection of Church and State," which we are compelled sometimes to use is very misleading and is calculated often to give quite a false impression, as it seems to confirm the common notion of the matter. For if we listen both to the friends of the Church and to its enemies we find that nearly all of them have some such idea as this. They believe that the Church and the State are two distinct institutions, which at some time or other, nobody seems to know when, made a bargain with each other. The terms of this bargain are variously represented; all parties agree that the State, on its part, gained control over the Church, but they differ as to what the Church gained; some regard this connection with the State as conferring chiefly favour and support, whilst others consider it as little else than incurring subjection to trammels. But whatever opinions there may be as to the terms of the bargain and as to whether or not the Church gained by the transaction, nearly all agree that there was such a bargain, and that the Church is, in itself, something quite distinct from the State. It is now sought to persuade the State to give up this bargain, and to let the Church go free.

Now this conception of the Church and the State as two distinct institutions thus treating with each other is so invitingly simple that we cannot help regretting being obliged to confess that it is quite untrue. We need not wonder at the general adoption of an hypothesis which clears away so many difficulties and justifies so many arguments, and we have good reason to fear lest this hypothesis may be still further accepted by those who do not care to take the trouble of being accurate. Therefore it is necessary plainly to declare that this idea has no warrant whatever in history, for the Church of England and the State of England are not now, and have never been, two separate institutions. There has never been a time when such a contract as is supposed could possibly have been made, or even thought of.

This mistake has arisen from confused notions of the meanings of the terms Church and State. We can readily understand the fertility of confusion produced by bringing together two terms, each of which possesses such a variety of meanings none of which are very definite. It is unnecessary to repeat all the meanings attached to the word "Church;" but there are two connected with our subject which should be kept carefully distinct. The word "Church" may mean either of these two things.

1. A spiritual brotherhood of those who hold the same faith. In this sense men belonging to any variety of outward communities may belong to the same Church. The only requisite is that the common faith shall be sufficiently strong and important. The Early Christian Church was at first something of this kind.

2. An outward organisation for religious purposes.

Now these two are not necessarily either opposed to, or identical with, each other, for it does not follow that those who hold one faith should therefore form themselves into one organisation, whilst numbers belonging to very different organisations may yet constitute one spiritual Church. Thus in one sense we speak of the Church of Christ, and in the other of the Roman Church, the Church of England, or any other of the too numerous bodies into which Christendom is divided. It is necessary to keep this distinction clearly before us, for one of the objections to a State Church is that Christ alone should be the Head of His Church, which is quite true when the word Church is used in the first sense, but manifestly absurd when it is used in the second sense.

Outward organisations for religious purposes may be divided into two classes, Self-controlled and State-controlled. To the first belong all the so-called Free Churches, as well as the Papal Church, for a Church which elects one of its members to rule it must be considered self-controlled even though the rule be autocratic. However great may be their spiritual disagreements, as far as our purpose is concerned we can recognise no difference between the Papal Church and any of the Protestant sects which possess an organization sufficient to deserve the name of Church ; in this respect the Wesleyan Conference is only a multiplied Papacy.

A State-controlled organization may arise in one of two ways—either the organization may first have existed by itself and the State have afterwards formed an alliance with it, or the organization may have grown up from the beginning as an integral part of the State. The first is generally represented to be the case of the Church of England, but the second is the actual truth.

That this is a real distinction may be seen by comparing even the different political organizations of the State. Thus the Telegraph Department was taken over by the State after it had been developed as a private undertaking, and this will also be the case with the railways if ever they become the property of the State; whereas the War Department must always have existed, in one form or other, as an essential part of the State, for a State ceases to be a State unless it can not only fight itself but can also, as far as its subjects are concerned, have a monopoly of fighting. A War Department independent of the State is only another name for rebellion.

This distinction is not only a real one but it is also a very important one in considering the question of the connection of Church and State, for if the Church be like the Telegraph Department then Disestablishment merely means the annulling of a bargain, and the Church would continue to be the Church after it was separated from the State just as it had been the Church before it was connected with it, whereas if it is like the War Department Disestablishment means the abandonment by the State of a duty which has hitherto been always an essential part of its functions, and it means also the annihilation of the Church.

If the preceding chapters give anything like a correct

L.

account of the history of the Church of England, it is plain that that Church has never existed apart from the State, but that, in the sense of being an organization, it came into being and has been entirely developed under State control.

But it may be said that even if the Church has always hitherto been connected with the State that is no reason why it should always continue so, any more than a child when grown up should remain in the same subjection to his parents. But the comparison is not at all correct, for whilst a child possesses from the first an individuality of its own, the development of which is the chief object of its life, the Church has no more individuality now than it had at the beginning, and it would be as reasonable to talk of the child existing without its brain as of the Church continuing to be the Church after it was deprived of the controlling power of the State. This is shown by the fact that those who wish to destroy the connection of Church and State but profess to wish the Church itself to continue do not tell us how that Church is then to be governed. If we look around we find that there would absolutely be no organization at all to fall back upon, and that a new one would have to be created. But according to the sense in which we, and those also who make this profession, are using the word Church, a new organization means a new Church, as it is the organization which determines the character of a Church. For the opponents of the National Church who are Dissenters are continually declaring that they do not differ from that Church upon any great question of doctrine, and yet Independents and Wesleyans and Baptists would each vehemently claim for their own organization the right to be called a Church as distinguished from the Church of England. They thus acknowledge that it is the organization which determines the character of a Church, and that a new organization means a new Church, and yet they can talk about the Church of England continuing the same Church after its organization has been destroyed. Every organization deserving the name of a Church must have a supreme authority lodged somewhere, whether it be in the State, or in a single person, or in the separate congregation, or in some assembly either clerical or mixed, and the character of that organization depends upon where this authority is lodged; all other arrangements are incidentals which can be altered in any way whilst the Church remains the same. This supreme authority for the Church of England has always been lodged in the State, and it is the Church it is merely on account of that fact. Convocation may be destroyed, as it has frequently been suspended; Bishops may be abolished, and the whole machinery of Church discipline may be changed, but as long as this organization remains under State control it will continue to be the Church of England, and it will cease to be that Church as soon as it is removed from that control, in fact the organization itself will cease to exist.

This is the reason why the separation of Church and State can only be made by the will of the State, and those who speak of the Church as a distinct body would be troubled to describe what that body is. That it is not the clergy is shown by the fact that even if all of them simultaneously refused to submit to the State's conditions, as we have seen that large numbers have sometimes done, the State, if it so decided, would only have to put fresh ones in their places, and the Church of England would continue even though the whole *personnel* of its officers had been changed. The separation of Church and State can only be brought about by the State determining to give up having anything to do with religion. Of course it can do this, just as it can determine to have nothing more to do with war, though whether it could long exist itself after such a decision is as doubtful in the one case as in the other. The staff of the War Office might hold together after such a change and take up some kindred business, as purveying or ordnance making, but it would be as reasonable to continue to apply the term "War Office" to such a private undertaking as it is to talk of the Church remaining the Church after the control of the State has been taken away.

It sounds very well, and has the additional advantage of assuming the whole matter in dispute, to describe the control of the State as a fetter from which the Church should be relieved, but it would be much more correct to speak of it as the wisp which binds up a sheaf of corn. Cut that wisp, and although the stalks which composed that sheaf would be there the sheaf itself would be gone.

It does not follow that every National Church must necessarily have always been an integral part of the State. On the contrary there are several State Churches now existing in different countries to which that language may correctly be applied which is used so erroneously respecting the Church of England, for these Churches existed as private societies before they formed an alliance with the State. This distinction is of great importance both to the Church and State, for such an origin implies a Church which has grown up with a sectarian organization and a State which has grown up without a religious organization.

We see the effects of this difference when we compare such countries with our own, for we may, without arrogance, affirm that the State of England is pre-eminent for its sympathetic earnestness, and the Church of England for its identification with social and national life. We are all of us very much disposed to overestimate ourselves, but there is good reason for believing that Englishmen, even allowing for all their renowned boastfulness, do not on the whole properly appreciate their highest national blessings. They talk a good deal about little superiorities, but they are too apt to ignore great ones; they are fully alive to their industrial advantages, but they do not seem to understand how much they have to be thankful for in the character of their State and the temper of their Church.

There is something to make us thoughtful, as well as cheerful, in the reflection, forced upon us by a review even of the last fifty years, that nearly all our great political struggles have turned, not upon some selfish object but upon some principle of kindly justice, and no measure which is not based upon such a principle can yet hope to gain for itself in England popular enthusiasm. How different, too, would be the feelings towards the Church of England, even of those who are now attacking it, were the Church, as it is in other countries, an isolated society submitting unwillingly to State control, instead of being, as it is in our own, mixed up with nearly all the State's operations and nearly all the people's pursuits! It is well to know our shortcomings but it is also well to appreciate our advantages, not that we may boast about them but that we may learn their causes and be faithful to their requirements. If Englishmen understood how much they owe to that union of religion with politics which has all along so distinguished their history they would not lightly think of destroying that connection of Church and State which has been, and is, its principal cause.

We may then define a State Church as a Church under the control of the State, and we may describe the Church of England, which is a State Church, as that part of the organization of the State whose duty it is to offer the appliances of religion to all without forcing them upon any.

Many people, and especially those most impressed with religion—for enthusiasts are rarely discriminating—are disposed vehemently to cry out against such a definition on the ground that it is degrading the Church to describe it as merely a department of the State. And the charge would be perfectly just if this was put forward as a complete definition of the term Church. As previously explained, this inquiry has nothing to do with the spiritual meaning of the word Church and is only concerned with its organic. The distinction between these two meanings is like that between the soul and the body of a man. When we speak of a man we may refer either to his corporeal frame and the outward circumstances connected with it, or to his inner self, and these two subjects require separate treatment. Undoubtedly the spiritual aspect of the Church is its highest, but that is no reason why we should disregard the lower but still exceedingly important one. Indeed the words high and low are incorrect in such a connection, for that which, judged by our own vague internal standard, seems lower is, so far as importance is concerned, as high as that to which it is essential. And so far as we need consider this world, and here we do not profess to go further, the organic Church is as essential to the spiritual as the body of a man is essential to his soul. To complain, as a degradation, of the Church being here considered only in its organic sense is as unreasonable as it would be to complain that the science of medicine lowers the dignity of man because it does not profess to cure the soul as well as the body.

This comparison of the two meanings of the word Church to the two parts of man suggests an answer to the objection that by considering the Church as a department of the State we lower the position of the clergy and take away their guiding influence, so that they merely become servants, like office clerks, bound to do and believe what they are told. There is, in a sense, some truth in this, for in this world everything is so connected with everything else that they all act and react upon each other, but there is no more truth in this objection than there would be in asserting that the soul is the servant of the body. Of course the soul is largely dependent upon the body, for through the body the soul must receive its information and carry out its will, and it is itself affected by the body's passions and imperfections, but still no one doubts that the soul is the most important part of man, nor does any one assert that the soul ought to try to separate itself from the body. Just as in man the two parts combine to form one creature so the two parts of the Church should combine to form one religious organization. The old motto is as true of religious as of physical health ; we must not merely have the healthy mind by itself, nor the healthy body; we must not merely have a true spiritual Church by itself, nor an able organization, but the two must be joined together; *mens sana* IN *sano corpore.*

And this is one reason why Disestablishment would not, as is asserted, raise the character of the clergy but would lower it, for now, whilst free from the details of its management, they know that the action of the Church must follow their influence. By being required to look after an organization as well as to teach a faith, the clergy would be corporealised instead of spiritualised.

Another objection to this definition is that whilst it lowers the position of the Church, it unduly raises that of the State. We are asked what right the State has to regulate what the clergy shall do and to dictate what the people shall believe. Such notions arise from the confused and demoralised idea of the State which now prevails. People will persist in talking as if the State and the Church are each something distinct from the nation as well as from each other, whereas in reality they are only two different aspects of the same object ; the State means the nation as a political organization, and the Church means the nation as a religious organization. Even if there is no system of representation the State must still be considered as the nation because the people acquiesce in it. And there can be no more tyranny in the nation carrying out its opinions in religious than in social or political matters, provided it does so as named in the definition, "without forcing them on others," for as religion is not essential to the State's material continuance we are not justified in inculcating it by force. Religion bears pretty much the same relation to the duties of a State as education does to those of a private individual; for although we know that the cultivation of the mind is more important than that of the body, still we are compelled to find food for the body whilst we are allowed to please ourselves about the mind. The powers of thought and imagination, the high moral faculties, and the delicate perceptions of the senses are given to us all, in much the same degree, at first, but we are left free either to cultivate or neglect these; both the poet and the miser must have a dinner, and may both walk through the same field, but whilst the mind of the one is listening to the sweet teachings of Nature, that of the other may be thinking of nothing but savings and gains. Providence lays out before us two tables and bids us all help ourselves from both; of one, containing bodily food, we must partake if we mean to continue, but we can leave the other alone if we like. So the State, whilst it is bound to provide political necessities, should also offer religious opportunities, but must not force them upon any one.

In this way every condition of real freedom is fulfilled, for the State does not dictate to the people, but the nation carries out its own opinions.

If it is a reflection upon the independence of the clergy to consider them, in this sense, as servants of the State, then we must at once plead guilty to the charge, for in no other way can we hold any consistent theory of the nature of a National Church. The nation resolves to have an organization for religious purposes, as it has one for military purposes, and it lays down the conditions in each case which those who enter its service must obey. Before entering the Church, and before taking any position in it, a clergyman knows, or should know, the conditions to which he will have to submit as well as the advantages he will receive, and it is for him to consider whether he is prepared to enter into the contract. If the State alters those conditions, or if he alters his own opinions, it is for him again to consider whether he can still abide by the contract, and if he finds he cannot it is then his duty to withdraw from it. Of course the nation has the right to alter its conditions, and the clergyman, when he enters its service, knows that this is a right which the State retains over all its departments; if those conditions are altered unjustly, then the clergyman may justly complain, but he has no right to accept the advantages of being in the service of the State and then to refuse to abide by the conditions of that service. The objection that a clergyman is the servant of his Master Christ alone, and cannot therefore be the servant of the State, also arises from confusing the two separate ideas of a Church. Every Christian clergyman is understood to be, as a matter of course, a servant, in the spiritual sense, of the great Spiritual Master, but this is not a quality confined to the clergy for precisely the same may be said of every Christian man. In a Christian nation the conditions of religiously serving the State are supposed to be in harmony with the requirements of spiritually serving Christ. If any clergyman finds that to him they are not so, then two courses are open to him; either he can try, by convincing the nation, to get those conditions altered, or he must, if he is honest, abandon the service of the State, for every man is bound first to obey his own conscience, and has no right to remain in a position whose duties are inconsistent with his convictions. But in religion, as in everything else, if a man continues to occupy a position he is bound to perform its duties. There is no difference in this respect between clergymen and other people, and we must emphatically reject any claim of the clergy to be judged in this matter by a separate set of principles. Whatever may be the difference so far as spiritual obedience is concerned, there is no doubt that the clergy, considered as servants of the State, ought to be judged by precisely the same rules as are applied to all other servants of the State. If this is making the State a tyrant, then the idea of tyranny is inseparable from the idea of a State, for it is impossible to conceive of any State worth the name which does not manage its affairs on this principle.

As to the inquiry whether there can be several State Churches under one State, it must be said that there can, for a State which is resolved to supply the opportunities of religion for its subjects, and yet finds those subjects so differing amongst themselves that no single organization can be framed which would do this, is obliged either to only partially carry out its purpose, or else to provide several organizations. Of course every State must prefer to have only one organization if it can, for then the whole matter is greatly simplified, but if it cannot, it must make the best of its unfortunate circumstances. This strong desire to have only one such organization led, in past times, to many oppressive attempts at coercion, but now that this practice is happily abandoned the State is compelled either to convince the minorities, or to ignore them, or to meet their wishes. We see how this has been the case in our own country, for since both Scotland and Ireland would not accept the same organization as the rest of the nation, the State provided a separate one for Scotland supposed to meet the wishes of the people, whilst in Ireland the State has recently abandoned altogether the problem of providing any religious organization at all. Although there may be several State Churches under one State, and thus the national principle of religion be carried out, none of such Churches can be called the National Church, for that term cannot be used except the State provides only one organization, as a National Church must be one which offers to minister to the whole nation. Not that every individual of that nation need take advantage of it, but only that it must be managed by the nation in the same way and with the same unity that it manages every other national institution. Thus if we consider the whole people of the British Islands as one nation, although both the Churches under the control of the State are State Churches, neither of them can strictly be called National, but we are so accustomed to consider as distinct the different peoples composing the British nation that it is not incorrect to speak of the National Church of England.

There is one very common impression about the nature of a State Church which is manifestly incorrect if what has been already said is true. Most people have an idea that property is in some way or other essentially connected with a State Church. An Established Church has recently been defined as "the Church established in legal possession of the ancient ecclesiastical endowments of the country." (First Peek Prize Essay, cap. 1, sect. iii.) According to this, if there were no endowments, or something equivalent to them, there could be no State Church, and that Church which retained possession of these endowments would continue to be the State Church even though it was removed from all connection with the State. By this theory the Protestant Episcopal Church in Ireland has not been disestablished inasmuch as it has retained most of the property which it held as a State Church, and supposing the Church of England were to be separated from the State it would still remain the State Church or Established Church, for the words have the same meaning, unless it was deprived of the ancient ecclesiastical endowments of the country. Thus it is tautology to speak of the Disestablishment and Disendowment of the Church for we cannot disestablish unless we disendow, and a Church which was deprived of the ancient ecclesiastical endowments would cease to be the State Church even though it continued in precisely the same relationship to the State. If this theory be correct we are met at the outset by a very delicate difficulty, for before we can know what language to use about a Church we are compelled to ask what proportion of the ancient ecclesiastical endowments entitles a Church still to be called "Established." Churches, like other institutions, are liable to many vicissitudes as to property, for they cannot claim exemption from the dangers of exacting tyrants or rapacious mobs. Their fortunes ebb and flow according to the sentiments and circumstances of the nation to which they belong; when a nation is enthusiastic and obedient, and also possesses means, the Church is made richer, and when that nation becomes sceptical and angry, and is also needy, the Church is made poorer. History is full of instances and we need not go out of our own country to find them. We may take, for example, the reign of Henry VIII. There is no doubt that under that monarch the Church of England was permanently deprived of a large part of the ancient ecclesiastical endowments of the country. Yet surely it would be absurd to say that the Church was made less a State Church when, at the very time, it was, by the Reformation, being brought more completely under the control of the State.

If this theory is correct, either there must be some proportion of the ancient ecclesiastical endowments the retention of which entitles a Church to be called "Established," or else no Church can be disestablished unless it is deprived of all such endowments. If the first be true, then it would be well to know what that proportion is, for perhaps since the Church of England has already been deprived of so much, we need only take from it a little more to make it cease to be a State Church. Thus the question of Disestablishment, about whose importance we hear so much, would become reduced to a paltry matter of financial detail, and could be settled by accountants. But if the second be true, and the Church, to be disestablished, must be deprived of all the ancient ecclesiastical endowments, then there is no need to discuss this question at all, for it is certain that such a method of disestablishment will never, in any time worth considering, have any chance amongst an honest people but will always be scouted as oppressive spoliation.

It may be said, however, that although the ancient ecclesiastical endowments may be diminished, still that Church which retains possession of them, such as they are, is the Established Church. But it is easy to conceive how, as was done to the Catholic Church in Ireland, a portion of these endowments may be taken from one Church and given to another Church, instead of to private individuals, but it would surely not then be said that both these Churches were Established, although in different degrees.

In opposition to this theory that a State Church is that which is established in possession of the ancient ecclesiastical endowments of the country it is here maintained that the idea of property has nothing whatever to do with the essential idea of a State Church. A State Church means simply a Church under the control of the State.

Since the only two motives for obedience are rewards and punishments, and the State is not allowed in this matter to use punishments, it can only obtain obedience by rewards. Thus it is found, as a matter of fact, that the clergy will not submit to the State's control unless they receive some advantages in return, and of such advantages money is the principal. But this is merely an accidental circumstance connected with State Churches, and has nothing to do with the essential principles of their existence; it arises from the imperfections of human nature, for it is easy to conceive how a religious organization might be so convinced of the advantages of State control as to be willing to accept it without receiving anything in return. On the other hand the State might, as has indeed happened, be so convinced of the danger of leaving a Church to itself, that it would insist upon assuming control over that Church without feeling called upon to give any inducement to obedience as an equivalent. It is obedience to the State which is the essential principle of a State Church, and in defining such a Church we have nothing to do with the means by which that obedience is obtained. It may be by preference, or compulsion, or property, but it is not our business to inquire into motives; we have only to ask whether or not the Church is under the control of the State.

Thus that instinct is sound which leads the popular mind to consider as distinct the questions of Disestablishment and of Disendowment, for a State Church can be disestablished without being disendowed, and disendowed without being disestablished. There is just now a tendency to consider State control as an evil, but if it were decided to separate the Church from the State there is no doubt that the Church would be left in possession of much of its property, for the nation would not allow this to be turned away from the service of religion. But it is quite easy to conceive that the time may come when a contrary disposition may be felt; when the nation may wish to retain its control over the Church but may think fit to deprive that Church of much of its property, either to meet its own necessities or to weaken a too-powerful rival. At the time of the Reformation the current ran in favour of Disendowment, but not at all of Disestablishment, whilst now there is a tendency to Disestablishment but not to Disendowment. These two questions are necessarily so connected that they must suggest each other, and be in some degree treated together, but they are in themselves essentially distinct.

Having thus laid down that State control is the essence of a State Church whilst property is only one of its accidents, an invariable one, it may be, but still only an accident, it may next be asked what is the nature of this State control? Does it mean that the State takes the whole direction of the Church and manages it as it does any State office? Not necessarily so, but only that the State has the supreme power, and is the ultimate authority to appeal to. Like an old-established and well-arranged business, the organization of the Church works generally without the interference of the master, but owes most of its smooth working to the fact that there is a master who both can and will take the direction if necessary.

To exercise authority without showing it is one of the highest feats of all government, and this is the character of the present relationship between the State and the Church in England, for whilst so many people are disposed to ridicule the reality of the State control everyone who wishes for a change finds out that he has to appeal to Parliament alone, and that the nation governs the Church by the same means as it uses for exercising all its other State authority.

Having thus tried to explain what is the National Church of England, and what has been the character of its growth, we have next to consider the objections which are now being so persistently urged against its continued existence.

It is necessary, in the first place, clearly to understand that these objections are of two totally distinct kinds, namely, objections to the principle of a National Church, and objections to specific details in the National Church of England. Now this distinction is very rarely observed, and apparently almost as rarely perceived, by most of those who are now so vehemently attacking the Church, for we constantly find these people inferring, when they have pointed out some flaw in its system or some failure in its discipline, some individual or collective scandal, some special instance of the law being defied, or oppressive, or ineffective, that therefore they have made out a good argument in favour of the destruction of the Church, whereas they have really only made out one in favour of its reform. And it cannot be too plainly laid down, that in this, as in everything else of the sort, destruction and reform are two totally opposite processes, for we only take the trouble of reforming that which we wish to preserve. A man who has a machine which he cannot replace, and of the principle of which he approves, does not order it to be broken to pieces because it is not working quite to his mind, but sets about to discover the causes of its imperfection and to rectify them. So with the Church, we have first to ask ourselves whether or not the national principle is sound and worth preserving ; we may afterwards go on to consider whether that principle is properly carried out in England, and if it is not, what should be done to make it so?

It is the principle of the National Church which needs now chiefly to be insisted upon for this is the centre of attack, and it is about this that the people generally are so ignorant and so uncertain. We are told that the National Church of England is now upon its trial, and those who defend an institution which has existed continuously for more than a thousand years, blending inextricably with the whole history of the nation, and which, if once put away, cannot again be revived, have a right to insist upon two conditions ; firstly that the institution shall be tried not upon its accidental imperfections but upon its essential character ; and secondly, that the burden of proof shall lie upon those who wish to destroy it. For according to the doctrine, now so much in favour, that experience is the source of knowledge, we are justified in believing that the longer an institution has existed the stronger is its right to continue, for the more it has been tested the greater is the probability that that which has approved itself to the judgment of so many generations will also be good for us. In order to favour such an institution it is not necessary for us always to understand its merits ; its age is a sufficient argument for its continuance in the absence of stronger arguments against it. Life is so short and so occupied, and our faculties are so weak, that it is impossible for us to understand the reasons for everything we accept, and even if it were possible it would be very foolish to try, for then either we should accept next to nothing or else we should have to content ourselves with very partial reasons. Good old customs are very much better guides than poor new reasons, and we shall generally be much more likely to go wrong if we submit ourselves to the tentative arguments of our own generation than if we follow the test of Time, which is only the purified reasoning of many generations.

Not that we should follow custom in opposition to reason but only in the absence of it ; not that we should stick to an old institution when it is proved to be a bad one but that we should not destroy one unless it is so proved. Therefore in considering the Church of England it is not for its friends to explain its character and prove that it ought to continue, but it is for its enemies to show why it ought to be destroyed. If they fail to do this, however thoroughly we might defend it on other grounds, it is sufficient for us to say that because the Church is now, and has been so long, therefore it should remain.

Accordingly we will not here attempt to elucidate more fully the principle of the National Church and to prove its excellence, but we will try to answer the objections which are now being made against it. Nor will we allow our attention to be distracted by those objections which merely refer to incidental imperfections, feeling sure that when once the English people understand how weak are the arguments against that principle they will soon clear away these imperfections. No doubt the national principle of religion, like every other great principle, is a very difficult one to carry out properly, but difficulty has never been a terrifying word in the English Dictionary, and he who supposes that on its account his countrymen will abandon a principle which they believe to be good is a traitor to the national fame and a friend to cowardice and indolence.

CHAPTER V.

RELIGIOUS OBJECTIONS.

THE objections which have been, and are now, urged against the continued existence of the National Church are so numerous that it is necessary to adopt some sort of division in order to understand them clearly. But these objections are so complicated and so mixed up with each other that it is impossible to find any method of classification which can separate them with anything like scientific accuracy, and it is also impossible to treat the several objections when so separated with sufficient fulness without being obliged to go frequently over the same ground. It seems that for our special purpose no better division can be adopted than that into religious, social, and political, which has the great recommendation of being familiar, but has also the great drawback of fostering that most mischievous, and now very prevalent, idea that human affairs are, or can be, as a matter of fact, really so divided. The principle of the division of labour, which has been so largely and successfully applied to trade in modern times, is now being more widely extended to other departments of human life, and probably, as far as labour is concerned, this is necessary, but if it comes to be carried out too far in thought also, nothing but disaster can be the result. The field of human life is now so extended that no man can work in all parts of it if his work is to be good for anything, therefore each has to choose his own plot and stick to that, but he must remember that this plot is joined to others, and is still only a part of one great field, and that he himself will not be able properly to do his own duty, with due regard to the whole result, unless he knows something of what is being done in the other parts. Some men must chiefly devote themselves to religious, some to political, and some to social matters, but no man will be really great in any of these who does not know something of the rest, or who forgets that all these are intimately and inextricably connected with each other. Politics which have nothing to do with religion become degraded; religion which has nothing to do with politics becomes unreal; and social life when not connected both with religion and with politics soon sinks into meanness and demoralization. It is the mistaken idea that religion and politics are, or ought to be, or can be, separated from each other which lies at the root of many of the objections to the National Church; therefore in speaking of these objections as religious, social, or political, we would have it most clearly understood that this division is for the most part arbitrary, and is here assumed merely for the sake of temporary convenience. Also in those objections which separately taken do not seem to be sufficiently treated or answered, it is only fair to claim that reference shall be made to the general principles which underlie the whole treatment, and also to the answers given in other cases of a similar sort. It must also be premised that the National Church of England is not here held to be a perfect institution, or anything near that, for perfection is a goal very far short of which humanity must be content to stop even at its best. It is not necessary to show that the Church has no faults in order to prove that it ought to continue, but it is sufficient to require its enemies to suggest something better. Therefore, to begin with, it is acknowledged that many of the objections urged against the Church are true, and that many others have much more to be said in their favour than there is space here to explain. It is not pretended that the objections named are completely treated but only that something is said on one side to be weighed against what is so often said on the other.

All the objections, both religious, social, and political, are, in the first place, either essential, relating to the principle of the National Church, or accidental, relating to its practice. The first are of course by far the most important, for if they are true the whole cause must be given up, whereas the truth of the second only implies the existence of some faults which ought to be remedied. We may rest assured that if the people are only properly convinced of the soundness and value of the national principle, there will be no difficulty in getting them to rectify, as far as possible, whatever defects there may be in the carrying out of that principle.

Turning to the religious objections we find that these may be divided into those which specially refer to the Bible and those which do not, and which may therefore for convenience be called general. These will be considered separately.

Biblical.

It must first be understood that no attempt is made in these pages to discuss the religion to be taught by the National Church. That is a totally distinct question to be handled by the theologians and settled by the people's convictions. We start with the assumption that the people have a religion, and we have only to consider whether or not that religion should have a National Church. Most of the arguments here advanced in favour of the national principle would be equally good even though the religion to be so professed were Mohammedanism or any other system of belief. But since objections have to be considered which refer merely to the Church of England it is necessary to assume that Christianity is the truest form of religion, and would continue to be accepted by the people whether or not there was a National Church. Therefore we have nothing to do with the objections of those who do not believe in the Christian religion, as generally accepted, or do not care for it. It is easy to understand why such men should be opposed to a National Church, but this is not the place to consider their objections; here we are only concerned with those who hold, in the main, the same religion as the Church of England, but object to a national profession of that religion. Therefore we assume that the Bible is not an ordinary book, but possesses that special authority accorded to it by those who hold the religion it teaches.

Still it is necessary to understand how far this authority is to extend, for the greatest differences of opinion on this point prevail amongst Christians themselves. The Bible is the most unfortunate of all books; it is well able to defend itself against its enemies, but it has the strongest reasons to wish to be saved from its friends, for it suffers most from those indiscriminating enthusiasts who do not distinguish between the accidental details of its separate parts and the essential spirit of the whole. Let the Bible, like any other book, be taken altogether, and there are few men capable of understanding religious truth and of feeling religious impressions who will not acknowledge to themselves, even if they do not confess to others, the force of its matchless beauty and the authority of its unique inspiration. But those who would readily yield to its claims if asked to look at it like men, will be the first to turn up their faces and search for some flaw if commanded to fall down before it as an idol to be worshipped with averted eyes. We hear much of the antagonism of science and philosophy, but those who have proper faith in the grand purpose of the Bible should welcome every increase of real knowledge, feeling confident that no science which is true can help adding to the lustre of that Book whose special mission is to declare the glory and love of God, and no philosophy which is sound can help strengthening the influence of that Book which alone satisfies the deepest needs of the mind. It does not help to win others over to believe in the impregnability of a citadel when they see its defenders panic-stricken with terror if only some disconnected stone is disturbed or a breach is made in some extraneous wall.

As these are the two ways in which the Bible is generally regarded, namely, either as a whole or in single passages, it seems advisable to consider in these aspects its bearing upon the question of the Union of Church and State, although it must be understood that little value is set upon the test by isolated texts. No one thinks of judging any ordinary author from detached sentences, and it is equally unfair to apply this method to that Book which specially expresses the Divine Mind. The Bible is like a great and varied building whose character can only be learned by looking at it altogether and from every side, but its effect is quite destroyed by those who pull away its separate stones in order to fling them as weapons at each other.

In the first place we would have it understood that we do not think that the Bible teaches anything definite either for or against the principle of a National Church, and greatly as we value that principle, we should feel that the dignity of the Bible was lowered if it did. For the main object of the Bible is to reveal the cardinal truths of religion, and the value of that revelation would have been limited, and the chances of its universal adoption would have been lessened, had definite regulations been given of how it was to be carried out in each country. Christ was content to call into being the living spirit of religion, knowing that this would in each country find its own most appropriate body. The Bible was written not merely for the Church of England but for the whole of Christendom, which is ultimately to be the whole earth. Therefore, were our object to prove positively that the national principle ought to be adopted we should not bring forward the Bible at all, partly because there is ample proof without it, and partly because the temper of our age is such that arguments of this kind have little weight. But as long as the Bible is put into the witness-box by the enemies of the Church, the defenders are compelled to ask what evidence it has to give. Mr. Miall (*Standard Essays on State Churches*, No. xi. p. 3) says:—" Our main objections to every kind of " alliance between the Church and the State spring out of our " views of man in his religious capacity. Our strongest argu- " ments are derived directly from the Bible." We must then consider what these arguments are and what they are worth, and in doing so we will first take those derived by general inference from the Bible and afterwards those consisting of definite quotations.

Any impartial reader can scarcely avoid confessing that the general drift of the Old Testament is decidedly in favour of the national principle; so much so, indeed, that the whole ecclesiastical polity of the Book is based upon it. Consequently there are not many specific declarations which can be quoted, for people do not think of talking much about anything which is accepted as a matter of course, any more than writers on statistics think it necessary to talk about the multiplication-table. Considered as a mere book the Old Testament is little more than a history of the Jews, together with a collection of their literature, therefore the real question is to get at what was the practice of the Jews in this respect. Of this there can be no doubt, for from the earliest times the Jews had no idea but that the Church and the State were, and ought to be, merely the same thing looked at in different ways, merely the names for two sorts of functions performed by one body. In the patriarchal days the head of each tribe was at the same time its lawgiver and its high priest, and in the divine instructions by which these were ordered to regulate their conduct, what may be called State rules were so mixed up with religious commands that it is quite impossible to separate the two. From the time of the captivity in Egypt the identity of Church and State is more decidedly authenticated.

Moses was pre-eminently a statesman, but he had complete control over the religious as well as over the political affairs of his people, for although Aaron was made head of the priestly order, we feel that he was merely an instrument in the hands of his brother; indeed we are surprised, considering his high position, to find how small was his initiatory influence. The position of the Church under Moses was almost exactly like that now advocated for it under the national ideal, only less dignified, for then the religious inspiration, as well as control, came from the State, whereas now this inspiration is looked for from the Church. Then, as now in England, the Church was an organization under State control to minister to the religious wants of the nation, and this was the ideal always standing before the Jews. Their times of greatest prosperity and highest divine favour were those in which they carried out this ideal most closely; their greatest rulers were those who most concentrated in themselves political and religious authority. The Almighty, in his communications to the Children of Israel, did not recognise any distinction between the religious and the political; He did not countenance any division between the Church and the State, but those to whom He committed the greatest political trusts were also those through whom He communicated the highest religious inspirations. In their literature there was no separation of religion from politics; not only the historical books, but also those of the greatest of the prophets, have politics for their subject-matter, and the books in the Old Testament which are the least political are those which were composed for the services of religion by the most active rulers of the State. The Jews had, from the earliest times, a distinct organization for religious purposes, governed by most precise rules, but there was no such thing as what is now meant by a Church, that is, a separate body having control over religion. The Jews had throughout their history but one centre of power, and that was the State, though we might, of course, considering its religious side, call it the Church, but then there could be no State. Whatever was its name, this one authority was supreme alike over politics and religion; the times of the Jews' greatest prosperity were those in which this dentity was most complete, and in their adversity they were punished for their unfaithfulness to religion by the loss of their political position. They had no idea of religious revival apart from political restoration; they would not have believed in any return to divine favour which had not included return to political greatness. Perhaps they were wrong in this, but it is certain that this feeling was not confined to the ignorant masses but was held most strongly by those who are believed to have been most fully endowed with divine inspiration. If the combination of religion and politics, the union of Church and State, be a mistake, then the greatest ideal of the Jews was a delusion and the Old Testament, considered as a book, is based upon a blunder.

It is objected that the Jewish Theocracy is no type for us, for we ought not to guide our conduct by that of a people who lived in such different times, and were subject to such different influences. One is inclined to think that people have very exaggerated ideas about the differences between nations of different times, and between those of the same time in different places. Although time changes all things, it operates very slowly, and most slowly of all upon the character of man; for if we go down to the moving depths of his being and consider his essential wants and characteristics, we are forced to confess that, as far as these are concerned, it is indeed true that a thousand years are but as yesterday, and as a watch in the night. Looking closely, and pulling away the superficial differences which so often deceive us, it is hard to see how we of this age and country differ much from the ancient Jews in the true essentials of civilization; in fact there is reason to suspect that perhaps the advantage is on their side. However, it is not for the supporters of the

Church, who do not bring forward the Bible, to follow up this consideration, but its opponents, who do appeal to that Book, are called upon to explain what are the reasons which make unfit and untrue for us a union of religion with politics which was carried out so successfully by one of the most civilized nations of history, and the soundness of which was always one of their strongest and most cherished beliefs. It is for those who bring the Bible into court to get over the difficulty of its evidence being apparently so much against their case.

It is said that the Jews were so specially under Divine care that they must not be judged by the regular canons of history, nor be put forward as an example for ordinary nations. Granting this, still it cannot be said that the Jews were under more special Divine influence than was the early Christian Church, called into being by the Presence itself, and endowed for so long with miraculous gifts. Yet those who refuse to accept the Jewish type are the foremost to order us rigidly to follow the Primitive Church. It may be said that until this time the Jewish type was right, but that the Primitive Church was meant to displace it. Had this been one of the missions of that Church, it would have given some definite teaching on the subject, but there is nothing to show that it wished to set up another ideal in place of that of the union of politics and religion.

There is room for reflection in the fact that a government in which the State and the Church were thoroughly united is the only government which Christians believe to have been developed under the direct superintendence of God, and to have received His special love and care. It is plain that, whatever may be thought of its advisability for us, a union so sanctioned cannot be wicked in principle, as we are so often told, for such principles remain always the same.

It seems that we may go back to the Jews, not merely to learn a true idea of the duties of the State but also a broad and charitable conception of what should be meant by a

Church. Notwithstanding all their faithlessness and sin, the Children of Israel were still called a holy people on the strength of their corporate relationship with the Almighty, and so, on the strength of common obligations to one faith, the people of one nation should be considered to belong to one Christian Church. The word Church should be used very mercifully, so that the chances of its influence may be as wide as possible, especially if it is a Church claiming the name of that religion whose tender compassion is limitless.

States of civilization are the results of so many and such complicated causes, and depend so largely upon character, that the one developed by each distinct nation must necessarily possess certain peculiarities distinguishing it from all others. Thus it is only in a limited sense, and with regard only to fundamental features, that we can compare the civilization of any one nation with that of any other. Still, as the forms of human beings, although differing so greatly from each other, are all supported upon bony structures which have many characteristics in common, so if we look beneath the outward differences we shall find numerous resemblances which connect certain civilizations with each other, and separate these from all the rest. Treating in this way the present state of civilization in England, and comparing it with all those of which history gives us any adequate knowledge, we shall find that in its leading features it most resembles, not the Roman, not the Greek, not that of any Eastern people, but the Jewish. The fundamental part of a nation's civilization is its law, and ours is derived, in its leading principles, almost entirely from that of the Jews. Take the Decalogue and fill it in with no more expansion than may fairly be given to all such essential principles and you have a foundation large enough to hold nearly the whole superstructure of English law; nay, if that foundation was only properly built upon, that law would have to be a great deal better than it is. From the Jews we derive those principles which regulate our legal relationships to each other, and from the Jews also first came those principles which govern our moral conduct. We shall realize the extent of this resemblance between the Jewish and the English, or we may call it the modern European, civilization if we consider how greatly the Jewish differed from all others. The doctrines of the rights of persons and the rights of property, which we accept as axioms and which so largely mould our condition, first sprang up as we have them amongst the Jews, and for a long time were unknown elsewhere. Considering, then, that the two main forces determining the character of a civilization are its laws and its religion, and considering also that both our laws and our religion are chiefly derived from the Jews, we may fairly assert that there must be a strong family resemblance between our civilization and that of the Jews. Now as family resemblances imply common family necessities, and as the principle of national religion was an essential part of the Jewish civilization, we may well suppose that it is also an essential part of a civilization which, like ours, is so largely modelled after the Jewish. If we choose a model, we must take it in its essential entirety; if we adopt the human skeleton and afterwards draw out the backbone our whole structure will tumble down in a heap, and so if, after building up a civilization on the form of the Jewish, we take away from it that which was one of the determining principles of the Jewish, we may look for surprising disasters. In the constitutions of nations, as in those of individuals, we cannot with impunity violate the laws of common necessities.

But it will be said, probably with indignation, that we have no right now to follow the Jewish model because the Christian model was meant to displace it, and that the abandonment of the national ideal was meant to be one of the consequences of that displacement. To this it may be replied that Christianity never claimed to be any displacement at all, but, on the contrary, a development; the Master did not come to destroy the Law and the Prophets, but to fulfil them; His two new commandments were not put forward to be instead of the Decalogue, but to be added to it; indeed one of them was but the repetition of the first old commandment and the other was but the enlarged spirit of the rest. Christianity was not meant to destroy the old body but to breathe a new spirit into it. This reanimation did not, however, alter its formal conditions, and since we have adopted that body we may still consider ourselves subject to those conditions.

But although the old tree was not pulled up but made to throw out fresh boughs and grow vastly in size and alter vastly in shape, although Christianity was not a revolution but a reform, not a displacement but a development, it is possible that the destruction of the national ideal was meant to be a consequence of that development. To convince us that this destruction was so meant we are pointed to the practice of the Early Christian Church, and to the sayings of its Founder and of its first supporters. And first as to the practice, the principal facts brought forward respecting the Primitive Church are—

1. *That it was not Established, that is, connected with the State.*

Recalling the two meanings of the word "Church," the spiritual and the organic, it must be remarked that although spiritually the Christian Church was governed by its own marvellous and unique forces, organically it always professed to follow the ordinary laws; its Master, although of course endowed with such supernatural gifts, refused to use them extensively, and left the propagation of His faith to be carried on by ordinary human agencies; He did not create a new means of development, nor have we any reason to suppose that He wished for a new form. Christ is identified with the spiritual Church, and Establishment concerns merely the organic, but if we may, without presumption, venture to draw an inference on this matter from His conduct, we should say that it was decidedly in favour of the national ideal. For He knew that this ideal was one of the strongest convictions and intensest yearnings of those to whom He spoke, and that by claiming to be the Messiah He identified Himself in the most complete and marked manner with this ideal, yet He said nothing plainly to discourage it. The idea of the Messiah universal amongst the Jews was that He would be both their priest and king, that He would both raise their Church and restore the State, that He would be supreme both in religion and in politics. It is true that when Christ claimed for Himself this position, He told the Jews that the ideal they had formed of their Messiah was wrong in many particulars; but He also pointed out what those particulars were, and therefore we may fairly assume that He did not disapprove of those leading particulars which He did not condemn. In a principle of this sort, which was of so much importance that it gave the tone to the whole religious thought of those whom He was trying to teach, silence may fairly be supposed to imply acquiescence. He who claimed for Himself, and over whose head was inscribed in His last supreme moments the title of "King of the Jews," cannot fairly be supposed to have been averse to the union of politics with religion.

To say that if the national principle is true the Primitive Church ought to have been established by the State is to cast a serious reflection both upon that principle and upon that Church, for it implies that the principle should have been carried out in opposition to its fundamental requirements, and that the Church should have violated those laws of natural promulgation which it always professed to follow. It would be just as reasonable to expect that the fowls of the air should be able to shelter themselves under the tiny mustard-seed, for National Churches and seeds obey the same laws of growth. A National Church means a Church teaching the religion which the nation actually holds, and not that which the nation ought to hold. No matter what may be the claims of the new faith, that faith has no right to be adopted by the State unless it is also adopted by the nation; a State which so organized its Church would be violating the first requisites of the national principle, and such a Church would have no claim to be considered a National Church. It is one of the great merits of this principle that a new faith has thus to fight its way up to national acceptance before it can receive national adoption, and is thus obliged to show what it is made of. Christianity did not claim for itself then any exemption from this natural law, nor have its supporters any right to claim such an exemption now. Instead of the example of the Primitive Church being opposed to the national principle, as far as we may reasonably infer the evidence goes the other way, since this Church carried out the two leading conditions of that principle, for it did not seek union with the State until the proper time, and then it gladly accepted it.

2. *That the Primitive Church was self-supporting.*

This objection has nothing to do with the national principle, for there is no reason why National Churches should not be self-supporting. If the people properly understood and appreciated the value of this principle there would always be sufficient means forthcoming without trenching upon the resources of the State. This is not the place to discuss the origin of the revenues of the Church of England, only on the method of simply answering objections we may say that no one has proved that these revenues were ever derived, in any appreciable degree, from the State. In the absence of such proof we may claim that these revenues are, what they seem, the result, for the greatest part, of accumulated gifts of private individuals, and that in the proper sense of the words the Church of England is thoroughly self-supporting. There is no difference in this respect between the endowments of the Church of England and those of Dissenters, except that whilst both are derived from private benevolence, those of the Dissenters are under their own control, whilst those of the Church are under that of the State.

Even if it was granted, as it is not, that Churches should be self-supporting, not only would the national principle remain untouched, but also by no reasonable extension could it be asserted that Churches should be self-supporting at each particular time, that is, that in religious affairs there should be no providence. The stream of religious enthusiasm and consequent religious benevolence is like a mountain torrent, sometimes overflowing and at others almost dry, so it is wisely directed into the mill-pond of endowments out of which it comes in an even course. Without such a reservoir the wheel of religious activity would at one time be spinning madly round and at another scarcely moving at all.

Even if we confine ourselves to the Primitive Church it cannot fairly be said that that was self-supporting, for it was not supported at all in the sense in which anyone now can apply the word support to a Church. For there is no evidence that the early promulgators of the Gospel received anything worth calling regular support from those who might be supposed to constitute the Church. On the contrary, it seems most probable that, like St. Paul, the chief supports of its ministers were their own labour and their few wants. Whatever they did receive from their followers was evidently as nothing compared with what even the most modest ministers now require. To return to the model of Primitive Christianity might perhaps disestablish the Church but it would also certainly reduce Dissenting ministers to a condition from which they would soon ask to be liberated. The Primitive Church furnishes no warrant for the ministrations of religion being intrusted to any separate body of men who thus earn a living; on the contrary, if we follow its example this duty must be performed by some who are also otherwise engaged like other men. It is possible that this method, which is only followed in England by a few obscure congregations which are too poor to maintain a minister, is the right one, but that is not the opinion of most of those who are opposed to the Church. It should therefore in common fairness be remembered that imitating the Primitive Church involves other changes besides destroying the National Church.

3. *Amongst the Early Christians the pastors were supported only by believers.*

This is an objection which does not affect the Church of England, for almost all its revenues are derived from either the past or present gifts of those who would be called believers. It may be said that most of those who have endowed the Church in past times did not believe in many of the doctrines now taught by that Church, and that if the principle of a Church being supported by believers only be true, the best part of the revenues of the Church of England should be handed over to the Roman Catholics. To this it must be replied, that Roman Catholicism, as now understood, had no existence when most of these endowments were given. Whatever changes have occurred, the Church of England now agrees in doctrine quite as nearly as the present Church of Rome does with that Church which was thus endowed, and in polity it agrees much more nearly. But doctrine is not the governing principle of endowments to a National Church. He who endows such a Church is really making over so much to the State, to be used by it for religious purposes. He may hope that those purposes will include the promulgation of certain doctrines, but he must naturally expect that some changes will be made in the course of time, for no endowments can be held absolutely to forbid all change. The condition requisite is that such changes shall be made in substantially the same way as they would have been made at the time when the donor was living, that is by the State. Faith is kept so long as the endowments given to a National Church continue to be used by the State for the purposes of religion, the character of such religion to be determined by the State, and faith is broken whenever such endowments are taken for any other purpose.

Thus the Church of England substantially accords with the idea that the pastors of a Church should be supported only by the adherents of that Church, but there is good reason to believe that this idea itself is as a requirement unsound, and even mischievous. It is best at once candidly to acknowledge that there is a radical discrepancy on this point between the opponents and supporters of a National Church. Nearly all those who are opposed to such a Church seem to take it as a matter of course that it is the duty of pastors to minister chiefly, and almost exclusively, to their own flocks, by whom therefore they should be maintained in return. As this idea lies at the root of so much of their reasoning it is necessary to ask whether it appears sound, and we are bound to confess that it does not. That is a narrow and spiritless conception of the office of the Christian minister which represents him merely as the pastor of a company of believers. Is it the neglected or the well cared-for who most need ministering to? Is it the ignorant or the instructed who most need preaching to? Is it unbelievers or believers upon whom the forces of religion should most be brought to bear? Let us go back for the answer to that Master whose miraculous benevolence was exercised almost exclusively for the good of the suffering and despised, and whose great boast was that by Him the poor had the Gospel preached to them.

If the Primitive Church had followed the method now advocated by the opponents of the National Church Christianity would never have extended beyond the eastern shores of the Mediterranean, and if it is degraded now into being merely the delusive luxury of private societies its days will soon come to an end. The propagation of a religion must chiefly be carried on by its ministers, and how can they perform this their most important duty when they limit themselves chiefly to those who are already supposed to be converted?

Although in comparison with the spiritual enthusiasms and eternal purposes of a great religion it is of trifling consequence how or whence its ministers receive their material subsistence, still we may grant that they shall derive this from those to whom they minister provided only a sufficiently broad and elevated conception is formed of who these really are. If the minister of religion has any claim to that title he must be regarded as the benefactor of society at large, and that society may therefore be justly expected to support him. This it can only do by means of a National Church. Instead of its being a cause for just pride that a minister is maintained only by his intimate associates it seems much more reasonable to consider that the more support he receives from those less identified with him the greater is the testimony of his influence and the stronger is the promise of his success. Thus the abandonment of the national principle in religion would encourage a narrow and degraded idea of the ministerial office.

4. *The Early Christians discarded worldly distinctions.*

It is easy to point invidiously to the large incomes and social and political advantages possessed by the bishops and deans and other officers of the Church of England, and it is also true to say that the apostles and leaders of the Primitive Church received no such distinctions, but it is probable that the inconsistency, if there be such, lies in the supposition that such things could have been associated with the Primitive Church rather than in the fact that they are associated with the English Church. Such organic details are no part of the essential character of a religion but depend upon its outward circumstances, and must vary with these. The great ends which ought to govern such arrangements are the elevation of the character of the religion and the strengthening of its influence. In the early days of Christianity not merely were these worldly advantages impossible, but they were also unnecessary, for the power of miraculous gifts and new enthusiasm was sufficient; but as a matter of fact it has been found in later times in every country that these advantages are on the whole a benefit to religion, and Dissenters recognise the truth of this principle by giving the highest salaries to their best ministers. Bishops and others with large incomes are no essential part of a National Church; they could all be abolished and the incomes of the clergy could be reduced to the lowest point consistent with getting any persons at all to take their positions, and yet the national principle would be preserved in all its integrity, if not in all its effectiveness. It is believed that these worldly advantages have a tendency to bring better men into the service of religion—that is, men better able to strengthen its influence. If the opponents of the Church believe that this idea is wrong, the best proof of the honesty of their belief will be given by their congregations abolishing all connection between the quality of ministers and their salaries, and by the ministers themselves abandoning the habit of changing congregations chiefly on account of these worldly advantages.

But instead of acknowledging the truth of this belief we venture to assert that it is founded upon a mistake, and that wealth and influence, instead of being inconsistent with religion, are meant to be amongst its greatest helps. There can be nothing more mischievous nor more calculated to degrade the character of influence generally than the idea that wealth and power are to be considered principally as advantages and rewards. The Great Teacher does not tell us that those who become His followers must separate themselves from worldly interests and duties; He does not command us to refuse wealth and neglect power, but that we must use wealth and power, and all other worldly advantages, not as means for our own self-indulgence and pride but as instruments for the general good and for the promotion of His cause. Wealth and power are considered great helps to every other cause, why not then to religion also? Bishops receive, it is true, large incomes and possess considerable social and political power. Is it therefore right to take it for granted that the office of bishop is desired or conferred merely for the sake of these advantages? Is it not, on the contrary, much more Christian-like to consider that these advantages are meant to strengthen the bishop's power for good, and to increase his duties and responsibilities? Bishops, like every other class, are subject to human frailties, but it may safely be affirmed that the majority of the bishops of the Church of England use their advantages not chiefly for their own selfish purposes but for what they believe to be the good of religion and the benefit of the nation.

One of the greatest difficulties of Christianity consists in reconciling it with the world, meaning by the world not that spirit of selfishness to which Christianity is essentially antagonistic but the ordinary requirements and conditions of material life. The body must be clothed and fed and the regular necessities of existence must always absorb the chief attention of the largest part of mankind. No religion which does not acknowledge these claims and make itself compatible with them can ever permanently exercise a proper religious influence, nor ought it to expect to do so, for it is impossible to believe but that Providence has subjected us to these necessities in order that we may receive our best discipline by learning to reconcile our religion with them. There is undoubtedly a radical antagonism between Christ and that spirit of self-satisfaction and self-seeking which is called "the world," and this antagonism needs setting forth much more plainly than is usually done, but he who teaches that the service of Christianity ought not to be associated with the possession of what are called worldly advantages is an enemy both to the progress and character of that religion. For it must be remembered that the bulk of people can continue to exist without regarding their spiritual nature, but that none can do so without attending to their bodily. The majority will turn away from a religion which teaches that these two are inconsistent, and many even of those who accept it will soon rob it of all real worth by separating it from association with their daily lives. Indiscriminating enthusiasts have done great harm to Christianity by urging impossible claims, and the great want in these days, when material considerations have so much influence, is a religious system which will teach us how to use the things of this world without abusing them; how to compel the needs of our bodies to minister to the discipline of our souls; how to make wealth and power the means for promoting our own lasting good and the glory of God. As long as there must be wealth it is for the Church to teach men how to use it, and it cannot do this in any better way than by intrusting some of it to its principal officers. Teaching by practice is far more effective than by theory. He who says that the Church has no concern with wealth hands over to the devil the largest part of life.

5. *The Early Christians refused to meddle with such business details as are necessary in a National Church.*

This objection is usually expressed by saying that the Early Christians would not leave the Lord "to serve tables." But if we inquire what "serving tables" in this sense means, we shall find that this is more likely to be done when Churches manage themselves than when they are under the control of the State. For however sentimentally we may be disposed, and however greatly we may like to think of religion as something quite apart from business details, there is no use in shutting our eyes to the fact that there must be such details in connection with every Church, and that therefore somebody must attend to them. This is one of the drawbacks of our earthly condition which we are compelled often to realize, for whoever tries to give practical expression to any charitable enthusiasm or intellectual aspiration finds himself brought face to face with unsympathetic details and imperfect organizations; he must get up committees, treat with societies, and submit to numberless practical disappointments. It is just the same with Churches. No sooner does religion try to go beyond being an individual sentiment than it is compelled to incorporate itself with some body of organization, and from that moment it must submit to the drawbacks which necessarily belong to such bodies. Churches must be managed in one way or another; appointments need making, funds need administering, discipline needs exercising. There are only two possible means for doing this; either the State must do it for the Church or the Church must do it for itself. Leaving it to the Church always means eventually leaving it to the ministers of that Church. We cannot find a single Church in history sufficiently extensive and organized to be entitled to the name of a Church in which this has not occurred. And the same is true at the present day, as we perceive if we look at the Papal Church, the Presbyterian Church, the Wesleyan Church, or any of the numerous self-governed Churches in America. The reason is not far to seek, for we could not expect otherwise when we consider that whilst the ministers are all interested in the affairs of their Church as matters of the greatest importance, the laity generally care comparatively little about them, as they do not come within the range of their regular occupations, and the few who do take a part in them are usually those most subject to ministerial influence. Thus whether they desire it or not the business details of a self-governed Church are sure eventually to have to be managed chiefly by the ministers themselves, whereas in a

National Church the State attends to these, and leaves the ministers to perform their spiritual duties with less distracted attention. It may easily be judged which method is most in harmony with that exemption from business details so often commended in the Early Christians, or which is most conducive to the spiritual elevation of the ministers themselves.

6. *The Christian Church declined after it became connected with the State.*

At this distance of time, and with our present limited and distorted information we should have some diffidence in speaking on a matter of this sort, were not the evidence too plain to leave any reason for doubt.

The early spread of Christianity is one of the most remarkable events in the whole range of history. Neither in the religion itself nor in its circumstances was there anything to promise such a result. Here was a religion promulgated only in casual conversations which had not been thoroughly reported with no organized system and no distinct body of doctrine, which appealed to none of the ordinary motives but made the most rigid exactions without offering any definite rewards, and this religion was put forward by a despised carpenter, who was supported only by a few humble women and by a few ignorant fishermen, the most promising of whom turned coward at the first difficulty, whilst this carpenter himself, instead of trying to gain popular support, apparently went out of his way to provoke the bitterest hostility of the influential classes and persistently asserted for himself the very claims most calculated to rouse the indignant disappointment of the populace. And just when the cause appeared almost utterly defeated, the leader, who had so far been its whole life and who alone seemed capable of giving it any help, was put to death amidst the triumphant exultation of His multitudinous enemies and the brokenhearted dismay of His handful of friends. After this tragical act the curtain went down in darkness and the drama seemed ended. But quickly the light came again, and the curtain rose on a very different scene; that religion instead of being extinguished, was spreading far and wide on every side; soon it was girdling the eastern Mediterranean and taking captive the imperial city of the world.

All this is sufficiently marvellous without the exaggeration implied by saying that Christianity declined after its connection with the State. For if we look calmly at the facts we must acknowledge that although this religion had spread so rapidly, it yet possessed only a number of scattered Churches on the shores of the Mediterranean; it had not been accepted by the people of any country, nor had it won over a single great city. The first spreading of Christianity, wonderful as that was considering its apparent means, was almost as nothing compared with its extension after it became adopted by the Roman State; indeed, if we may venture to pry so far into Divine purposes, we should be inclined to believe that as the ascetic Baptist was the harbinger of Christ's spiritual Church, so the Roman Empire was its organic forerunner, for it seems as if by that Empire the various parts of the then civilized world were first politically connected in order that by Christianity they might afterwards be spiritually regenerated. The conviction is true which acknowledges Rome to be the spiritual as well as imperial mother of the Christian world, but it would be false if the new religion had suffered by her adoption. The map alone is sufficient to refute the assertion that Christianity was injured by being connected with the State, for if we turn to it we find that this religion has only retained its vitality where it has been spread under State influence, whereas it has died out in all those parts even where it was originally promulgated but where it did not form any State connection. Let the present religious condition of Palestine and Asia Minor, of the eastern islands of the Mediterranean and of its southern shores, speak on this point.

But we are told that apart from any general arguments which may be drawn from the Bible, the connection of Church and State is emphatically condemned in specific passages. Let us turn to these and try to find out what they may fairly be supposed to mean. Those usually brought forward are nearly all taken from the New Testament and chiefly consist of sayings of Christ. The most frequently urged and the most important are the following:—

1. "*My kingdom is not of this world.*"

We naturally shrink from picking out isolated passages and presuming to apply them to a question to which when first uttered they had in all probability no reference whatever. As named before, we do not pretend that Christ ever intended to teach anything either for or against the national principle in religion. His mission was merely to reveal the religion itself, and He left all questions of organic detail to be settled afterwards. A sense of grating profanity comes upon us when expressions of the most sublime and universal truths are dragged in to give evidence about earthly and temporary disputes; it is like imploring the gods to settle the paltry squabbles of men. Words like these, whose application is spiritual and whose reach is eternal, ought not to be applied to so transient and comparatively unimportant a matter as whether or not our religion shall in this earthly condition be nationally organized, and he is no friend to the dignity of the Gospel who so narrows and degrades its meaning. Much, however, as our intense reverence for every word uttered by the Master makes us shrink from such a task, since many of His sayings are so often quoted in this connection we are compelled to inquire whether they will really bear the interpretation which is so frequently put upon them; but it must be understood that we do not presume to explain at all fully what those sayings were actually intended to mean.

The sentence now quoted is represented as expressing Christ's wish that His Church on earth should not accept such worldly honour and power as are involved in its being connected with the State. Granting that this sentence condemns the assumption of temporal power by the Church, it does not follow that it also condemns the union of that Church with the State; on the contrary, it seems to encourage it. For Churches cannot remain mere spiritual fraternities; they must have outward organizations, and nothing is more certain than that such organizations must, if left to themselves, exercise great temporal influence. Much is said about the separation of religion from politics but a very slight glance at history, to say nothing of our knowledge of human nature, teaches us that such a separation is utterly impossible, and that if it were possible it would immediately deprive politics of their power and religion of its reality. Religion has always been the moulding power of history and is now, as much as ever, by far the largest factor in the sum of human life. Men's outward actions as citizens are but the results of their inward convictions as men, and most of these convictions are formed by their religion, and all of them are affected by it. To confess that religion exercises great temporal power is one of the highest tributes to its value, for it is only another way of saying that it is a living religion and not a dead superstition. Religion is one of those things about which there can be no compromise; half-and-half religion is no religion at all. Religion will not be treated as a lodger to whom certain exclusive apartments of the human mind are let off, but will go away altogether unless he receives the run of the whole house.

Since, therefore, temporal power is inevitably associated with religion the question is whether that power shall be exercised by the Church itself, or by the State connected with the Church. The State is the proper instrument for the exercise of such power, but a Church which is separated from the State is sure to assume much of this power to itself, for there is no dividing line between religion and politics and men's strongest emotions gather about their Church. Therefore it seems that the union of the Church with the State is the only means of preventing that assumption of temporal power by the Church itself which Christ is understood in these words to condemn.

The choice of the word "kingdom" does not suggest that Christ wished to encourage the opinion that religion and politics ought to be separated from each other, since He thus connected with His own spiritual influence the associations which belong pre-eminently to the highest political entity.

2. "*Render unto Cæsar the things which are Cæsar's, and unto God the things which are God's.*"

This often-quoted passage is supposed to inculcate the doctrine that obedience to the State ought to be kept distinct from obedience to the Church. We must ask what were the circumstances under which this sentence was uttered before we can pretend to understand its meaning, and if we do so we find that it was not obedience to the Church which was then in danger, but obedience to the State. The Pharisees are like the bad characters in a drama, and therefore generally receive equally scant justice. Instead of being so utterly wicked and hypocritical as they are often represented there is no reason to suppose that they were either better or worse than many respectable men similarly trained and situated are now-a-days. One great evil of considering the Pharisees as so peculiarly bad is that we fail to apply to ourselves, as we ought to do, those words of scathing scorn with which Christ immortalized their weaknesses. The habit of thinking more of givings and fastings and prayings than of the weightier matters of the law did not die out in the first Christian century; in our own country at the present time there are plenty of earnest people who, like the Pharisees of old, mistake ritual for religion, and who also, like these, are often amongst the first to question the authority of the State. It was to such people that this saying of Christ was addressed, with the object of vindicating the claims of the State, for the Pharisees had no doubt about rendering to God the things which are God's, as they understood the expression; indeed, their difficulty was whether their duty to their religion did not make it wrong for them to render anything to their State. Christ rebuked this mistake, declaring that His religion did not aggrandise the claims of the Church at the expense of those of the State, but combined these two together, "and unto God, &c.," and it is rather significant that "Cæsar" comes first in the sentence. If this passage has any application to this subject it surely then seems to teach that the State and the Church ought not to be rival claimants for obedience. They have always eventually become such rivals when separated from each other, and they always must, for it is impossible to distinguish the claims of religion from those of politics. In a great matter of this sort we must not be guided by temporary circumstances but by the ultimate tendencies which history proves to be inevitable, and the history of England strikingly shows the utter impossibility of such a separation. That it is no more possible in the present than it has been in the past is evident to any one who knows what a national difficulty Roman Catholicism is now, and who reflects upon what would be the effect of the education question, after disestablishment, upon political parties.

The separation of the Church from the State ultimately always leads not to the supremacy of the State but to that of the Church, and it was against such a result that Christ's words to the Pharisees were spoken.

3. *It is said that Christ's declaration, that His truth is hidden from the wise and prudent and revealed to babes, suggests the idea that religion ought not to be under the control of high State dignitaries but should be left to the people themselves.*

But who were "the wise and prudent" who were referred to by Christ? The clergy of a self-governed Church. There is a very common mistake made in reference to this side of the question, for people seem to think that pomp and dignity are the determining characteristics whereas these have really nothing to do with the national principle at all. The dignitaries of the Church of England, although resembling them in name and social circumstances, really differ much more from those of the Church of Rome, in this respect, than do the poor and humble ministers of some small self-governing sect. The only dividing principle is that of obedience; all those who are under national authority must be placed together in one class, and all those who are under no authority but their own must be placed together in another class. It is to this second class that the words "wise and prudent" thus used refer, as we must acknowledge if we consider what was the position of those to whom the words were in the first instance applied. There was at that time practical separation between the Church and the State in Palestine; the Romans did not care anything about the religion of the Jews and left them to manage it themselves. The Jewish Church was then controlled by its own clerical organization, and those to whom with most reason we may suppose that Christ referred in these words were just those who had always been most in favour of such a government, and who, as the High Churchmen of Judaism, had always been most jealous of the power of the State.

These words, then, besides teaching us that we ought not to intrust the control of religion to the clergy of a self-governed

Church, if they apply to this question at all teach us also to whom we should intrust it, namely to the people themselves, who are supposed to be the "babes." But there is no way by which the people can exercise such a control except through a National Church, for by no other means can they save themselves from that clerical dominion against which they are warned. All schemes for combining lay control with clerical eventually and necessarily fail, though it is possible to join laymen with clergymen in the government of a Church but the laymen who take such a part are always those most disposed to form clerical opinions and to be subject to clerical influence. Laymen, most of them probably of very limited cultivation and chosen under clerical initiation, who take up Church affairs as a hobby are no match for the clerical body which feels strongly, speaks intelligently, and acts compactly. The facts of history verify the conclusions of reasoning, for no self-governed Church of long standing can be found in which the lay element has not ultimately been subjugated by the clerical. Real, courageous, representative lay influence can only operate through one organization, because lay interest is only capable of attaching itself permanently to one, and that is the State; this is the only abiding lay entity in the land. Lay influence must act in religion by the representative system which it uses for everything else, or it must not act at all.

Those who think that this opinion is derogatory to the character of the clerical body must remember that in this world work has to be divided because no one can do everything, and that it is not usual to consider the dignity of a class lessened by its being relieved of its lower functions. In ecclesiastical affairs the best system of division of labour seems to be for the clergy to attend to the spiritual guidance and the laity to the temporal management. The figure of St. Paul is peculiarly applicable to a National Church for no part can assert that it has no need of the others, and it certainly seems unreasonable for the head to complain because it is not allowed to do the work of the feet and the hands as well as its own; a man standing on his crown or carrying with his teeth is neither really nor figuratively a dignified spectacle.

4. *The Parable of the Tares is interpreted to mean that a Church should consist only of the good, and should therefore have some means of keeping out the bad which cannot be possessed by a National Church.*

But we are told that the tares and the wheat must grow together until the harvest. When is the harvest? Surely not in this life. And who are the harvesters? Surely not weak and erring human beings, many of whom will probably themselves turn out to be tares. Men are not meant thus to judge each other and be the ministers of God's final purposes.

But if "the harvest" is to be in the future, after death, surely an injunction to let both good and bad, or those who are considered such, grow up together can only be considered as a recommendation for a religious system which allows such a blending of both. A National Church can alone afford such a system, for all others are essentially founded on exclusiveness.

Of course it is thoroughly true that a man cannot enter Christ's spiritual Church unless he "be born again," but neither a Church which is National nor any other which it is possible to organize can be made to correspond with that spiritual Church. This fact of second birth is one which lies quite beyond all human tests, and the Church of those who have been so born again is not meant to be an earthly organization but a society which will gather itself together hereafter. Human Churches ought to be organizations for offering the means of this second birth; if they turn themselves into mere societies of those who think they have already experienced it, they make Christianity ridiculous and become nurseries of self-deception and intolerance.

5. *The teaching about Christ's kingdom coming "not with observation," that is, with show of power, as well as that which warns His followers not to seek who shall be greatest, is supposed to inculcate upon the Church the duty of refraining from such a position of worldly importance as is involved in connection with the State.*

But there is no reason for supposing that anything more was intended by these teachings than a warning against that assumption by the Church, so strongly and frequently condemned by Christ, of temporal authority, and union with the State is the only means of preventing this assumption.

6. *Christ's injunction to His missionary disciples to provide neither scrip nor purse is sometimes taken to imply a condemnation of those settled incomes which the Church of England supplies.*

What this injunction really seems to mean is that the needs of ministers of religion ought to be provided for by those who receive the benefit of their services. If such ministers carry out the spirit of Christ's religion and so bring themselves within the range of His injunction it is not merely, nor chiefly, the few who listen to them who receive good from their influence, but the whole nation is the better for it. The true way to carry out St. Paul's injunction about those who preach the Gospel living by it is not to narrow the area from which the living is derived but to widen that to which the preaching is addressed.

Before England can ever be properly won over to that real Christianity from which it is now so distant the conception of the clerical office must be lifted out of the unhappy position into which it has fallen, and must be broadened and purified, and this must be done, not by the clergy becoming the ministers of little private societies, but by their being set forth as the teachers of the whole people.

Other passages from Christ's sayings are often quoted to prove the unscripturalness of the union between the Church and the State, but sufficient has already been named to illustrate the character of the principal arguments drawn from this source. Before leaving this part of the subject, however, it may be well to call attention to the following facts.

Whether or not Christ inculcated the union of Church and State it is certain that He always upheld that religious character of the State which is one of its principal consequences. If ever there was a people which might be considered justified in refusing, if not to obey the commands at least to recognize the claims, of the government, it was the Jews of Palestine under the Roman Empire, for not merely were the Romans heathen usurpers but they made no religious pretensions for themselves and grounded their rights exclusively upon force. Yet Christ not merely refused to resist this government, even when lending itself to an iniquitous persecution, but He also distinctly pointed out the high source of its authority, as when He said to Pilate "Thou couldst have no power at all against me except it were given thee from above." He also worked a special miracle in order to pay the tribute money for Peter and Himself. Good people are led to commit many distressing eccentricities through failing to observe that although Christ was a spiritual revolutionist He was also a social conservative, if such an expression may be used of One who only believed in those changes which proceed from within and work outwards. It looks so much more heroic to be prominently differing from others than to be quietly minding our own hearts, and singularity has such a strong fascination for weak minds, that in every age and country there has always been a number of people who have thought that to prove themselves the followers of their Lord they must set at defiance some law or fly in the face of some custom. This is not to follow the example of Christ, who even in His religious observances, as well as in His social habits and political conduct, always carefully conformed to the usages of His nation. His actions justify us in giving the widest application to those pregnant words—"Think not that I am come to destroy the Law and the Prophets; I am not come to destroy, but to fulfil." St. Paul inculcates the same principle when he says—"Whatsoever things were written aforetime, were written for our learning." And the broken outlines of that picture of the millennium sketched for us by Christ do not suggest that we shall be working towards the realization of that time by disconnecting religion from the State. In that future towards which Christ bids us look governments are not to be degraded by being separated from religion, but are to be ennobled and elevated by being thoroughly identified with it. "The kingdoms of this world" are not to be cast away but are to become "the kingdoms of our God and of his Christ."

The other fact to be noted in connection with Christ is that His death, considered as a civil outrage, was plainly a result of the separation of the Church from the State. For, as named before, the Romans, although retaining the complete control of the State, allowed the Jews to manage their own religious affairs. Because the State refused to have anything to do with religion Christ was allowed to fall a victim to ecclesiastical enmity and popular frenzy. The multitudes who arrested Him were sent by the chief priests and elders; it was to the high priest's palace that they bore Him, and He was condemned by an exclusively clerical tribunal. The State, when appealed to, merely lent its Roman soldiers to carry out the will of the Church. Poor, weak Pilate, washing his hands in court before the multitude, is a true type of the condition to which the State is brought after it becomes separated from the Church.

We must now turn to those objections which, although to be considered as religious, do not specially relate to the Bible, and which may therefore be called

GENERAL.

The following are the principal objections of this class which are urged against the existence of a National Church :—

1. *It puts the State in the place of Christ.*

We are told that as Christ is the Head of His Church no other is needed, and that by making the State the head of the Church we commit an act of disloyalty to our Master. This objection arises from confusing the spiritual meaning of the word Church with its organic. Considering a Church as a spiritual society Christ is of course the Head of each Christian Church, or rather of that one great Church of which all such Churches are merely parts ; but to say that He should be the Managing Head of all Churches considered merely as temporal organizations, is to talk nonsense and to make Christianity ridiculous. It would be as reasonable to say that we need no political government because Christ is the Head of the World, and that as He is the Bread of Life we may give up all material provision. Indeed both of these mistakes have frequently been committed. The Fifth Monarchy men under Cromwell fell into the first, and at the present day there are several societies in America and England founded upon the second. The national principle so fully recognizes that Christ is the Head of the Church that it objects to the degradation of that Headship by His being expected to perform the duties of the hands and feet and rest of the body as well.

2. *It is said that as religion is a matter for each individual conscience the assumption of its control by the State is a violation of the rights of conscience: also that as religion is concerned with absolute truth, and the State only with relative truth, there can be no proper union between these two.*

This objection arises from that common misconception of the State which represents it as a separate entity in itself; people often talk as if the State is some power apart from the nation whereas it is in reality only the instrument by which the national will is carried out. This is true whatever be the form of the State, whether the people have delegated their authority to a few, or even whether they have allowed a single person to seize it, for acquiescence must be considered a representation. The State being merely a tool in the hands of the people can have no conscience of its own as opposed to that of the people, for even when the State takes the initiative it can merely do so by the people's will. Conscience causes and guides action and in any matter of combination the line of action followed is the resultant of the various individual consciences in operation. The instrument of that action does not assume a conscience of its own, nor can any individual conscience complain that its rights are violated because the action adopted is not just in accordance with its own dictates. The utmost claim which can be justified is that each individual conscience shall have free play to exert its fair influence in determining the resultant action. Complete freedom of action for each individual conscience is only another name for anarchy. The truth then, as far as conscience is concerned, about the national principle of religion is, that a State Church does not control the religion of the people nor interfere with their consciences but is merely an organization for carrying out that religion which has been approved by the individual consciences of the people in the same way as they determine about every other collective matter. We may just as reasonably complain that committees of chapels, and all other organizations in which it is not possible for every man to have all his own way, are violations of the rights of conscience, as make this charge against a National Church.

And as to religion being concerned with absolute truth this may be correct so long as religion is confined to each individual soul, and in that sense a State Church has nothing to do with it, but it is not correct as soon as religion comes to require any outward organized expression. There is no such thing as absolute truth where human organisms are concerned; we cannot truthfully utter a single thought of our minds or feeling of our hearts; not a word that we speak is absolutely true, and it is impossible to express the doctrines of religion in any language which shall convey exactly the same ideas to any two minds who think about it. The features of a truth may possibly be plainly seen as long as it remains naked in the chambers of the mind, but they become more or less enigmatic as soon as it has to clothe itself to go out into the material world. All Churches, as outward organizations, are relative institutions, and a National Church is no more so than any other.

3. *It is objected to the national principle that it implies a distrust of the intrinsic power of religion.*

Many zealous Christians assert that they have too much faith in their religion to think that it needs the help of the State. The spirit of this objection is expressed in that aphorism so frequently used and so very misleading that "Truth will prevail." Of course those who have faith in the good ultimate destiny of the world believe that error must finally go down before truth, but that "finally" is often deferred for longer periods than history can grapple with or human arrangements reckon for. He who from the mountain summit of thought gazes at the world as it now lies beneath his feet and then carries his eye over the plains of the past as far as the dim horizon of antiquity is forced to the melancholy conviction that truth at best makes but very slow way. He is also forced to admit that even this progress would not have been made had not truth allied itself with organizations able to give it material help. The spread of Christianity is an instance. Since its first extension by the mechanism of the Roman Empire it has not, through all these long centuries of increasing facilities and growing intelligence, won over a single great nation; it has only been spread by the emigration of its followers, and Christians have now fallen into such a state of unacknowledged hopelessness that they welcome with surprise the supposed conversion of a little savage island. Yet we are told that truth will spread itself. This assertion is not true even when confined to ourselves, but if we are to get at the truth of those great principles which apply to all peoples we must look beyond the little circle of our own nation, and beyond also that of Christianity itself, for we are too apt to forget that a very large majority of the population of the earth reject altogether that religion about whose trifling minutiæ we squabble so much amongst ourselves. Taking this broad view we find that the truth of truth is one thing and the spread of truth is another, and that however true a truth may be it cannot become more than an isolated sentiment until it has received some embodiment. Organizations are to religion what speaking and writing are to thought ; a revelation made to a single mind cannot become useful until it has expressed itself in sound or on paper, and a religious faith cannot operate upon the world except by means of an outward organization. Since, therefore, religion must have some organization it remains to be proved that the one afforded by the State implies such a distrust of the intrinsic power of truth as is not implied by the others. This cannot be done, but until it is done it is just as absurd to say that we have too much faith in religion to think it needs the help of the State as it would be to boast that we have too much faith in the power of thought to believe that it needs the help of a tongue or a pen.

4. *It is said that the connection of the Church with the State prevents the spread of truth, and for two reasons amongst others.*

a. The machinery of the State is too cumbersome.

At first sight there seems to be some truth in this objection, for considerable force must evidently be required to overcome the inertia necessarily belonging to the machinery of a great State. But when we consider that religion is chiefly concerned with doctrines and practices which are independent of change this very impediment turns out to be an advantage, inasmuch as it acts as a buffer upon which sudden and evanescent emotions can expend themselves. A Church whose organization is too easily moved is sure, in times of temporary excitement, to adopt changes which subsequent experience condemns and which have ultimately to be given up. But if any good and substantial changes are required it seems that the machinery of the State is the most likely to carry them out, for as it is concerned chiefly with political matters, in which constant changes are required, it must necessarily acquire an elasticity which purely Church organizations, confined to the permanencies of religion, cannot possess. Exclusively Church organizations have two radical defects; they make rash changes in times of excitement, and at other times they will make no changes at all; they are too revolutionary or else too conservative. The State provides an organization comparatively free from these defects, for whilst it will not yield to proposals which have not commended themselves to general approval, it is too much accustomed to making changes to refuse such proposals when they have so commended themselves.

If the machinery of the State is defective and does not answer to the national will, that is a reason, not for taking away the religion but for improving the machinery; indeed, the religion ought in that case to be more tenaciously retained in order that the defects of the State may be more glaringly exposed, and more quickly remedied.

b. The interests of the State are opposed to change.

This objection arises from the mistake of considering the State as possessing a personalty distinct from that of the nation, whereas it is only the nation itself in its organic aspect. The interests of the State are those of the people, and therefore cannot be opposed to changes except when the people are, and then such changes ought not to be made.

A great objection to the national principle in many people's minds is that although its adoption in our own country may be right because the religion is true, it would be wrong in other countries where it would be allied with error. It may be as well to acknowledge that this objection is a most fundamental one, for the national system is not put forward in these pages as an arrangement suitable for one or two nations only but as a principle which, with certain necessary variations, is generally applicable. Whatever be the character of the religion accepted by any nation, whether it be Christianity or Mohammedanism or any other religion; whether it be Protestantism or Catholicism or the religion of the Greek Church, it is here maintained that that religion ought to be united with the State. We frankly confess that this wide extension of the principle suggests many difficulties, but if this principle is what we claim it to be it must be capable of this extension and therefore those difficulties must be met.

The principal and most obvious objection is the one already named, that if religion is helped by alliance with the

State, when that religion is false we are, by advocating such an alliance, assisting error, and so violating one of the primary demands of our own consciences.

In reference to this objection it must be stated in the first place that religions are not so easily divided into true and false as so many people seem to suppose. Of course everyone who is honest must believe that his own religion is very much nearer the truth than any other, but that is no reason why he should put down every other as utterly false. Such a principle as this is not merely irreligious in itself but it is also the greatest impediment to the spread of our own religion, for whilst it arouses the enmity of those who differ from us, it prevents us from understanding their religion sufficiently to have a chance of replacing it with our own. It is easy to consider ourselves all in the right and every one else all in the wrong, and this is the faith held by the bigots of every religion all the world over, and held always the more intensely the more ignorant they are; but this is not the faith of Christianity, which teaches a higher and more difficult truth; it is easier to believe that "in this mountain" alone, or "at Jerusalem" alone is the proper place to worship, than it is to realize that "God is a spirit, and they that worship Him must worship Him in spirit and in truth." A little more knowledge of other religions and a little more real sympathy with the cardinal virtues of our own soon lead us to the conviction that no religion, as generally held, is completely true, and that none is completely false. Religions are like pieces of marble; some are whiter than others, but it is impossible to find the perfect purity of truth, for all are more or less streaked with the lines of error. In acknowledging this we do not derogate from the high claims of Christianity but rather pay a tribute to them, for whilst we believe in the perfection of that religion itself, we must confess that even the best of us very imperfectly realize and express it. If we compare the Christian religion as embodied in the doctrines of the most enlightened Churches with the teachings of Christ Himself as given to us in the Gospels we must feel how very far human nature yet is from being able to grasp the fulness of that marvellous and adorable revelation. Even if our doctrines are all true they are at best but very partial and fragmentary. Mankind is yet but in its religious infancy, and so its eyes cannot bear the full glory of the sun; we are like shepherds on the mountains watching the coming of the day; our light is but "the flaky darkness breaking in the east," and it ill becomes us to think slightingly of those who have not yet climbed high enough to catch a glimpse of the dawn. It is not the religion itself which has to be developed but our capacity for appreciating it; the sun is there in all its fulness, but we cannot yet bear its meridian glory.

But even if the religion of a people be utterly false it is still for the interests of truth that that religion should be nationally organized. For it must be remembered that this religion, whatever be its character, is already the religion of the people or it could not be nationally adopted, and therefore its national adoption does not in itself make it the religion of the people. But the national principle has this remarkable advantage, that whilst it strengthens truth it weakens error, and for the simple reason that it lays open that error more fully to the action of truth. The great difficulty in fighting with error is to get at it; we have the best chance of conquering a country when it has a nationally recognized army with which we can bring our own forces into decisive conflict, but conquest is most difficult when our only opponents are independent guerilla bands. So when the religion of a people is in the charge merely of private societies we do not know how to attack it; we cannot penetrate the ambush of independency, and even if we do, we never know when we can claim for ourselves the victory. But if that religion is nationally organized we have the following advantages in contending with it. We have, in the first place, the right to attack it, for this is involved in the position, and in the second place, we can claim in so attacking it the protection of the law, for a State Church is a national institution and those who attack it are subject to the same general legal conditions as the opponents of any other national institution. This advantage may be understood if we compare the freedom of those who are now attacking the Church of England with the punishments which can be inflicted, without the chance of appeal, upon those who offend the Roman Catholic Church.

Besides having the right of attack we have also the advantage of knowing exactly what it is that we have to attack, for the religion of a National Church must be openly defined. A private religious society need have no acknowledged statement of belief, and even if it has one, it is its own private property and no one can claim the right to make it a matter of public dispute. But a State Church must have a creed drawn up with legal definiteness and just as much open to public knowledge and criticism as any other State document. This act of defining is also in itself a great help to truth, for there is nothing so inimical to error as a definition. Definition is the sun which melts the snow of misunderstanding and lays bare the surface of truth; it is the chemical test which shows, as nothing else can, the presence and amount of error. In public disputes, and in private arguments, half the difficulty is mastered if we can only get the opponents to come to a definition. Religion is the subject in which above all others definition is most needed, for it is the one in which people are most apt to be led away by vague phrases and indiscriminating enthusiasms. If we wish to attack the religion of a people it is of the utmost importance that that religion should be openly defined. This advantage is secured to us by a National Church, and by that alone in its full sense.

Therefore, even if we consider the religion of a people to be false it is better that it should be nationally organized, for thereby those who wish to replace it have the advantage of its being plainly defined and openly declared. The law also lays down the conditions to which they are subject, and they have besides the advantage of appealing to the heads of the State, who are in general likely to belong to the most intelligent and advanced portion of the people. That National Churches are not obstacles, but aids, to the spread of a new religion is proved by the fact that Christianity has yet only gained a permanent footing in countries where such Churches previously existed.

5. *It is said that connection with the State is degrading to the Church.*

This objection lies at the root of a great deal which is said against the National principle; we constantly hear the control of the State over the Church spoken of as a "fetter," and many of those who are now working to separate the Church from the State profess and believe that they are thus trying to do the Church a service ; hence they use the word "liberate" to describe their object, and call their Association "The Society for the Liberation of the Church from State Patronage and Control." It is therefore necessary to examine as carefully as we can this objection about degradation, and if we do so we find that it consists of two parts, one referring to the character of the Church, and the other to its position.

And first as to character, we are told that connection with the State degrades the Church in the following ways:—

a It prevents any demarcation between the godly and the ungodly, for a National Church must be open to all.

It is quite certain that there is a radical discrepancy between the national and what may be called the private ideal, which is that representing a Christian Church as merely an association of those who are, or are considered, godly; but it is not so certain that the fault lies with the national. Undoubtedly the tendency of the present age is strongly in favour of this private ideal; almost everyone who speaks or writes on the subject seems to take it as a matter of course that a Church, if properly constituted, ought to contain only those who hold one common faith, and the only difference seems to be as to the possibility or means of organizing such a Church. But the popularity of a tendency is a very small proof of its truth, and instead of accepting the idea that a Christian Church ought to be merely a society of the godly, that is, of those who may be considered as converted to the Christian faith, we venture to believe that this idea has no warrant in Scripture, and is contrary to Christian wisdom, and opposed to Christian progress. For although the word Church is often used in the Scripture to denote merely those who have accepted the Christian faith, we must remember that this is but a very small portion of the meaning which can fairly be supposed to correspond with what we now understand by the word. For Christian Churches are in these days not merely associations of those who have accepted the Christian religion, but they are also the only means of offering that religion to those who have not; if we look around we are bound to confess that beyond what are provided by the Churches there are no organizations of any value for spreading the Christian religion. The spreading of that religion therefore depends upon the Churches, and, considering the limitations of Christendom and the present religious condition even of our own population, we maintain that this spreading is the principal work of these Churches, and should be their determining characteristic. Taking this large view we see the folly of limiting the application of the term "Church" to those little societies of early Christians who banded themselves together for sympathetic fellowship, and we acknowledge that this word must be understood, as a Scriptural comparison, to include the whole organization by which the new religion was offered to the world. The ministrations of this Church, first provided by Christ and His Apostles, were open to everybody, and such a Church finds its nearest modern counterpart in a National Church, which is open to all, and yet allows the function within itself of private associations like those which gathered together within the first Christian Church.

The mistake of considering the Primitive Church only in the narrow sense of a collection of private societies instead of in the broad sense of a varied organization for the spread of religion has done incalculable harm to Christian progress and brotherhood.

But setting aside Scriptural example and analogy, we may safely ask whether this broad conception of the true character of a Church is not much more in harmony with the spirit and purpose of Christianity than the narrow one now so much adopted. For one of the fundamental moral doctrines of the Bible is that this life is not meant for selfish enjoyment but for unselfish work, and no more repelling and contemptible picture of Christian duty can be given than that which represents that our only religious aim should be the securing of what we believe to be our own salvation, and our only religious exercise should be in the fellowship of those whom we consider to be like ourselves. It must be confessed with shame that this is the substance of what is now being largely taught as Christianity, and there is therefore no wonder that so many people stand aloof altogether; indeed we are inclined to respect the honesty of those who remain in acknowledged unbelief rather than accept a religion such as this. The fundamental principle of the religion taught by Christ Himself was pure unselfishness, whilst that of the religion now·set forth by many who believe themselves His followers is selfishness as complete as that of any paganism, although more refined. From this wrong and selfish conception of the Christian religion has arisen that equally wrong and selfish conception of the Christian Church which represents that it should be merely a private association of believers. It is high time that this foundation, upon which sectarianism rests, should be tumbled to the ground. If Christianity is to live and grow and be worthy of itself it will not be by our abandoning the national ideal and adopting the sectarian, but by our abolishing the sectarian. The Temple of the Lord must be an open Church and not a private club; the waters of religion must not be served out to an exclusive few but must flow in public fountains freely for all.

That the sectarian ideal is contrary to the wisdom of Christianity is plain as soon as we ask ourselves, "Who are the people for whom Churches are principally intended?" Is it the godly who most need their services, or is it not rather the ungodly? Those who are converted may be considered to be already provided for in the main, so that if the Church is to obey the command of its Master and go out into the highways and hedges it is to the unconverted that it must chiefly direct its attention. But if Churches are to be merely associations from which the ungodly can be excluded they at once cut themselves off from what is infinitely their most important and highest work.

But it may be replied that although a sectarian body is in itself a private society, that is no reason why such a body may not preach to those who are outside it, and that, as a matter of fact, the various sectarian bodies of England are just as active as the Church in missionary efforts. This may be quite true and yet the difference is a most fundamental one, for whilst such missionary efforts are works of supererogation to a sectarian Church they form an essential part of the duty of a National Church. We see this difference if we consider that the minister of a Dissenting Chapel is not expected to attend to any but his own congregation whilst a clergyman is bound to be at the call of everyone in his parish; although of course others are welcome, still the services of a chapel cannot be joined in as a right except by its members, whilst those of a Church are open to all who choose to come. It is one thing for work to be done or not as we choose, and another for it to be a part of our duty. If the National Church does not do its duty properly it should be made to do so. The destruction of that Church would be a great blow to the future spread of Christianity, for there would then be left no organization bound to minister to the unconverted as well as to the converted.

But even if it were wise for Churches to be enabled to turn out those who are not considered godly, it is practically impossible to plan any arrangement by which this can be properly done. Human nature seems to resent the assumption of men thus making themselves judges of others, for it furnishes no means by which any reliable judgment can be formed about such a matter as godliness. Real, deep, religious feeling most of all shrinks from public observation and criticism, and the more real and deep it is the more likely is it to find itself unwilling to take verbal expression because the more strongly it feels the utter inadequacy of all language. Thus in the matter of what is called conversion —the most radical revolution which can happen to our condition even here—although we would not deny that dispositions vary greatly and that in others modes of expression may be honest which would be dishonest in ourselves, still we cannot help believing that if a man really comes to feel his own sinfulness and to look to Christ, he will be much more likely to become silently self-distrustful and to let his new state work itself out in his life than to proclaim it from the housetops. All men, and especially Englishmen, are so reserved about their deepest feelings that no man with much experience of the world will venture to say that he can judge with certainty the religion of his closest friend. How impossible then must it be for societies of men to judge the godliness of those about whom few of them can know much? In fact, although it is objected to the National Church that it cannot keep out the "ungodly," the sectarian Churches who raise the complaint are just as impotent in this respect. Godliness is a quality which eludes all their tests, and so in fact they do not look for it, but they can see the professions of it, they can test the creeds which men say they hold, and so they fall back upon these. But professions and creeds ought not to be the sole tests of Christian membership as they have comparatively little to do with the Christian religion, and to make them such tests is to encourage hypocrisy, and what is still worse, self-deception. As a matter of fact, "turning out the ungodly" resolves itself into turning out heretics, and to give such a power to the Church of England would only be to transform it into a sect from which all would be excluded who could not profess to believe in a certain creed. We believe that such a transformation would greatly lower the religious character of that Church and lessen its usefulness.

Indeed it is impossible to introduce such a power and yet preserve the national ideal. In a National Church there is no "in" or "out," for as named before such a Church is merely an organization for religious purposes; clergymen can be discharged from its service but they cannot be excluded from such advantages as are open to all the laity.

In conclusion, in answer to the objection that in a National Church there is no demarcation between the godly and the ungodly, we would say that it is not the business of a Church to provide such a demarcation; also that it is impossible to provide one, and that the attempt encourages hypocrisy and intolerance, and also that, even if it were possible, the character of the Christian religion would thereby be lowered and its progress hindered.

β. Another objection is that the character of the Church is lowered in consequence of the encouragement given to nominal Christianity by the national principle.

It is said that where there is a National Church all those who are not connected with other religious bodies are considered to belong to that Church, and thus many are called Churchmen who know nothing and care nothing about the Christian religion. In this way there is encouraged a purely nominal Christianity, which leads to deception and often prevents the adoption of the real religion.

It must be replied that if the national principle is properly carried out, there is no reason why the word "Churchman" should be used at all, for that would be implied in the word Englishman or whatever was the national name. It is sectarianism which has introduced the habit of calling men according to their religious opinions and habits, and the national principle must not be blamed for the consequences.

But even if large numbers of the population are now called Christians who possess no religion at all, it does not follow that harm is done. For we must remember that these people are presumed to be actually irreligious, and therefore no name we give them makes them more so. Besides, those who have disregarded the warnings and teachings of religion are not likely to care what name they receive. If a man does not heed your religion he will not care whether or not you call him by its name.

But whilst there is little chance of harm in applying the term Christian with charitable freedom, there is much chance of good. The Church prefers to call people according to what they should be rather than according to what some of them actually are; thus there is kept before them a testimony of the great inheritance to which they are born and a reminder of their duty respecting it. We learn both from the practice of Christ Himself and from general experience that the truest way to reform the wicked is not to keep telling them of their wickedness but rather to remind them of the goodness to which they may attain; honest servants are not made by suspicion but by confidence. Most of us try to live up more or less to the expectations which we know are formed of us, and there is nothing more inspiriting to the downcast man than the thought that others have better hopes for him than he has for himself. The best way to bring those back who have strayed away is not to shut the door, but to keep it open and hang out everything to remind them that they ought to return. If we cannot always obtain Christian practice let us at any rate always hold up the Christian ideal. The prodigal would probably have become merely a degraded farm labourer had he not kept up within him the remembrance of the home which he had left and the opportunities to which he had been born. Even when eating the food of swine he was still called his father's son, and so let those who are born in a Christian land still be called Christians, and Churchmen too if such a name be used, even though they are indifferent and degraded. The more degraded they are, the more are we bound not to give up any chance of raising and reclaiming them.

γ. Another objection is that the character of the Church is lowered because in the national system there are no openings for individual enthusiasm and no opportunities for private fellowship.

It is said that even if Churches ought not to be merely private associations still those who hold the same faith do desire, and even need, to meet together for the strengthening and refreshing of their own souls, and that as dispositions and capacities differ, there ought to be a greater freedom of action than can be allowed in a National Church.

There is no reason why in a properly constituted National Church there should not exist together any number of private associations. The business of such a Church is to inculcate the simple truths of religion and to cultivate the spiritual welfare of the people, but it ought not to include amongst its requirements any but the most fundamental doctrines or the most general practices. Beyond these the people, and the clergy also, are left to differ amongst themselves, and there is no reason why those who join together for the ordinary ministrations of religion should not form themselves into separate societies for the mutual encouragement and spread of such opinions and practices as they agree about amongst each other. There is no reason why those who hold strong opinions about Baptism, or who are attached to the methods of Wesleyanism, should not gratify their own preferences and yet also join in the ministrations of the Church. The mistake has been that those who have adopted peculiar opinions have been too ready to break away into schism instead of trying to find room for those opinions within the Church itself. If the Church would not have adopted those opinions as a part of its creed, it might have allowed them in its people; it is absurd to suppose that the body of doctrine of a large Church should include all the opinions held by every section of its followers.

And the same is true concerning practical outlets for individual enthusiasm. A National Church provides certain organizations for religious purposes in which all who wish can take a part, some in one and some in another, but there is no reason why those who are not satisfied with any of these should not strike out a new way for themselves, provided that they do not thereby interfere with what is being done in the ordinary manner. Just as the Roman Church has its various orders of monks and friars, and is ready to welcome any new one which promises to further its cause, so a National Church should allow the widest latitude for religious activity consistent with the preservation of its own character and of freedom from excess.

Of course a National Church must have a definite creed

and a definite system, but that creed ought to be broad and that system elastic. If they are not sufficiently so, if there is some belief or practice which is objectionable to a number of the people, the proper course to pursue is for those people to try to get the conditions of the National Church altered accordingly. But instead of this unhappily their general course has been to separate themselves from that Church. Thus there has grown up in England a number of sects which have since been blaming the Church for not possessing a latitude which they themselves have done nothing to procure. A change is not likely to be made if those who wish for it go away instead of trying to bring it about. There is no reason why the Church of England, whilst retaining all the essential characteristics of a National Church, should not afford opportunities for all such expressions of enthusiasm and activity as the history of any of these sects has shown to be necessary or desirable.

Respecting the position of the Church, the following objections, amongst others, are raised, viz. :—

a. The national principle lowers the Church by placing it under the control of politicians.

We hear a great deal about the absurdity and inconsistency of the Church being ordered what it must believe by a Parliament containing, as the phrase goes, "Jews, infidels, and heretics," or, in other words, men of almost every belief and of none; and the Church is exhorted to liberate itself from this degrading thraldom. We are told that in matters of religion our undivided obedience is due to our own consciences, and that by allowing the interference of the State we fail in our loyalty to Christ, and permit our religion to be dishonoured.

Undoubtedly there is something very taking in phrases like these, and their takingness is of a sort which has especial force in these days. Whether it be from the immense spread of newspapers during the last few years, or from the political changes which have so greatly enlarged the constituencies, or whatever be the cause, there is no doubt that the decision of great public questions is now referred to a public which is in a large degree ignorant and indiscriminatingly impulsive. Such a public is prone to be readily led away by ear-catching phrases, vaguely suggestive of sentiments which, although very good in themselves, have really nothing to do with the question at issue. Happily this danger is less here than probably in any other country, for there is in the English people a strong practical instinct which leads them to take the right way, although they do not know why themselves, and if they did, could not explain to others. In the present state of public feeling on this matter, there is probably no other nation in which the masses possessed the same political power as they do here which would keep up the National Church for a year. Everywhere else amongst the body of the people there prevails a strong, though vague, sentiment that the Church and the State ought not to be connected together. The English people refuse to give way to this, although the continental philosophers, and their English imitators, set them down as stupid for refusing to follow logic which they do not seem able to answer. It is the object of these pages to show in some degree that this logic, although apparently so conclusive, is wrong, and that this instinct, although apparently as stupid as it really is dumb, is right.

The phrases about each man choosing his own religion, and the like, are, when applied to this question, listened to in pretty much the same frame of mind in which too many people generally hear the public reading of the Scriptures. If we tell the truth we must all confess that to many of the chapters most familiar to us we attach meanings which do not properly belong to them, but which are made up of associations set going in our minds by particular words and verses. The majestic roll of Isaiah, the sweet flow of the Psalms, the pithy picturesqueness of Christ, are dangers in themselves, for too often they so carry us along with them that we fail to notice the real meanings of which they are the vehicles. The Bible is like one of those eastern caskets of fragrant opiates whose opening throws those about it into a condition of virtuous somnolence. We are continually startled by finding what we call new meanings in passages of Scripture, but if we come to look closely we shall generally have to acknowledge that these are but the natural meanings making themselves seen for the first time through the mists of delusive associations and sentiments. So in the matter of the union of Church and State, we hear a number of phrases continually used which convey false impressions and produce in many of those who hear them a state of mind which prevents them from understanding the real question.

Thus all that is said about Parliament ordering what the Church shall believe is not true, and its untruth would be detected at once if the associations connected with religion were set aside. If the Church is to be regarded merely as a sect which only differs from the other sects in being under the control of the State, then perhaps this objection might be partially true, but then also the Church would not be national and would not come within the application of what we have said about the national principle. But if it is really a National Church then it is only the nation in its religious character, and Parliament no more orders what the nation shall believe in its religious character than it orders what the nation shall believe in its political character. Nobody ever thinks of saying that Parliament dictates what political beliefs the people shall hold, yet it exercises a much greater control over their political condition than over their religious, for it determines entirely the political, which moreover is continually changing, whilst the religious is chiefly under another influence, and remains comparatively fixed.

Of course Parliament exerts a strong influence in forming the nation's wishes, and it will be an evil time for this country if ever the belief becomes general that statesmen ought merely to obey public opinion and ought not also to lead it, but this formative influence has nothing to do with the objection before us, which concerns merely the legal powers of Parliament. Considered in this light what does Parliament do? It simply carries out the wishes of the nation. Before Parliament can take any such action as can be called control it is supposed that the opinions of the nation on the matter in question are already formed, and Parliament has only to carry them out in such a way as the nation wishes. In politics if it is desired by some to bring about a change they do not first ask Parliament to enforce it, for that would be Parliamentary tyranny, but they set about and try to convert the opinion of the nation. And so in religion, the nation first forms its own beliefs and then Parliament merely gives those beliefs adequate embodiment.

And as to giving this embodiment it does not follow that this work should not be shared in by those who do not agree with the beliefs. The primary requisite in this respect for a member of Parliament is that he shall be able to understand the national wishes and to carry them out. Of course if he is not capable, either through ignorance or prejudice, or from any other cause, of comprehending what those wishes are he ought to keep out of the matter, whatever be its nature, whether political or religious, but if he can comprehend them, it is as unreasonable to say that he cannot carry them out when religious as it would be if they were political. No one thinks of saying that a capable member of Parliament because he disagrees with the principle of the Ballot ought to be excluded from discussing the details of a Ballot Act, neither is even a Jew, properly qualified in other respects, unfit to carry out the ecclesiastical wishes of a Christian nation. And as to Dissenters, unless they are opposed to the national principle so strongly as to feel that they ought to try in every way to impede its operations, there is no reason why they should not be just as capable as anyone else of deciding about the organisation required by the religious decisions of the people, especially as nearly all Dissenters agree with the majority respecting all such opinions as are of sufficient importance to come within the scope of real religion.

But indeed it may reasonably be doubted whether for such functions as Parliament exercises towards the Church indifference is not a better qualification in some members than sympathy. Assuming that there is no ill-will towards the Church, and no desire but to carry out legally the wishes of the nation, there are many reasons why a man who has no feeling either way will be more likely to decide disputed points fairly and to frame a suitable organization. Looking back over the past, most people capable of judging history will allow that in England the government of the Church by Parliament has been more reasonable and successful than the Church would have received had it been under the control of its own clergy; at the present day the nation generally has an instinctive feeling that Parliament is much more likely than Convocation to be right about matters of ecclesiastical government. And why is this? In a great measure because members of Parliament are not so much interested as the clergy in these questions. Warmth of feeling testifies to our sincerity but it says nothing for our fitness to legislate; in fact, if it passes a certain point, it completely unfits us. One chief qualification for a juryman is that he knows nothing and cares nothing about the case he has to try. Although in a less degree, the same holds good respecting Parliament and legislation for the Church. Parliament has not to dictate beliefs but to carry out opinions, and all that we have a right to look for in such members of Parliament as take a part in ecclesiastical legislation is that they shall have intelligence enough to understand those opinions and honesty enough to carry them out. Considering that Parliament consists for the most part of those who are attached to the Church and who are therefore liable to be influenced too much by feeling, it is probably an advantage that it contains also a few who may be presumed to be less interested and who will therefore have a tendency to keep the others in the paths of sober judgment.

What the State therefore does for the Church is to provide and watch over its outward organization. The Church must have an organization provided for it by somebody, and the nation entrusts the work to the highest power in the country, that power to which it confides its own complete political welfare and which is believed to be best able to create and manage great organizations. Yet we are told that the Church is thereby degraded in position. Presumably its honour would be spared if its organization was under the control of a committee of laymen or of divines, although it is well known that in nearly all committees the least worthy are likely to be most prominent, and that divines are the last people to whom business management of any sort should be entrusted. The nation is likely to get the best organization it can to manage its own affairs, and having done this, it then gives the Church the benefit, so to speak, of that organization. Yet we are told that the Church ought to feel itself dishonoured by this.

Instead of considering itself dishonoured the Church ought to feel grateful for this union with the State because thereby religion is enabled to exercise a far greater influence over the State than would otherwise be possible. The Church is not merely governed by the State but it also governs the State in return. Indeed it may safely be said that the Church exercises a far greater influence over the State—meaning by the Church the organized national religion—than the State does over the Church. For the relationship between the State and the Church is very similar to that between a man and his wife who are happily and wisely married. For although the man possesses all the paraphernalia of government and the law confers upon him the authority of a despot, in most cases, and in nearly all those which are as they should be, it is the woman who really rules, the man being merely the obedient, though unconscious, instrument of her will. So the Church, which in its organization is under the control of the State, may by that connection make its influence far more fully felt upon the State, and through the State upon the nation. The Church is honoured and the State is elevated.

Another objection is that—

β. The national principle lowers the position of the Church of Christ by giving it geographical limits.

We are told that Christianity is not intended to be limited in its true form to any particular country, and that we ought not to attempt to impose upon it such geographical restrictions as are involved in the national principle.

But it is not true that any such restrictions are so involved, for to give to each nation the control of the outward organization of its religion is to put no limit upon the religions of different nations being the same. Just as the principle of constitutional government is a single principle which may be adopted by different nations, each in its own way, so Christianity is a single religion which may be adopted by different nations, each in its own way.

6. *The next objections to be considered are those which relate to the assertion that the connection between the Church and the State is lowering to the clergy.*

And first, as to character, it is said that—

a. The worldly advantages offered by a National Church induce men to enter the ministry from unworthy motives.

We are told that the large incomes and high distinctions conferred upon bishops and other chief dignitaries of the

Church, and the rich livings enjoyed by many of its clergy, are inconsistent with the Christian spirit and impart a worldly and irreligious tone to the Christian Church. It is said that no man ought to enter the ministry who does not feel himself specially called to the work and who is not actuated by the purest motives, and that therefore when we add worldly inducements we draw in many who are not thus qualified and whose infusion lowers the tone of the whole body.

This objection is one amongst many instances of that unreasonable method of discussing this question, now so much followed, which judges the Church of England by a standard so ideal and impossible that it is absurd to apply it to any human institution, and the test of which would prove just as damaging to any of the Churches which are not national.

Undoubtedly it would be much more in harmony with our highest conceptions and would save a great deal of the friction now involved in the working of religious organizations if all the ministers of religion adopted this calling purely from enthusiastic devotion, and if none of them ever allowed themselves to be influenced by worldly considerations; it would simplify our practical problems immensely and would do away with those occurrences which so constantly jar upon our finer feelings, if the clergy had nothing to do with money, or position, or anything of the sort. And undoubtedly it would be a great relief to the clergy themselves if this could be done; but unfortunately they happen to be men, and are therefore subject to the conditions and necessities of ordinary humanity. And is there any layman touched by the influence of religion who does not sometimes long for himself for this same immunity from worldly embarrassments? Do we not all of us often feel weighed down by the material exigencies of our earthly condition? Does not the dull drudgery of our everyday life often make us so discontented and hopeless that we almost sympathise with the Frenchman who committed suicide because he was tired of putting his clothes on and off? And is it not true that this dejection comes upon us most frequently at the times when our better feelings are uppermost? How hard do we often find it to bring back our minds to our daily work after the elevating rest of Sunday! The word "black" so long applied to Monday has a spiritual as well as a physical significance.

There is great meaning in the saying that life would be tolerable if it were not for its pleasures, for to most of those who join in them the pleasures which belong especially to our material life, the enjoyments of fashion and custom, are delusions which do not delude; people follow them because they suppose that they must give happiness, but if we could hear the voice of their hearts it would tell us that they do not find in them what they seek. This deep longing, this constant unrest, produces many of the most opposite effects; it causes some to shut themselves away from the world, whilst it leads others to give themselves more vigorously to the world in order that they may accumulate such wealth as they believe will relieve them from anxiety; monasticism and money-making have much more in common than appears at first sight.

Most of us will confess that our lives would be lighter, and that it would be much easier for us to attain to that higher condition after which we so often long, if we were relieved from our material necessities, if we could carry out strictly Christ's injunction to take no thought for the morrow, and could be fed like the sparrows and clothed like the lilies.

But if we ask ourselves whether this desire to be quit of earthly necessities, although apparently so elevated, is really a religious one, we are bound to confess that it is not, and that therefore it ought to be resisted. For God has not made a mistake in putting us here; he has not imposed labours and cares upon us to bear us down but to lift us up; and we may depend upon it that those who give way under them and allow them to crush out their higher life, would have had their weakness found out in some other way; whilst those who carry the load with religious manliness will get from their earthly pilgrimage a discipline which will do them more good than anything else could. The cares of this life are not to be avoided, as by many ascetic people, nor to be merely endured, as by many pious people, but they are to be turned into blessings.

The great problem of life, the solution of which makes Christianity the highest form of philosophy revealed to the world, is how to reconcile the material with the spiritual; how, whilst not being taken out of the world, to be kept from the evil. It is this problem which lies at the root of many of the most disturbing social questions, and which also each individual soul feels to be its greatest difficulty.

It is religion alone which can work out this problem; this is, indeed, its chief task, and a religion which cannot do this, which cannot conquer this difficulty, and so either avoids or ignores it, is not worth calling a religion. The highest duty of ministers of religion, then, is not to preach, not to pray, not to work, necessary though these are, but it is to show practically in their lives how the material conditions of life ought to be reconciled with its spiritual aspirations; how the necessities which Providence has imposed upon us in this world may be made to minister to our highest good and to fit us for the world which is to come.

How, then, are the ministers of religion to be qualified for this, their highest vocation? Surely not by relieving them from the cares of this world or the deceitfulness of riches, but rather by making them subject to the same temptations as other men, so that they may become living examples by resisting them. The ministers of religion must feel men's difficulties before they can teach how they should be overcome.

It is therefore maintained that it would not be wise, nor in accordance with the true requirements of religion, for the clergy to be exempted from worldly cares, even if it were possible, but, as a matter of fact, it is not possible. Clergymen, like other men, must live; they must have food and clothing and shelter; their bodily wants must be provided for unless in the future this is to be done miraculously as it has never been in the past. Nay, we may go further and say that unless the possession of wealth is in itself irreligious there is just as much reason why ministers of religion should have it as anybody else. Indeed there is more, for laymen justify their pursuit of it on the grounds that wealth gives greater means for cultivation and refinement, and evidently there are no persons who need cultivation and refinement more than the ministers of religion.

Worldliness and covetousness are so commonly associated with riches that we are apt to forget that these are vices of kind and do not depend for their degree upon the amount of that to which they are directed. Men may be just as covetous with one pound a week as with a thousand, and a man in the position of a small shopkeeper is just as likely to be given to worldliness as a duke. As a matter of fact, the man with large means and a large expenditure is less liable to be covetous than he who receives little and spends less, and the man of a high, assured position will in all probability think less about worldly importance than he who, with humble surroundings, is according to the common phrase "making his way in the world," or "getting on."

The difference between a national and a sectarian Church is in this respect merely one of degree. Granting that the incomes received by the clergy are larger than those of what are called "the ministers of all denominations," the only conclusion reasonably to be drawn is, not that these large incomes should produce more worldliness but that they should bring forward a better class of men. For it is a fact, the frank acknowledgment of which by all sides would greatly help the discussion of this question, that with ministers of religion, as with everybody else, the amount of salary, with its attendant social circumstances, regulates the quality of the supply. If a Dissenting minister receives a hundred a year and the corresponding clergyman five hundred, the real truth is, not that the clergyman is subject to worldly temptations from which the Dissenting minister is free, but that, as a general rule, this minister will come from a class to which one hundred a year is just of as much importance as five hundred is to the class from which the clergyman comes. Differences of salary do not imply differences of worldliness but only differences of social condition.

It is not pleasant to have to talk about such matters, but since they are so frequently raised it is better to go into them properly than to pass them over with deceitful amiability, and therefore we are compelled to call attention to the fact, plainly apparent to all who are qualified to judge, that as a general rule the Dissenting ministers of England come from what is called a lower social class than that from which most of the clergy come. It is a significant fact that wealthy Dissenters do not, as a body, think of sending their sons to the ministry, and that if any one of these sons is so determined to devote himself his friends are greatly surprised, and often feel, if they would confess the truth to themselves, that he is doing a foolish thing. The common sarcasm about the fools of good families being put into the Church implies more than is thought of by those who use it, for it is something that such families think of putting even their fools into the Church. Rich Dissenters must have a higher idea of the social status of their own ministers before they will, as a class, think of doing even so much.

Of course it is quite open to assert that it does not matter what is the social class from which the ministers of religion come, but that does not touch the point at issue, which is that the larger incomes and better positions of the clergy do not promote worldliness but only bring forth men of a higher social

Q

class. The sale of livings and the more open way in which these matters generally are treated in the Church as compared with the euphuisms which prevail too much amongst sectarian bodies tend to convey a false impression. When a clergyman is promoted he is said to have got "a better living," whilst the Dissenting minister, to whom the same thing happens, is spoken of as having "received a call."

There is no intention here to comment on the fact that such "calls," if favourably considered, are generally from congregations offering better positions. On the contrary it is maintained that ministers, like other people, are fully justified in trying to increase their worldly means. Souls in one place are just as important as souls in another and therefore, all other things being equal, the balance inclines to the larger salary because that gives better opportunities for cultivation and enjoyment to the minister and his family. Either money is in itself an evil or else it is unreasonable in laymen to consider it an advantage for ministers of religion to be stinted of that the pursuit of which they feel justified in making their own chief occupation.

As to social training being of no consequence in ministers of religion, a word of caution may be given against the often repeated remark that only ability and right feeling are needed. Undoubtedly a sound heart is the first requisite, and compared with this all social considerations are trifling, but still they are not to be ignored altogether. A man who is not what is really called a gentleman but who has a sound heart will make a better minister of religion than such a gentleman without that heart, but he who has the heart and is also a gentleman will be much better than either. Apart from the fact that social culture tends to make the mind more capable of appreciating the richness and delicacy of religion there is no doubt that social position gives to a teacher great additional influence over the minds of most men.

It is no essential part of a National Church to offer worldly advantages, but even where, as in England, it does so we hold that these do not tend to lower the character of the clergy but that, on the contrary, they elevate it.

β. It is said that the character of the clergy is lowered because in a National Church there are no means of preventing the ministrations of ungodly persons.

The word "ungodly" carries with it in ecclesiastical discussions two totally distinct meanings which are much too often confused together; one of these is intellectual and the other is moral. Many zealous bigots, and indeed most of those who may be called polemically religious, for the most part apply the epithet "ungodly" to those who do not believe in what they hold to be the doctrines of Christianity. This incorrect use of language has done more than is dreamt of to poison the well of charity and stop the march of progress, for it stirs up against intellectual differences that sort of bitter antipathy which is only justified by moral delinquencies. Undoubtedly in this sense of the word a National Church does permit the ministrations of a good many who are considered "ungodly" by those who differ from them, for the creed of such a Church, whilst setting forth clearly the plain fundamentals of religion, must possess that liberality and simplicity which are essential to its being fitted to be the creed of a nation. There is no inherent reason why a National Church cannot be as strict about secondary matters as any of the sects, and indeed it ought to be able to enforce them more effectively since it has the law at its back, but no wise National Church will attempt anything of the sort, nor will any other Church which comprehends the true meaning and liberal temper of the religion taught by Christ Himself.

But as to the plain fundamentals of the Christian religion, ungodliness in this respect can be prevented better by the national principle than in any other way, for by this alone can we be sure of being able to obtain the two principal requisites for such prevention, namely a simple statement of what those fundamentals are and an open legal trial of any person who is accused of not adhering to them. In the Church of England, in spite of all that is said to the contrary, it would be hard to find any case of importance in which the system has not been found able to deal with avowed unbelief in any of the doctrines which even the religious majority of the nation would permanently consider to be fundamental.

There are waves of feeling which pass over the religious world and lead most people to attach a fictitious importance to some popular doctrine of the hour, but it is the function of a National Church to resist and not obey such impulses. Many doctrines have been thought fundamental for the time, and the Church has been blamed, and schism has been caused, because it would not adopt them, yet afterwards even their supporters have confessed them to be either untrue or unimportant. The plain truth about most of the complaints of "ungodly" ministers in the Church is that a number of people, many of them often opponents of the Church itself, take up with a new doctrine, or a new interpretation of an old one, and then call those "ungodly" who do not think as they do, and that Church system ineffective which will not insist upon these opinions as fundamental.

As to moral "ungodliness" that is certainly a vice which no Church ought to allow but it must be remembered that it is not one which it is very easy to bring home. If a nation claims for itself, as the English does, great personal liberty, it must allow the same to its clergy, and therefore it cannot expect to keep up in its Church such a system of surveillance as might be an effective check upon most moral shortcomings. When we consider the great power of hypocrisy, the indefiniteness of moral faults, and the extent to which each man's conduct must be left to his own control, we may understand how difficult it is for any Church system to keep out this "ungodliness." Of course if a congregation, as often in the sectarian system, feels itself justified in exercising a controlling watchfulness over the private affairs of its ministers, it may sometimes prevent such open scandals as occur occasionally amongst the clergy, but this advantage must be obtained at the cost of lowering the character of the body, for the men who would submit to such interference are not those whom it is desirable to have as ministers of religion. It is better that the clergy should have liberty, even if some of them go wrong, than that they should allow their congregations to be always keeping them right.

There is no reason why the National Church of England, or of any other country, should not be able to check all such " ungodliness," whether intellectual or moral, as it is desirable for any Church to have control over. If there is, however, a deficiency in this respect, the proper cure for the evil is for the nation, which controls the Church, to exercise that power and not to gloat over the scandals of the clergy or rejoice over the helplessness of the Church. It is neither manly nor consistent for those who have withdrawn themselves from the Church and probably thrown obstacles in its way, to point as proofs of the failure of the national principle to occurrences which would never have happened had they done their share as loyal citizens in helping to carry out that principle properly.

Secondly, as to position it is said that in a National Church—

a. The clergy are lowered by being placed under the control of politicians and not allowed to choose their own dignitaries.

Acknowledging that the appointments of bishops, and of many other dignitaries of the Church, are really made by the Prime Minister at the time, we are told that such a system is manifestly contrary to the spirit of religion and unjust to the clergy. Much merriment is often occasioned by supposing the case of such appointments being made by a Jew, or a Dissenter, or an Atheist.

But the justification of this merriment vanishes when we come to look calmly at all the bearings of the question. For, as explained before, such appointments in any Church cannot be made except in one of two ways—namely, either by the clergy themselves or by some power which is over the clergy, and which can only in any large organized Church be the State, for all attempts to combine laity with clergy in such matters necessarily result either in the clergy being made to submit, and then this objection comes into force, or else in their decisions being merely assented to by a number of laymen who in no sense properly represent true lay feeling.

And is there any man who is acquainted with the ecclesiastical history of the past or who understands what is almost invariably the conduct of ministers of religion in such matters, who will maintain that appointments made by the clergy would be likely to be better than those now made by the State? For if we suppose the clergy of any diocese gathered together to choose their own bishop we can form a pretty correct idea of how they would set about it. They would themselves, like every other large body, be divided into parties, upon some principle or other, as they now are into what are called Low, High, and Broad, and the majority would be almost, if not quite, certain to choose one of its own party. No one can believe that a man having High Church opinions or Broad Church leanings would be chosen as their bishop by any body of clergymen of whom the large majority were attached to the Low Church party. As affairs are at present, the consequence of the clergy choosing their own bishops would probably be that every diocese in England would be ruled by a Low Churchman.

It is not our business here to say which of the so-called parties in the Church deserves most encouragement; it is very painful indeed, when we think of what the Christian religion is, to have to talk about such parties at all. All that we have to maintain is that it will be an evil day for the Church, for religion, and for the nation, if ever a system is adopted which will allow any one of these parties to monopolise the government of the Church.

It must be understood that this description of what would happen is not to be taken as implying any condemnation of the conduct of the clergy. On the contrary, looking at the matter from their point of view, the course which they certainly would, is the only one which they conscientiously could, adopt. For there is this peculiarity about ministers of religion that they, as a body, are apt to attach too much importance to secondary matters and to raise questions of practical management into the dignity of conscientious principles. The more enthusiastic they are the more prone are they to this fault, for in the brilliant light of burning piety the minor details of religion stand out in unnatural prominence. We have no right to expect that one who feels thus will vote for a man as his bishop who holds opinions which he believes to be heretical and dangerous. What we have to do is to see that the power of choosing bishops is not entrusted to such hands, and if we do so entrust it we can only hold ourselves responsible for the consequences. The unfitness of the clergy for this office is one proof of their integrity and zeal, for if they were less conscientious or more indifferent they would in all probability be better qualified.

Three evil consequences may here be named out of the many which would result from allowing the clergy to choose their own dignitaries. In the first place, the character of the clergy would be lowered by their differences being embittered, and their attention distracted, by partisan conflicts. In the second place, the character of the dignitaries would be lowered, for it is well known that it is not the ablest nor the most conscientious who are best qualified for gaining votes but those who are most partisanish or most pliant. In the third place, the character of the Church would be lowered because freedom of thought and variety of opinion would be discouraged and suppressed. It may also be named that schism would inevitably soon follow, for a powerful minority would not long be content to see itself completely and hopelessly excluded from power.

In these days when theoretical consistency is by many people so much more sought after than practical efficiency, it is necessary to remind ourselves that that organization which works the best is the best although it may not seem to be the most reasonable. It is unwarrantable conceit in any generation to suppose that it can understand everything, and that therefore any institution for which it cannot find a satisfactory reason must be unsound, for the truth will turn out to be that in most cases the fault lies not in the institution but in the generation. As far as the Church is a spiritual brotherhood we must be guided in our conduct towards it simply by conscience, and must leave the consequences in other hands, but as far as the Church is a temporal organization we must follow that course of action which is most likely to produce permanent practical success. It is a sufficient answer to all the objections about its being wrong for the State to appoint the dignitaries of the Church if we can show that this method actually works better than, or even as well as, any other would be likely to do. And when we come to look at the matter in this way nearly all the objections seem to vanish. For without entering into details, which would be unpleasant because personal, we may safely say that the dignitaries of the Church of England are, taken altogether, of a character which does honour to the Church and which no other system of election has ever been able to excel or even, we might add, to equal.

But setting aside practical results there is good reason to believe that the method of the dignitaries being appointed by the State is also theoretically sound. Even supposing that the Prime Minister is a Jew the case is not so unreasonable as it appears to many people. For a man is made Prime Minister not because he is a Churchman, or a Dissenter, or a Jew, but because he is believed to be best able to manage the affairs of the nation. Now one most essential part of such ability is the power, either in himself or in his associates, to choose the best men for the service of the State, no matter what may be the particular character of that service. In order that the Prime Minister may choose well it is not necessary for him to be personally interested in the particular work to be performed; the administrative functions of a government are distinct from the speculative, and the Prime Minister who personally disapproves of a Ballot Act, or a Coercion Act, or any other measure, may still be thoroughly qualified to carry out properly the decisions of the nation respecting it.

In addition to there being no inherent disqualifications there are several reasons why a Prime Minister, as head of the government, is especially qualified for such an office. If he does not care about the religion he is, as long as it is national, interested in the welfare of the Church as a political institution. No man in the land can have a greater desire that the nation should be well governed, and therefore that the affairs of the Church, as an integral part of the nation, should be wisely administered. He is also presumably the leader of a great party, and since that party is large enough to have put him into power it must necessarily contain a great many adherents of a Church which can be national. A man who has had the tact requisite to gain such a position would be very unlikely to affront a large number of his supporters. A Prime Minister who, although himself indifferent about the religion of the National Church or even opposed to it, did not administer the affairs of that Church to the best of his ability would be committing political suicide.

There is another great advantage in the fact that the actions of the State are done openly and are subject to public criticism. Where the dignitaries of a Church are elected by its ministers their votes are generally given in secret, and even if not, they themselves always resent any interference from the outside public, and indeed that public itself also generally believes that in such circumstances it has no right to interfere. But this is a most mistaken, and also a most mischievous, idea, for it must be remembered that the Church does not exist for the sake of the clergy but for the good of the people, and it would be almost as reasonable for workmen to choose their own overlookers as for the clergy to do so. In a National Church it is the nation which has to be satisfied, and therefore the appointments should be made under national supervision. This is only possible when such appointments are in the hands of the State.

The present method works pretty much in this way. If the head of the Government is ignorant or indifferent he seeks the help of those whose advice he believes to be most in harmony with the wishes of the nation, but if he himself understands ecclesiastical affairs, and takes an interest in them, whilst endeavouring to choose qualified men so as to avoid national opposition he probably allows himself to be influenced in some degree by his own particular feelings. Thus the leanings of a Liberal Government being towards certain schools of thought and those of a Conservative Government being towards others, the succession of political parties furnishes the National Church with a body of dignitaries who, whilst holding in common the simple fundamentals of religion, fairly represent the varieties existing in the nation.

If this method of election is wisest for the Church it must be most conducive to the elevation of the character of the clergy, for that elevation is best promoted not by conferring showy personal power upon the clergy but by increasing the respect and affection of the nation for the Church whose welfare it should be their highest wish to promote.

The next religious objection which it is desirable here to consider is that—

β. The connection between the Church and the State is lowering to the position of the clergy because they are thus fettered by Articles.

It is said that the clergy of the National Church are bound hand and foot; that by signing the Articles of the Church of England they give up their freedom of thought, and that many of them are in consequence afterwards obliged to stifle the promptings of their own consciences and to preach what they do not in their hearts believe.

If we look fairly at this objection we find that it involves a question of more importance even than that of the existence of a National Church, for the real point at issue is whether or not there should be any definite creed in religion. This is a question which underlies a great many of the discussions of these days and which must sooner or later come to the front for decision. The feelings respecting creeds of civilized humanity have always greatly ebbed and flowed; in some periods religious-minded men have been so keen in this respect that they have fought and suffered and died for differences of creed which seem to us almost ridiculously insignificant. But the characters of these men and their other works amply prove that they were no more likely than we are to get so excited about trifles, and therefore we must believe that they felt that there was an importance in these matters which we cannot even conceive of. During other periods the world generally has fallen into almost total indifference about creeds, most people having a feeling, too indefinite and easy to be called an opinion, that it does not matter what is a man's belief so long as he lives up to it, nor even whether he has any religious belief at all provided he conducts himself properly and enjoys life reasonably. It is in one of these second periods that we have lately been living, and we shall find that the objection now before us is mostly urged by those who have no definite belief themselves, and for whom sentimental liberality is often, although it may be unconsciously, merely a cloak for sceptical indifference.

Those who do not care about religion at all are of course quite consistent in putting down creeds as unnecessary, but it is well for those who really value and cherish religion to consider whether there can be any abiding religion without a creed. It would not be appropriate here to attempt to explain the workings of the human mind, but we may go so far as to say that it is very doubtful whether there can be any continuous sentiment without a corresponding intellectual belief; even sudden outbursts of emotion must, unless they are to be considered irresponsible, be founded on something which, expressed in language, would be their creed. Even if religion had merely to do with the emotions it must have a creed. But we know that all religion necessarily is largely concerned with the intellect, and there can certainly be no intellectual operation without a belief, the statement of which is a creed.

Undoubtedly the first simplicity of Christianity has been lamentably disfigured and hidden by the addition of so many extra and unnecessary beliefs, still we must acknowledge that from the beginning belief has been an essential ingredient of Christ's religion. To understand the meaning of that mysterious and much-abused word "faith" we must go back to the unity of human nature and forget those distinctions between feeling and thought which may have served the purposes of philosophy but which have darkened the face of religion. If we may be bold enough to venture to inquire what all those who, coming into personal contact with Christ, were pronounced by Him to possess that faith which leads to salvation had in common we should say that it was a bending of their whole nature before Him. We cannot help feeling that this is in large measure what Christ Himself meant by faith, and that all those who since then, when the Gospel has been put before them, have felt that it revealed to them something infinitely higher and better than they had any conception of before, and something which their souls must reverence and submit to, these are real Christians whatever be their names. This faith may in individual cases find expression, as in the language of St. Peter: "I believe that thou art the Christ, the Son of the living God;" or it may not be able to express itself at all; a man may have it and not acknowledge it to others or even to himself.

But this faith, although principally coming from the heart, cannot be separated from the intellect; the intellect is the door of the heart through which it must pass in and come out. Religion must have a belief, and as soon as religion requires expression that belief must become a creed. This is necessary even for communication between one individual and another. But a Church as a temporal organization is founded entirely upon the outward expressions of religion, for it knows nothing of religion except from expression. A Church is a unity not because it is a single organization but because that organization is for a single religion; and the singleness of that religion can have no existence for a Church except through a singleness of expression—that is, through a creed. A Church without a creed, either written or implied, is no Church at all.

As a matter of fact all Churches have creeds. There is no place of worship in England, no matter what may be its name, the congregation of which does not expect its minister to hold certain opinions. Would any Trinitarian congregation retain a minister who openly and continuously preached Unitarianism—or any Unitarian congregation one who taught Trinitarianism? The difference between the National Church and other Churches as far as creeds are concerned is that the creed of the National Church is plainly written out and must in cases of dispute be legally interpreted, whilst that of other Churches is either not written out but left to the decision of the individual members of congregations, or else, if written, its meaning is subject to clerical interpretation. Bearing in mind how changeable are the moods of what is called the religious world; how at times its temper is lax, whilst at others it is exacting even about secondary matters, few people will deny that the liberty of the law is better than that of congregational surveillance or clerical judgment.

Many people talk about creeds as if there was something humiliating about them; as if we may fairly pity those who acknowledge them, and pride ourselves on our own exemption from them. But in spite of this notion, now so prevalent, we venture to say that creeds have the best of the argument. For if a man has a belief on such an important matter as religion it is surely more manly to say so. The attacks which are now being so freely made against religion amply prove that unbelief has no hesitation about expressing its creed, and it is hard to see why belief should not do the same. In politics every man is expected to have a creed, and many of those who speak against religious creeds are the first to condemn those who will not openly avow a political one, calling them vacillating, and careless, and ignorant. The truth appears to be that creeds are to be required on subjects about which we are ourselves interested but are to be condemned on those to which we are indifferent or opposed.

But it is said that even if creeds are necessary they ought not to be made binding, and that it is wrong to compel young men on entering the Church to bind themselves to go on believing in a set of opinions which they probably do not then understand, and from which they may afterwards feel obliged to dissent. This is one of the evils, if an evil it may be called, which are essential to the conduct of human affairs. Nearly all positions of life are taken up on certain conditions which we are expected to adhere to. A man who takes upon himself the office of a minister of religion enters into a bargain by which he is to receive certain advantages on condition that he performs certain duties. One of the most important of these duties is that he shall teach certain doctrines which those who engage him believe to be of primary importance, and it is naturally understood that he will not teach those doctrines unless he believes in them himself. Therefore if he does not believe in them he has no right to enter into the bargain, and if he ceases to believe in them he ought to retire from a contract of which he can no longer perform his part. It is difficult to see how a National Church—and especially that of England—deviates from this simple rule of commercial integrity. A nation adopts a religion, an essential part of which is belief in certain doctrines; an organization—the Church—is established for this religion, and the nation not unnaturally expects that those who enter that organization and receive its rewards will teach this religion. Whoever undertakes any secular office to which a reward is attached is required to promise to perform the duties of that office, and this is all that is meant as far as the Church is concerned by the clergy having to sign the Articles. If afterwards they find that their opinions have so changed that they are no longer in accordance with these Articles they ought to consider themselves unable any longer to carry out their part of the contract and therefore obliged in honour to give it up. If they do not do so the State has to decide, and it is generally accepted that the law is the best authority to which questions of breach of contract can be referred. To deprive a clergyman of a position whose conditions he can no longer conform to is not persecution, as it is so frequently called, but is merely the enforcement of one of the most rudimentary principles of honesty, and the reflection, if any there be, lies not upon the system but upon the clergyman.

The same practice in all important characteristics prevails in every other Church, for if a minister of an organized Church like the Wesleyan ceases to profess the opinions which are considered essential he is subject to deprivation by his fellow-ministers, whilst in what is called the Congregational system he is expected by his congregation to retire, and if he does not do so voluntarily, there are many ways in which he can be, and is, removed. And this is only perfectly reasonable, for those who build and support a place of worship on the condition that a certain system of religion is to be inculcated there, have a right, and also a duty, to see that that condition is fulfilled.

It may be said that the worldly advantages which a clergyman must abandon by leaving the Church offer too strong a temptation and prevent many men from following the dictates of conscience. This is undoubtedly true, for we cannot help fancying that there are clergymen remaining in the Church whose opinions are not in accordance with the requirements of the nation, whilst others do violence to their moral natures by smothering the first suggestions of doubt through fear that if openly treated these might so grow as to make the retention of their clerical position inconsistent with integrity. This is one of the drawbacks of all positions which involve moral considerations. In politics we often see men obliged to give up what they most value for the sake of conscience; occupation, position, ambition have to be sacrificed, but we do not therefore say that these things should be done away with, or that political creeds are evils. In religious affairs such sacrifices are more frequently required simply because conscience enters more largely into religion. But the difference is only one of degree, and if we object because a change of religious creed often involves the loss of worldly advantages we must not blame either the creed or the advantages but must lay our complaints at the door of inevitable law. And undoubtedly this law is a good one, especially in these effeminate times, for it tends to give to the service of truth the robustness which comes from difficulty. Singularity is now so much esteemed that he who denies what the majority believe is much more likely to be made a hero than a martyr.

But it is said that even if a Church ought to have a creed it does not follow that this creed should be stationary, as in the National Church. We hear a great deal in these days about the influence of science upon religion; we are told that modern discoveries have so enlarged our knowledge that we can no longer accept the doctrines of our forefathers, and that as the rate of progress is now so great we may expect that before long most of our religious opinions will have been changed. It is said that we ought not therefore to bind ourselves to any permanent creeds.

Theology has usually been considered the study most guilty of bold assumptions and unwarrantable hypotheses but it must now yield the palm to what is called modern science; the greatest achievements in this way of theology, its wildest flights of imagination, its extremest exactions of dogmatism, seem humble when compared with what is now done by its modern rival. Universal laws are assumed on the strength of accidental coincidences, and the examination of a few superficial phenomena is supposed to afford sufficient material for dogmatically laying down explanations of the whole system of nature. Scientific men seem now to follow seriously the method suggested in those jocular problems, such as the one by which we are invited to infer all the particulars about a ship from knowing the age or complexion of its captain. One axiom of this sort of science seems to be that the oldest and most general beliefs are the most likely to be untrue and may be denied upon the least evidence. And it is thought that there is no sphere of

R

knowledge into which this science may not enter as the arbiter; the man who can split up a ray of light, or offer a theory about the history of a rock, supposes himself fully qualified to analyse the operations of the mind and explain the deepest intricacies of the soul. Science and religion are like the Borderers of early times; for a while those on one side were the strongest and ravaged the territory of the others, and then the reverse came. Science is now having ample revenge; if in past days religion has encroached on its domain, it has never overrun it; it has interfered in some parts, as astronomy, but has left the rest alone. Science, however, is now sweeping over all the fields of religion, and claiming for itself universal dominion, shaking its despotic sceptre even over the most distant and most foreign regions.

If, however, we look through the clouds of dust raised by the chariot wheels of science and keep ourselves from giving way to the prevailing excitement, we are surprised to find how very little substance there is in all that is said about the influence of science upon religion. Science is like a foreign conqueror—it may assume outward dominion, but can have little real effect upon the people themselves; like Alexander, it may sweep over whole nations yet leave no influence behind; there is all the show and noise of power but none of its reality. If we take the Bible and read it carefully in the newest scientific light, with the aid of all the knowledge which science has in any degree substantiated, we find that the great text-book of the Christian religion remains just what it was—not a doctrine of any importance, not a feeling of any strength, is affected in the least. We might go even further and say that there is not a fact worth considering which does not remain where it was, but it is sufficient to find that our religion, in so far as it has any reality, and our Bible, in so far as it has any value, come out completely untouched from all attacks. Not only so, but our affection and faith in them are increased by the revelations of science, for all true knowledge must bring out more clearly the fundamental principles of creation and display more fully the benevolence and marvellousness of God.

And, indeed, if we reflect calmly we see how impossible it is for science, when developed to the utmost, to exercise any permanent control over religion, or even any considerable influence upon it. For when we survey the whole extent of being we see that matter, with all its connections, occupies but a small portion of it, and it is as absurd to extend to the whole the inferences derived from this portion as it would be to assume that the conditions of a single province apply universally to a great empire. Even excluding all thoughts of a future state, there are few men of correct judgment and proper feeling who will not acknowledge that the sum of what they would call life is made up much more largely of that which has nothing to do with matter than of that which has. But science cannot go beyond matter without ceasing to be science, and therefore all that realm of being outside the bounds of matter must be under another rule. This rule is chiefly that of religion, to which are subject our highest thoughts and feelings, our affections and hopes, and all our purest sources of such pleasure as does not depend upon material things. We may therefore, without being frightened for religion, give up to scientific men all that they can ever think of claiming, and even more; we may listen calmly whilst they assume as scientific truths hypotheses for which they can offer no scientific proof; we may allow them to demolish, if they can, the material beliefs which have associated themselves with the spiritualisms of our religion. For instance, even if the theory, lately brought forward by Darwin, about the origin of the human frame be true, the religion cannot be affected of those who feel that this frame itself is but a passing accident, and has no permanent part in man's real being; we may consider quietly all those suppositions about atoms which are now disturbing men's minds when we reflect that these atoms themselves are but fleeting appearances and will vanish after a duration of time which, compared with eternity, is but as yesterday or as a watch in the night. We will gladly let Science search out to the utmost the innermost secrets of nature, but we also bid it remember that this nature itself is but a transient expression of the Creator's will, and is also but one such expression amongst many. Every day, from this earth alone, there are thousands of individual souls being summoned to shake themselves loose from all material conditions, and the time must soon come when the whole of humanity shall be liberated from them; when Nature itself, with all that Science can take any cognizance of, shall be folded up as a garment and as a vesture shall be changed.

There is one question which we must settle in our own minds before we attempt to decide whether creeds ought to be stationary or not, and this is whether or not we believe that the theory of evolution still holds good for religion. It is not for us to determine whether the religions which previously prevailed in the world were meant to bring man into a fit condition to receive the Christian revelation, but we do believe that for any period such as we have a right to consider that revelation was meant to be complete and final. The whole meaning of that revelation could not be apprehended at once, for even after this lapse of time we feel that we only very partially know it, but the fault is with ourselves; the changes of mankind bring with them changing interpretations but the revelation itself remains the same.

Those who consider that Christianity but marks one stage in human development and that this religion will be replaced by another are consistent in objecting to settled creeds, but it is only in such people that this objection is consistent, for those who believe that the doctrines of Christianity will be lasting must wish to have those doctrines embodied in a lasting form. Doctrines can only be embodied in words, and such an embodiment is a creed.

As a matter of fact there is no reason why the creed of a National Church should be considered as especially fixed. Undoubtedly there is more promise of stability in a faith which is plainly expressed and legally interpreted than in one which is left to individual understanding or sectarian explanation, but still there is no reason why the National Creed cannot be modified, when necessary, as easily as any other; it is merely the creed of the nation and can be altered by the nation whenever it likes. History shows that nations have been much more ready to alter their creeds than private religious societies have.

Another objection to a National Creed is that since the doctrines of Christianity were meant to be the same for the whole world, we have no right to give them geographical and national limitations. But we do not limit the universality of religion by giving its doctrines a separate expression for each nation, any more than the universality of a political principle is limited because in various countries this principle is embodied differently. In fact, the necessities of language, imposed upon us by Providence, compel us to find a separate expression of this religion for every separate language. And the national plan has this advantage that it is found to correspond more nearly than any other with the divisions of language. In addition to this, we can claim for it that we thus adopt the largest unit under our control, whereas by the other system each sect is left to make out its own creed, and thus the universality of Christianity is, in this sense, much more broken up.

7. *The last objection which it is necessary in this chapter to consider is that a National Church cannot uphold a definite religion.*

In the attacks now being made upon the Church of England probably no argument is more frequently urged or more widely accepted than the one asserting that the divisions in the Church itself warrant its disestablishment. We are repeatedly told how wide are the differences separating what are called the various "parties" in the Church from each other, and how strong are their mutual oppositions; how "High" are arrayed against "Low," and both against "Broad;" how "Ritualists" despise "Evangelicals" and "Evangelicals" hate "Ritualists," and how the earnest men of all parties are chafing under the control of the State and longing to be able to follow their own conscientious convictions and to liberate themselves from the scandal of Church fellowship with those to whose opinions and practices they are so strongly opposed. It is said that many of the clergy are crying out for liberation from State bondage and that many more are secretly longing for it, so that those who are called "Liberationists" ought not to be spoken of as trying to destroy a Church, but only as wishing to break open the door of a prison; roused by the cries of its inmates they are rushing—in unselfish enthusiasm —against the ecclesiastical Bastille.

We are also told that this Liberation movement will, if successful, only anticipate by a short time the ordinary course of nature, like a draught given to carry away a suffering and hopeless patient. For we are expected to believe as a matter of course that a Church so divided against itself cannot possibly long hold together but must soon fall to pieces without being attacked from outside, like a ricketty old ship going to the bottom in calm weather.

The positive movement for disestablishment is said to be justified because a Church so demoralised should not be allowed to remain, and because the many excellent ministers whom it contains ought to be set at liberty and enabled to follow their own convictions.

In reference to this objection it is necessary in the first place to call to mind a fact which needs constantly repeating because it is so constantly forgotten, namely that a National

Church is not the Church of the parsons but of the people; it exists for the benefit of the people and is under their control, therefore it is for them to decide what latitude ought to be allowed in it. Of course the clergy exercise a great, and indeed the principal, influence in forming the opinion of the people in this respect, but they have rightly no power beyond that, and are bound themselves to conform to the decisions resulting from the opinion so formed. If this opinion is in favour of exact uniformity and of allowing no differences amongst the clergy, there is no reason why a National Church cannot uphold as definite a religion as any other Church can, but if this opinion is not thus disposed, it is a proof that such differences already exist amongst the people and are not caused or fostered by a National Church which permits them. A true National Church reflects the feelings and opinions of the nation; it is the mirror which tells us what is the religious condition of the people, and if we see differences of which we disapprove, our proper course is to alter the condition which is reflected and not to smash the glass which reflects it. As we cannot destroy these differences by preventing ourselves from seeing them, we should be thankful for that which shows them to us and so teaches us our duty respecting them.

The truth is that if the nation is in favour of what may be called a rigid religion, the National Church will uphold such a religion, and if the nation is not in favour of such a religion, it would be wrong and absurd for the National Church to uphold such. If in the Church there are differences which are to be condemned, the fault lies not with the national principle but with the people, and it is to the people that the cure ought to be applied.

It may be said that we can only affect the people through the Church but, granting this, we must remember that it is much easier to exercise this influence through a Church under our own control than through a number of private Churches with which we have no right to interfere. If there was no National Church we may be quite sure that the causes of the differences now existing in that Church would not be removed, but instead of that they would become intrenched within a number of private Churches and would thus be strengthened and perpetuated. Opinions with which we disagree are not likely to be more easily conquered by being made inaccessible, nor will that unity which we desire be most probably brought about by the sectarian isolation of those who differ from each other. The best way to get rid of differences is to bring together those who hold them, and not to send them off by themselves into separate corners. He whose ideal is the agreement of an exclusive sect has a poor and cowardly conception of what is meant by Christian unity. Grieved at the differences existing amongst the people, he invites those who agree with him to shut themselves up together and let down the blinds and forget the general differences in the enjoyment of their own little unity. This is not the conduct of a Christian or a patriot, for the nation, which is the largest brotherhood on which we can bring our influence to bear, is the one whose ideal we should keep before us. Christian fellowship is to be brought about by promoting freedom of intercourse and not by raising up in the national territory a number of isolated fortified towns at war with each other.

So far as differences are concerned, a National Church has, then, these two advantages, that it shows what these are and also provides the best means for overcoming them as far as is desirable.

Turning to the particular case of the Church of England we must ask ourselves whether the differences in it are not such as exist amongst the people, and whether these differences must not on the whole be considered beneficial rather than otherwise.

Two explanations must here be given. In the first place, by the people is not meant the majority of the whole population, or even of those who exercise control by voting, but only of those who may be said to be included amongst what are called religious people, that is, people who take an interest and part in religious affairs. For we cannot help knowing that large numbers of the population of England are completely indifferent about religion, and others are even opposed to it. But indifference and opposition are not qualities which ought to be represented in any Church. It may be said that we have no right thus to limit the term people, but this objection disappears when we remark that it is not the indifferent or opposed who govern the religious policy of England, but the others. In the present attack upon the Church an attempt is being made to rouse into activity the indifferent and opposed, but so far these have been content to leave the conduct of religious matters to others and therefore it is with those others that we have to deal. And, as a matter of fact, this is the course adopted in almost all national business. When Parliament passes any new law of importance or repeals an old one we choose to say that this is done in accordance with the will of the people, but the truth in almost every case is that a small active portion desires the change whilst the large passive portion merely acquiesces in it. In every community the many are led by the few, and we cannot get rid of this necessity by any schemes for making all men equal; what is called the public feeling of a town is formed by a score or two of its inhabitants, and action is taken obediently to that feeling in matters about which a large numerical majority know absolutely nothing. So nationally we say that the voice of the people is in favour of a certain course when, in reality, by far the largest number of the people have expressed no opinion and in all probability have formed none. In all such affairs, and in religious ones most of all, the uninterested must be led by the interested, the ignorant by the informed, and dark will be the future of any nation in which this is not so.

Considering the people in this way, we cannot but acknowledge that the differences in the Church no more than represent the differences existing amongst the people for whom that Church exists. This is so even if we limit the term to those who may be supposed to have an interest in a Protestant Church such as that of England, for Roman Catholics are at the outset obliged to draw themselves away, but Protestant Dissenters must be included; and indeed there is good reason to believe that even taking Dissent as a whole, its varieties of thought and tone are more accurately represented by the Church of England than by its own fragmentary societies.

It would not be becoming here to attempt to enter into an explanation of what are the theological differences now existing in the Church, but we are obliged most earnestly to give one necessary warning, and that is that we must not allow our estimate of the importance of these differences to be formed from what the clergy themselves say about them. Those who study any subject much almost invariably think a great deal more of their small differences with other students of the same subject than they do of the great differences between themselves and those who do not study that subject at all. This holds true in philosophy, in history, in science, but most of all in religion, for that is the subject into which conscience, and passion, and all the feelings which help to embitter differences, most largely enter. The clergy, who are constantly busied about this subject, would not be men if they did not come to attach to the differences existing amongst themselves an importance quite out of proportion to that which really belongs to them, and the more earnest and conscientious they are, the more liable are they to do this.

But it is for others to judge as to the real importance of these differences, and when we come to do that we must take up a very different standard from that which the clergy, or ministers generally, use. We must shut our ears to the clamour of the hour and our eyes to its exaggerations, and must try to see these things in the proportions of eternal truth. A man may hide the sun with his thumb-nail, if this is only near enough, and so the closeness of apparent differences may deceive us as to their absolute size. But in religion it is this real importance which must be looked at, for partisan excitements are very temporal and have next to no concern with anything which, as religion, reaches through eternity.

Religion is like a great building whose complete proportions cannot be seen unless we stand a long way off; those who go too close begin discussing the little architectural details and fail to observe the general proportions of the whole. Looking at Christianity in this way, many of the differences about which its followers quarrel so hotly completely disappear, and many others, although remaining visible, sink into insignificance. Reading our Bibles in the natural light of calm sense, the conception of religion which rises in our minds and takes possession of our hearts is one upon which most of the differences about which we hear so much can have next to no influence. 'All through the Bible there is but one difference recognised and that is the difference between those who follow Christ and those who do not. This is not confined to the New Testament, but is equally true of the old, for there they followed the same leader, only less fully revealed to them; Abraham saw Christ's day and was glad. The unity of the Bible is most strikingly shown in the unity of the qualities which throughout its pages are displayed by those who are thus the followers of Christ. If we put all the Bible heroes together, from the first to the last, we shall find that they all possessed certain qualities in common and that their rank in the scale of heroism is determined by their possession of these qualities. We thus form an idea of what it is which constitutes a Christian, and then coming back to our own times we find that with this idea most of the differences which now separate Christians from each other have scarcely anything to do. We therefore say that Churches ought not to be split up, nor others organised, on account of these differences, for we have no right to create and make prominent distinctions which the Bible itself does not recognise.

Of course there must be different forms of worship adapted to the varied characters and states of civilisation of different nations, but we must not be led into attaching too much importance to these differences of form ; as long as the central feeling is the same we must allow great liberty of expression. Christ Himself did not look for any uniformity of confession from those who became His followers ; He was satisfied often with no confession at all, and often, too, with knowing that the right feeling was there although the possessor himself might be only very partially conscious of it.

Not merely must there be great latitude of expression allowed for different nations but also, on account of the same reason, for the people of the same nation. The Church of England recognises this fact. Whilst laying down such conditions as will ensure, as far as anything of the kind can, the acceptance by all its clergy of the fundamentals of Christianity, it allows the same liberty as the Bible does in respect to all such matters as are not fundamental.

When we come to compare all these differences in the Church with the great verities of Christianity we are ashamed that so much fuss can ever have been made about them. When we put together "Thou shalt love the Lord thy God" and " Thou shalt preach in a surplice," or "Thou shalt love thy neighbour as thyself" and " Thou shalt stand at the north side," we feel how liable men of every age are to trouble about mint, and anise, and cummin, and to neglect the weightier matters of the law.

But even judging them by a lower standard, the differences existing in the Church of England seem comparatively insignificant. We hear occasionally of a solitary clergyman who goes beyond what the nation approves, but these instances are so few that we can count on our fingers the names of all those who during the last ten years have come into any real prominence of this sort. When we think of the thousands of clergymen who are going on steadily doing their duty from year to year without a word of complaint we see what little reason there is for disaffection. As to differences of doctrine the cases are still fewer, for we scarcely ever hear of one worth notice. Instead of complaining about the differences in the Church of England being so great, we are surprised that, considering the liberty allowed, they are so small, and we are disposed to maintain that in comparison with the difficulty and delicacy of its task, there is no organization in the land which works more effectively. Probably the unobtrusiveness of its workings, which is usually considered a recommendation for other organizations, is the reason why the Church system is so often accused of impotence.

We say then that the differences in the Church of England are no more than may be reasonably expected, and that to split up the Church on account of these would be to distort the great principles of the Christian religion.

In the second place we would go further and maintain that these differences, such as they are, are an advantage to the Church and to the cause of religion.

For it must be remembered that compared with the great body of those who are attached to the Church, those who consider these differences to be of great importance are but very few, much fewer than we should suppose from the statements of the enemies of the Church or from the prominence which they give themselves in public attention, for they are like the men who play the part of soldiers at the theatre and who keep coming in and out so rapidly that we may believe there is an army. The truth is, however, that by far the great majority of the laity care very little about the differences amongst the clergy; they attend the services of the Church to satisfy their own spiritual wants and so long as those wants are reasonably attended to in substance, they are willing to allow considerable latitude about forms. The temper of the English nation is sensible and patient, and this temper finds its best expression in the Church. For it may without unkindness be said that the laymen attached to the Church are, as a body, marked by a religious moderation and quietness which are not found so largely amongst those who belong to the various sects.

Although this moderate temper is liable to be despised in times of excitement it is nevertheless that to which the English people must, from its inherent character, inevitably always return as its natural condition. The system of a National Church alone can meet this condition.

If we suppose the National Church destroyed there would then soon be left no religious organizations except private ones, most of them created to vindicate some isolated doctrine or practice. We can imagine what would then be the painful condition of those who, whilst personally attached to religion as a whole, do not care especially about these doctrines or practices, and in general have a strong dislike to the associations of sectarianism. They would be compelled either to ally themselves with some one sect or else to have no religious services at all. No doubt many would take the first course, some of whom would degenerate into narrow-minded fanatics, but the most would in all probability prefer to fall back upon their own resources, and in consequence their religion would gradually grow weaker, and often die out altogether. In spite of appearances to the contrary, we believe that those who would be placed in this position by the destruction of the National Church are not a small number, but comprise the large majority of what may be called the moderate and respectable classes, using the adjectives with their best significations.

Not only would those quiet and reverent laymen who want religion and not sectarianism be, after Disestablishment, like sheep without a fold, but the alienation between them and the different Churches would develop in a rapidly increasing ratio. For there can be no harm in stating the fact, which indeed follows from natural necessity, that the men who are willing to become ministers in a Sectarian Church are sure to be, on the whole, less cultivated and more narrow-minded than the clergy of a National Church, if only because of the difference of intellectual liberty. The religion taught by such men, and the tone they would give it, would provoke the neglect, or even sometimes contempt, of the more educated portion of the laity, who, having to choose between no religion and such a sectarian one, would decide against the sectarian. Thus the Church would lose the friendship of those upon whom it must depend for the supply of its most desirable ministers, and in consequence the tone of the Church itself would be lowered. The men who require such intellectual liberty as is allowed in the Church of England are those who are most capable of giving tone to a Church and to religion, but these are just the men who would not enter the service of a Sectarian Church.

But the effects of destroying the Church on account of its differences would not be so great even upon these classes as they would be upon the masses of the people, who seem to care very little about religion. We cannot deny, for the fact is being constantly and painfully impressed upon us, that large numbers, if not even a majority, of the masses of the people apparently go through life in complete indifference to religion. The disputes between the various Churches and the differences in the same Church are nothing to them; they do not even know about them, and all attempts to raise them to an interest in religion seem utterly to fail. No doubt a large part of the blame must be laid upon the people themselves, upon that weakness of human nature to which they are in bondage, but we may also ask ourselves whether some of the responsibility does not rest upon those who are considered the friends of religion, for this religion has been so broken up and distorted that it has lost its power of charming those who have not seen into its nature. If we would do our duty we must return to the breadth and simplicity of the Bible; we must teach a religion which is natural and sympathetic, which will commend itself to the plainest understanding and meet the commonest needs; we must banish or sink into insignificance the differences about which theologians quarrel and Churches divide, and must lift up again in all its glorious plainness and practicalness that Christianity which was given to us by the great Master.

A religion such as this, which can alone have any chance of winning over the masses of the people, must allow plenty of differences such as those on account of which we are now asked to destroy the Church of England. To hand over religion to the sects would be to abandon all hope of ever making it accepted by the people. Instead of supporting Disestablishment we must become convinced that the religion of a National Church is in this character the only one which is possible amongst the masses, and that the organization of a National Church is the only one which can bring that religion to bear upon them.

In concluding this chapter we may venture to make one appeal, and that is that this question of the National Church shall be judged less by political theories or social recriminations and more by religious consequences. Those who are attached to religion must feel that, compared with its welfare, all other considerations are trifling, and therefore they should consider with solemn carefulness before they join in a movement which may so grievously injure it.

CHAPTER VI.

SOCIAL OBJECTIONS.

THE first and most frequently urged of what may be called the social objections is that which is grounded on the assumption that the Church is a State-paid institution. This may be put in the form that—

1. *The State has no right to pay towards the support of one religious body.*

It is represented that the Church is only one amongst what are called "the religious denominations," and that it is manifestly unfair for the State to single out this one for its support. We are told that the money of the whole nation ought not to be given to a Church whose adherents are only part of the nation, and for two reasons, namely, that the money of the nation should not be spent at all for religion, and secondly, that even if it should be so spent, all the different religious bodies ought to have a fair share.

After what has been said it is needless to remark that this objection is founded on a fundamental misconception of the nature of a National Church. Still, as this objection is so repeatedly brought forward and pushed to the front, and as the attempt is constantly being made to rouse by it the angry cupidity of the multitude, it is necessary, even at the risk of repetition, to examine it at some length. This examination divides itself into the two questions of whether a State has the right to support one Church, and secondly, whether the

State actually does pay towards the support of the Church of England?

In reference to the first question we must repeat that a National Church is not in any sense a "sect," or "body," or "denomination" at all; and neither has, nor can have, any existence whatever apart from the State. The State does not single out any one religious organization to favour with its especial help but creates its own organization, and even if it adopts some particular form, that form is so altered by the addition of State control as to become virtually a new one. A National Church comes into being, not by the State holding a review of all the religious bodies and picking out one for promotion, but by the State deciding that the control of religion is an essential part of its duty; the means by which that control is to be exercised are then developed like any other portion of the organization of the State. The absurdity of talking in England about the State choosing one sect from many to receive its favours is seen at once when we consider that the National Church here is as old as the monarchy, whilst all the so-called "sects" have come into being during the last two or three centuries. Soldiers might as well object that they were not promoted before they were born as the sects complain that they were not chosen in preference to the Church.

The State having decided to include the control of religion amongst its functions, and having erected an organization for this purpose, has just as much right to spend the money of the nation upon that organization as upon any other. There can be no injustice merely because some people do not believe in the religion upheld by the State, or disapprove of its receiving State support; it is for the nation to decide upon this matter in the same way as it decides upon all others, and then those who disagree must submit without complaining until they can bring about a change. Unbelievers or Dissenters would have no more right to complain if they were taxed to support a National Church than Quakers have to object to pay towards the support of the army. We are nearly all of us compelled to pay taxes for some purpose or other of which we disapprove, but we do not think of saying that we are on this account unjustly dealt with. To those who say that even those who disagree share in the benefits of such measures whereas those who differ from the Church get no good from it, it may be replied that this disagreement with these measures presumably arises from the conviction that they will not be beneficial, and also that the National Church is maintained because it is believed to be for the good of the nation, in which good even those who differ from it must necessarily share. Therefore we maintain that even if all was true which is said about the Church being State-paid, there would be no injustice and no violation of the ordinary and necessary methods of national procedure.

But, as a matter of fact, it happens that the Church of England is not, and never has been, State-paid at all. In order to test this we must try to ascertain what are the sources from which the revenue of the Church of England is derived. This is an exceedingly difficult task, partly because the Church is one of the oldest institutions in the land, and therefore its possession of property goes beyond any reliable records, and partly because the law does not recognize the existence of any such body as the Church. The theory previously laid down that the Church has no individual existence apart from the State is confirmed by the fact that the law never speaks of the Church of England as an incorporated body, nor treats it as such. Each separate Church holds its own property as a distinct ownership; glebes and parsonages are invested in the incumbents as corporations sole, and there is, as far as property is concerned, no more connection between any two parishes than between any two landlords, both being subject to the law and to that alone. It is therefore very difficult to trace as belonging to a single institution the origin of property which has come into the possession of numberless isolated institutions.

Excluding the annual contributions in different forms to the Church, which, it must be remembered, exceed in amount all the other sources of revenue put together, we may say that the income of the Church of England is derived either from tithes or from possessions of land.

The custom of giving tithes is older than Christianity, and probably even than Judaism itself, for it seems to have been introduced amongst the Jews not as a custom new to the world. It is not important to inquire whether there is any philosophical reason for pitching upon this particular fraction ; even if no better can be given than the number of our fingers and toes a custom which has continued since man was so constituted may be considered to have justified its claim to existence. It is sufficient to point out that neither here nor anywhere else where this custom has prevailed can any date be found for its beginning.

But although there is no record of the way in which tithes first began in England we can form a pretty fair idea of their origin without claiming for our ancestors—" pious ancestors " as they are satirically called—the possession of any particular amount of religious fervour ; indeed self-interest alone will afford sufficient motives. For the material interests of all owners of land are involved in the preservation of order and the development of civilisation. Without order there can be no security for produce, and therefore no rents, and without civilisation there can be no prospect of such rents being increased. But the landlords of old times believed, as the landlords of times to come will have to believe, that religion is the strongest instrument for the preservation of order and the development of civilisation ; they knew that the parson was even for these objects more effective than the policeman and the Church than the prison. Therefore they took care that the people on their estates were provided with churches to go to and clergymen to look after them. In those days, as there was no middle class, these had to be provided by the landlords themselves, and so these landlords did provide them and set aside for their support a fixed portion of the revenue they received from their land.

The kings also, who were as much interested in the preservation of order and the development of civilisation over the whole kingdom as the landlords were over their separate estates, did all they could to encourage the landlords in thus bringing the influence of religion to bear upon the people. Hence we find that at a very early period the title of thane was conferred on every landlord who built and endowed a church.

The bishops also, as men of exceptional character and education, exercised great influence in those times and did their utmost to encourage the custom of granting tithes. Most of them made the concession of tithes a necessary condition before they would consecrate a new church.

Thus the granting of tithes came to be a custom. Instead of tithes being originally a requirement of the State they were for a long time inculcated by the Church before the State took any cognizance of them; they were mentioned in the "Excerptions" of Archbishop Egbriht, of York, in A.D. 740, and in the 17th Article of the Council of Calcuith in A.D. 785 the general payment of tithes was ordered. The history of tithes is marked by the following stages; they arose from the piety or self-interest of the landlords, they became a general custom through the encouragement of sovereigns and ecclesiastics, they were then ordered by canon law, and were finally confirmed by common law.

Many people now speak of tithes as a State-imposed tax and justify their language by pointing to an old charter or two in which the payment of tithes is inculcated by royal authority. It must be remembered, however, that there is the greatest difference between a law which creates a new tax and one which adopts a tax already customary; the phrase "State-imposed" can only be correctly applied to the first case whilst tithes come almost exclusively under the second case. Blackstone emphatically states that no time can be found for the beginning of tithes; in Bede's *Ecclesiastical History* there occurs, in the latter part of the seventh century, the mention of a payment called " Kirksest," which most probably corresponds with tithes.

The unreasonableness of representing tithes as a State exaction is shown by the fact that in those times the landlords, out of whose pockets these tithes entirely came, were very powerful whilst the State authority was very weak. Yet we hear of no disturbances on the part of the landlords, no such opposition as would certainly have been shown had they considered tithes as a State tax, and such as they did show against impositions quite trivial in amount compared with tithes.

After the payment of tithes had thus grown up to be a general custom confirmed by canon and common law, the invasions of the Danes occurred and disturbed the whole fabric not merely of the civil constitution but also of the social habits of the people. When this whirlwind had passed away the authorities began to build up again all that had been blown down. Amongst other institutions the custom of tithes was restored, and several charters are still extant, notably one of Ethelwulf, by which directions are given in this respect. But it is unreasonable to point to such charters as creating a new law when they only revived an old custom.

The remainder of the revenue from the old endowments devoted to the Church is chiefly derived from the land which at different times has been given over for the use of the Church. In these days, when money is so plentiful and land so scarce, we can hardly realize to ourselves the condition of those times when there was scarcely any money in England but plenty of disposable land. If the people in those days were poorer than we are now they were not less religious, and therefore we can understand that as money gifts to Churches are plentiful now so were land gifts then.

Not only did many landlords give up a certain quantity of land for the Church who were not in a position to grant tithes but many who granted tithes gave land also.

In addition to these private benefactions the Church received also large gifts of land from the State. These gifts were generally made out of the "folkland," or common land, by the king with the consent of his "Witan" or Parliament. The chief motive for these gifts most probably was that both the king and his Parliament regarded the Church as their greatest ally in the preservation of order, and were therefore wishful to increase the resources of that Church in order to increase its power for usefulness. We not unfrequently have sarcastic interpretations given of the motives which produced the gifts to the Church; we are told that private individuals, and even the State, gave land to the Church from superstitious fear or from a desire to stand well in the future world. It is not our business to inquire into such matters but we may express the opinion that these motives, which we laugh at as superstitious in our ancestors, prevail amongst ourselves quite as strongly, if less honestly. If all gifts given from similar motives during the last half century were taken away, many chapels, as well as churches, would be sadly impoverished.

Two considerations must be borne in mind in reference to the gifts of land made by the State to the Church. In the first place, they were made in return for services which the State believed itself to receive from the Church and with the expectation of increasing these services. Also the State had another motive, for the lands of the Church were, on account of their security and of the industry of their occupiers, in those days known to be the best cultivated, and it was for the interest of the State to increase the quantity of land under such cultivation. In the second place, these gifts of land by the State to the Church were made in precisely the same way and subject to precisely the same conditions as the gifts of land made to private individuals by the State. These Church lands were subject to the obligations required from citizens to the State and not to those from vassals to their lord, especially the three burdens—*Trinoda Necessitas*—of military service, repair of bridges, and repair of fortresses. As to the right of the Church to retain the lands thus given to it by the State it is sufficient to say that the Church is one of the oldest landowners in the nation, that its land was conferred upon it in the same way as nearly all the nobles received theirs, and that no principle can be suggested to justify the Church being deprived of this land which would not avail to upset the ownership of most of the land in the country.

Considering the great pretensions which are so constantly put forward about the people being in these days generally well-informed, we should think it would be almost impossible to believe that any one of decent education could now be found to assert that tithes can be in any sense a tax upon the people. Nevertheless it is true that not merely by those whose ignorance is excusable but also by many who are accepted as creditable leaders of the present movement against the Church, tithes are spoken of as if they were so much taken for the support of the Church out of the pockets of those who pay them. Therefore we are compelled, even at the risk of being thought schoolmasterish, to point out that tithes are not, and never can be, a tax upon any one except the landlord who first granted them and his heirs. For, as the well-known theory of rent teaches and universal experience confirms, the rent which a tenant will pay for land depends upon the net produce after all payments are deducted. Thus if, after deducting what is considered a reasonable return for the farmer himself, the net produce of a farm is one hundred pounds, this will go to the landlord for rent, but if a tithe charge has to be paid, this rent will be diminished by just so much. It does not matter to the farmer whether he pays all this net produce over to the landlord as rent or pays some of it to the Church as tithe and the rest to the landlord. The whole amount which he can so pay is fixed, and it is perfectly immaterial to him whether it is divided into two portions or not.

We thus see how absurd is the sentimentality which leads men to talk as if there was an injustice in those being obliged to pay tithes to the Church who do not agree with it. Tithes are purely commercial arrangements and it is no part of the payer's business to inquire into what is done with them ; he might just as well object to pay his rent to a landlord whose religion did not agree with his own. Many dissenting chapels, especially old Presbyterian ones, are partly supported by the rents of farms with which they have been endowed. The trustees of such chapels would be surprised if the tenants of these farms objected to pay their rents on the ground that it violated their consciences to be obliged to contribute towards the support of a religion of which they disapproved.

As tithes are no charge upon those who rent land, neither are they upon those who buy it, for they know that the land is subject to this charge and therefore they purchase it for a proportionately less price.

The substance respecting tithes then is that they are a capitalised gift made over to the Church by their original donors. As nearly all the land has frequently changed hands since that time subject to this charge, it may be said that tithes constitute, for the support of religion, a fund which does not now cost anything to any one.

Instead of the ancient endowments of the Church being described as grants by the State there are really only two to which this description can with any strictness be applied, and both of these have been made during this century. These are the following. About half a century ago Government received from a foreign power an unexpected payment of a loan of several millions. Parliament voted one million and a half out of this sum towards the building of churches in populous places. Also from 1809 to 1820 the State paid £100,000 a year to the Governors of Queen Anne's Bounty for the purpose of increasing poor livings. This, however, was merely returning in some measure the first-fruits and tenths which had previously for so long been paid to the Church but had since been seized by the State.

We thus see that the National Church is just as voluntary, so far as its material support is concerned, as any independent Church; there is no proof that its land was not obtained by just as voluntary means, making allowance for the difference of time, as the land now held by many dissenting chapels in England, and by many churches in the United States of America, where plots of land are often granted to encourage the building of places of worship. And even leaving out this consideration, it is certain that the lands of the Church are held by a title just as good as that of most of the landlords in the country, and no more than this need be said. As to the tithes, they are evidently equivalent to a money endowment by the landlords who first granted them, the only difference being that instead of making over a lump sum which the Church could invest for itself, they gave security that they and their heirs would for ever pay to the Church the income of such a sum. In ordinary endowments the Church invests the money, but in tithes the donor invests the money in his own land and gives the Church the income. It is easy to see how preferable tithes are in such cases to endowments, for not only does the Church obtain security without trouble and the benefit of sharing in the increased value of land, but the nation gains by the land being left under the control of those who, taken altogether, are sure to do it most justice. How strong is still the hold upon humanity of the principle of tithes is shown by the well-known fact that in these days many people, and Dissenters just as frequently as others, make a rule of setting aside each year for religious and charitable purposes a tenth of their incomes. The wisdom of this principle of tithes is confirmed when we reflect that most of those who are qualified to judge believe that no better rule than this can be laid down for the general guidance of mankind and for the performance of individual Christian duty. Tithes have this advantage over such a voluntary rule that when once granted they continue compulsory, and become a perpetual endowment. Such endowments are not merely a help to religion but are even essential to its continued existence, for the showers of enthusiasm are like tropical rain; for a while they are almost continuous and then for a while scarcely a drop falls. Endowments are the store reservoirs of enthusiasm by which the Church is enabled to subsist through a drought. The mill-wheel of the Church can never run properly or do good work if at one time the water is rushing over in torrents whilst at another there is scarcely enough to turn it. We approve in these days of irrigation in India and recommend our Government to spend large sums in carrying it out. We ought not to forget therefore that by their grants of land and of tithes our forefathers applied this same principle of irrigation to the spiritual fields of religious activity. And even if we do not recognise this principle we must acknowledge that these grants were so much taken from the private and selfish use of those who gave them and made over for purposes which they believed to be pious and generally beneficial.

But without disputing about the origin of ecclesiastical endowments, the following arguments, amongst others, are urged why these endowments should not now be used exclusively for the Church of England. Taking the annual revenue of the Church of England roughly at ten millions, we may say that half of this sum is made up of voluntary contributions, one quarter is derived from Pre-Reformation en'owments, and the remaining quarter from Post-Reformation endowments. Now it is said that at any rate these Pre-Reformation endowments belong by right to the Roman Catholics because they were made to their Church. But when these endowments were made there was no Church such as that which we now call Roman Catholic existing in this country, nor, indeed, anywhere else. The Church to which these endowments, in the Christian era, were made was the "English" Catholic Church, the fundamental condition of which was that it was under the control of the State. The very phrase "Roman" Catholic was unknown then, and for generations afterwards. All through English history we find that almost universally loyalty to the State has taken precedence of loyalty to the Pope, and this not merely with those who might be supposed to be indifferent about the Pope's authority but also with his devoted adherents. It must be remembered that up to a comparatively recent date there was only one Church in England. That Church, like all large organisations, contained various parties, but the doctrine of the supremacy of the State was all along held by such a preponderating majority in that Church as to be accepted as a fundamental article of the Church itself. Even those most inclined to favour the Pope's claims nearly always stood by the State when the Pope and the State came into collision.

We are very apt to lose sight of the fact that Roman Catholicism, as we now understand it, is quite of recent growth in England, and has very little in common with the old Catholicism of our history. Probably we owe this new form in a great degree to our connection with Ireland, and to the large immigration of the Irish. Settling down together, in large communities, as they always will, they have been able to keep up their old religion in their new country, and their numbers being so large and their obedience so complete, they have developed a powerful organization. In consequence of the schisms of Protestantism and as a reaction from the unbelief of recent times, some Anglicans of character have been led to join this organization. Through the dominant Irish influence which, as might be expected, has always been in favour of opposition to the State and of indiscriminating submission to Rome, helped by the enthusiasm in the same direction of Englishmen of superior culture, many of the old English Catholics have been led to join this Roman party, or rather to acquiesce in it, for there has been nothing like devoted adherence professed. This Roman Catholic party, Irish in its character and numbers but helped by English respectability and brains, although undoubtedly loyal in the general sense of the word, has always shown itself to have a tone very different from that of the old Catholics of England, or from that of any party with which our history makes us acquainted. We see this in its political conduct, both local and imperial. True to the old Papal idea of making the State the instrument of the Church, which never until now could find any party in England to support it, the Roman Catholics here seem to have given up nearly all individual political principle and to be guided in their political conduct simply by the consideration of what will be good for their Church. There can be no unkindness in stating a fact of which they themselves seem to be proud as a proof of their religious zeal, and it is certainly necessary for us to understand the causes and consider the consequences of there being now in England a large and well organised party using its political power solely for the assistance of a Church which claims unlimited authority and over which the English nation can exercise no control. Whatever may be the right course for the future we can certainly say for the past that our ancestors would have been the last men to give their substance to such a Church, and that it is manifestly unreasonable to say that property bequeathed to a Church of which the fundamental condition was submission to the State, should be made over to one which not merely repudiates all State control but also claims submission from the State.

But it may be said that this property was granted on the understanding that such a relationship as then existed between the Pope and the Church of England should be maintained. As is well known, during the early ages of the Church, when most of the property was granted, the Popes of Rome did not exercise any such authority as they now claim; in fact, during much of this period the name Pope was almost unknown. It is certain that during such times as need be considered in reference to the property of the Church the control of the Pope over the Church of England was so slight that instead of being a fundamental condition of these gifts it was most probably in the majority of cases never thought of at all.

Still it may be said that the later endowments, given when the Pope did exercise greater authority, ought to be given up to the Church of Rome. But the Pope never did possess any such authority over the Church of England as he now claims over all who are considered to belong to his Church. The Pope in these days will not be content with the power which satisfied his predecessors but insists, as essential conditions to membership in the Roman Catholic Church, upon demands which no Pope for ages ever dreamt of and which no people with the independence of the English would ever have allowed.

Of course it is impossible to come to any provable conclusion on such a subject, and every one is sure to be led much more by his own feelings which he does know than by facts which he does not know, but it may certainly be reasonably maintained that the present Church of England conforms more nearly than the present Church of Rome to such conditions as those who gave the property in question would have been likely to wish for.

Besides, endowed bodies have surely the right to reform themselves, or to be reformed without forfeiting the right to their endowments. A man who makes over property to an institution does so with the understanding that that institution must be continually changing. For there is nothing in this life which can possibly remain long the same; we may preserve the old forms and appearances of institutions but their real nature, that which makes them what they are, cannot be kept stationary; ancient dress and customs will not keep out new knowledge and spirit. Therefore in examining the right to endowments we have not to consider whether the institution is exactly the same as that to which those endowments were first made but only whether in its fundamental conditions it may fairly be taken as the heir of that institution. We maintain that, judged by such a comparison, the Church of England is much more nearly related to the Church on which these endowments were conferred than is the present Church of Rome.

But in addition there is the fact, usually in this country considered sufficient by itself, that the present Church of England has held continued possession of these endowments and that this possession has always been confirmed by law. The manner in which the old Presbyterian endowments are now used, under the sanction of the State, for the support of a system of religion which would have shocked their original donors, illustrates the wide margin which the feeling of the nation allows in respect to similarity of doctrine and the importance which is attached to continuity of possession.

As for the Church of England's claims being invalidated by the changes made at the Reformation, it may be remarked that but for those changes it is probable that the Church itself would have been swept away and the whole of its property confiscated.

The fact of property alone is sufficient to account for the Church of England having been all along so intimately connected with the State, for a State cannot help giving legal acknowledgment to an institution so richly endowed; even if the State exercises no control, it must define which Church is to have the income, as had to be done when the Irish Church was disestablished. Besides, land must always be subject more or less to public control and therefore the Church, as the largest landowner in the country, must be brought into constant connection with the State. In addition to these reasons the State cannot politically afford to ignore the Church, for apart from all other sources of strength, the influence arising merely from the possession of so much property must make the Church a political power always to be reckoned with as a desirable ally and often to be struggled with as a dangerous rival. There has never been a time in the history of England when the State could have afforded to let the Church keep its property and also to leave the Church alone.

The well-informed amongst those who are now asking for Disestablishment understand quite well that it would not be safe to take away the State control and yet leave so much property in the hands of the Church and therefore they insist upon Disendowment as well as Disestablishment. And undoubtedly they are consistent in this, for not only can no lover of his country think with comfort of an institution possessed of so much political power being free from all national control, but since by Disestablishment the Church of England would be immediately destroyed, there is no reason why property left for the support of a National Church should be handed over to any religious sect, however great that sect might be or however largely it might believe itself to have inherited the system of the original Church.

Hence we are told, and this is the position now most generally taken up by the opponents of the Church, that even if none of the Church property belongs by right to the Roman Catholics but has so far been properly used for the support of the Church of England, still that is no reason why it should continue to be so used. Since the Church of England is the National Church, its property, it is said, must be national property, and if the nation does not wish to use that property any longer for the support of a Church, it may devote it to any other purpose which the nation believes will promote the national good. Hence we are told that the nation has a perfect right to take the present revenues from the Church and spend them on national secular education or for the relief of the poor-rates. Ingenious schemes are now being put before the public by which the funds of the Church are to be used for the reduction of taxation whilst its buildings may be thrown open to all the different religious bodies or be turned into lecture halls and science schools ; the flame of religion is now flickering in its socket and so it must give way on the altar to the cheering and satisfying light of science.

As far as the settlement of the national principle itself is concerned it is almost to be regretted that there are any considerations of property connected with the Church, for we must consider that by rousing the cupidity of the ignorant and careless there is danger that this question may be decided not by its own intrinsic merits. If the majority of the people of England can be brought to feel that the Church is a useless institution and to believe that they have a perfect right to take its property and use it for the relief of their own burdens, it is very probable that the Church will be disestablished from motives which ought not to be allowed to have any weight in the decision of such a matter. Therefore the friends of the Church ought emphatically to insist that considerations of property have no essential connection with the principle of the national system of religion, and the enemies of the Church ought scrupulously to guard themselves against any alliance with improper motives and low passions. There is a famous speech of Lord Chatham's, familiar to schoolboys, against the employment of Indians in the war between England and the States of America. The same feelings by which we sympathise with the orator's denunciation of the introduction of savage tribes into civilised warfare should

T

make us protest against the forces of base cupidity and barbaric ignorance being summoned to join in the struggle about a great and high principle. We may rest assured that no settlement can be satisfactory or permanent which has been gained by the help of such allies.

Even if the funds of the Church might rightly be taken and used for the relief of national taxation we may well believe that the nation would not be better, but rather worse, for such an appropriation. For some time past, and especially during the last thirty years, nearly everyone seems to have been believing without any misgiving that the greatest object of a nation should be to get rich, to accumulate as much and spend as little as possible. In fact the phrase "national prosperity" has now come to mean nothing more than the increase of the national wealth, and "national happiness" has little reference to anything beyond national taxation. Happily there are signs of the fall of this despicable ideal. We are beginning to learn that increase of wealth does not necessarily mean increase of happiness for us either as individuals or as a nation. We have little to show for all our marvellous wealth except the division of society into two unfortunate classes, one with too much money to spend and the other with too little, and every addition of wealth seems to increase these classes proportionately. Instead of lessening the taxation we are sometimes inclined to think that it would be better for that taxation to be increased by some war or some other great national enterprise, for then not merely would a dangerous superfluity be removed but the tone of the nation would be raised. At any rate it is certain that if the funds of the Church were used for the relief of taxation neither the poor nor the rich would get any real benefit.

Thus it would not be advisable to appropriate in this way the revenues of the Church even if the nation had the right to do so, which as a matter of fact it has not. For let us ask what is meant by the National Church being "State-Paid." It does not mean that it is paid out of the funds of the State but merely under the direction of the State. As far as endowments are concerned, the State is merely the Trustee, who has to look after their management and pay over their funds for the purpose originally laid down. The State does not pay anything out of its own resources towards the National Church but is merely the executor for those who originally granted the tithes or land from which the Church is supported. That this is not a fanciful distinction but a very real one would be acknowledged by all those who having to administer a will or manage a fund found themselves obliged to pay all the disbursements out of their own pockets.

Since then the National Church is not State-Paid in any other sense than that its funds are under the control of the State, and since the State pays nothing towards its support out of its own pocket, it is difficult to see what right the State can have to seize the funds of the Church and use them for its own purposes. Those funds were left that the State should use them, not for any purpose it might choose but for the particular purpose chosen by those who gave them, namely the support of national religion. If any individual now was to make over a sum of money to be administered by the State for any specific purpose, as the increase of naval pensions, and the State accepted that trust, it would manifestly be unfair for the State afterwards to turn round and say that as the money was paid through its hands it might be taken and used for any purpose the State wished.

Of course the State has a perfect right to give up a trust of this kind at any time; it may refuse to act any longer as the administrator of any fund and may therefore retire from all control over the property of the National Church; but this is very different from taking that property for its own use.

It is not our duty here to say what ought to be done, in the event of Disestablishment, with the Church property. Of course it is not supposed that the State could possibly withdraw from all control over it. There is no reason why it should be made over to a self-governing body which might call itself the Church of England, although devoid of the essential characteristics of such a Church. Theoretically when a fund can no longer be used for the purpose for which it was given it should go back to those who gave it, but this is evidently impossible with property which was given so long ago as was that of the National Church. In such cases there is one rule which should chiefly guide us, namely, that such property ought to be used as long as possible for the purposes for which it was given, and that when this can no longer be done it ought to be devoted to purposes which most resemble these.

It is not for those who are opposed to Disestablishment to solve the difficulties of Disendowment, but they have a right to insist that the nation shall not be taught to believe that the money comes out of its own pocket which is merely paid under its control, and that the State has a right to spend in any way it likes funds which were given to be used, under its superintendence, for a definite and peculiar purpose.

As far as the assertion, now so frequently made, is concerned that the money would be much better spent in paying for secular education and scientific instruction, and in reducing the poor-rates, than in supporting a National Church, we may put forward this dilemma. Money either is or is not a help to religion. If it is not, how do Dissenters justify their universal desire to obtain it for their own purposes? But if it is a help to religion, how can this proposal be defended to take it away from the National Church and devote it to uses which are not religious? There is some reason why those who are opposed to religion altogether should wish to secularise the funds of the Church but such a proposal cannot be consistently supported by anyone else.

It is said, however, that even if this fund ought to be used only for religious purposes, that is no reason why it should be given exclusively to the Church of England. We are asked why the members of that Church should have their religion for nothing whilst all the other religious bodies have to pay their own expenses. To this it is sufficient to reply that this fund was left for the maintenance of a National Church, that is, of a religion of such a character and organized in such a way as the nation should from time to time decide upon. It is for the State, as the trustee of this fund and as expressing the will of the nation, to fix the conditions upon which this fund shall be enjoyed. If there are any who do not approve of these conditions it is their duty to convert the nation to their opinions and so to get these conditions altered. If they cannot do this they must submit for the same reason as minorities have to submit in all organized communities. We cannot all get everything we want, and therefore we have to give way when the feeling is against us, for the sake of union and civilised combination. This principle is universally accepted in political matters and there is no reason why it should not be extended to all the functions of the State.

But if the minority, instead of obeying this common and necessary law, chooses to set up a rival religious system of its own, it is only reasonable that it should pay its own expenses. This plan is followed in all the affairs of life. If a town lays down free water-pipes to every house, those who choose to draw for themselves are at liberty to do so, but if any insist on having pumps they must provide them at their own expense. So it is with the National Church, except that it offers its ministrations for nothing and asks for no water-rate. The national system of religion is like a free public feast ; such a bill of fare as is chosen by the nation is offered gratuitously to all, but if there are any people who insist on having extra dishes of their own they are expected to pay for them.

It is manifestly unreasonable to suppose that a fund left for the support of a religion under State control should be divided amongst religious organizations which reject that control. The conditions for participation in this fund are plainly laid down and there are only three courses open to those who disapprove of these conditions; they may quietly acquiesce, or endeavour to get them altered, or provide for themselves. They cannot expect to partake of the benefits without submitting to the conditions.

In conclusion we may say that so far as property is concerned the substance of the matter is that the National Church is an institution which costs no man a penny against his will but is bound to provide the ministrations of religion gratuitously for all who choose to take them. The difference in this respect between the National and the so-called "Free" Churches is that in the National the offices of religion are provided for nothing whilst in the Free they must be paid for.

But it is said that religion ought not to be provided for nothing; that those who care for it are quite willing to pay for it, and that we have no right to perpetuate a system which tends to weaken this desirable sense of independence. Those who are opposed to the National Church not unfrequently glory over their own self-reliance and boast that they at any rate are free from the taint of spiritual pauperism; they tell us that they are quite able to provide their own religion and do not care to be dependent on their ancestors or anyone else for it.

Undoubtedly this spirit of courageous self-dependence is a very admirable quality and ought to be encouraged as far as is reasonably possible, but like all other feelings of the sort it becomes absurd when carried too far. No man can possibly depend upon himself alone, leaving out of view any supernatural agency; his powers, his opportunities, his means, have nearly all come down to him from the past. A particular Englishman differs so widely from a negro not merely because of his own efforts but chiefly as the result of the efforts of generations of his ancestors. And not merely are we indebted to our ancestors for our physical and moral and intellectual qualities but also for the material resources to which we apply those qualities. Each generation as it passes can add only a little to the accumulated obligations of the generation which succeeds.

The impossibility of carrying self-reliance to such an extreme is universally recognised in material affairs. A son who refused to receive the inheritance left to him by his father on the ground that he could not thus sacrifice his independence would be considered a fool, and precisely the same principle applies to bodies of men as to individuals. The endowments of the National Church are an inheritance left to us by our ancestors in the same way as they left their land and money and everything else which has come to us from them. If we ought to reject these endowments to preserve our independence we ought also to cut ourselves in everything completely away from the past. This is plainly impossible, as we see in this case, for these endowments must go somewhere, and if we use them for education or any other purpose we merely transfer this so-called taint of pauperism. And not only so but we make it less justifiable, for if there is any object for the sake of which we may be permitted to feel ourselves under obligations to our ancestors it is religion. A man who conscientiously objected to receive an inheritance which was to be used for his own glory and pleasure might still very reasonably be glad of all he could get to help the progress of religion. Therefore the inheritance of a National Church is the last which we should have any scruples in accepting or with the use of which we should allow any feelings of impossible pride to interfere.

Turning next to the more strictly social objections the first one to be considered is that—

2. *A National Church promotes social dissensions.*

We are told that by this institution people are divided into two classes, Churchmen and Dissenters, betwixt whom there is an almost impassable barrier. Glowing pictures are drawn of there being two antagonistic parties in every town and village, not merely spoiling the gentle spirit of religion by the infusion of unholy rivalry but also weakening the strength of Christian usefulness by calling into being two disconnected organizations for purposes which would be much better served by one united one. We are told that Churchmen will not unite with Dissenters nor Dissenters with Churchmen; that not only are they divided from each other in religious work but that also they will not join together even for charitable objects. After looking on this picture of discord which is now before us, we are told to look on that of happy unity which would be presented when once the National Church was abolished; instead of party divisions and un-Christian isolations there would be a united brotherhood and a common sympathy; instead of good men wasting their strength in factious struggles they would all work together for the spread of religion and for the promotion of the general good.

If these pictures were drawn with the outlines of fact and painted with the colours of reason they would say a great deal in favour of Disestablishment, but we beg to dispute not merely their details but also their general accuracy, for the facts chiefly come from the imaginations of the artists and the reasons from their desires.

In the first place, the social barriers separating Churchmen from Dissenters are nothing like so great as we are asked to believe. Of course they worship separately, and have their own separate religious organizations, for all this is involved in the toleration of Dissent, but it does not follow that they are therefore socially estranged from each other. It is natural to expect that those who frequently meet together, no matter for what purpose, will be inclined to become socially connected. Churchmen associate more with Churchmen, and Dissenters with Dissenters, in so far as this is so, not on account of any antagonism but simply because acquaintance is much more likely to spring up between those who are brought together than between those who are not. And as to charitable objects, excepting those which are best promoted through the religious organizations, which the existence of Dissent often obliges to be twofold, it is not true that Churchmen and Dissenters are antagonistic to, or even estranged from, each other. Since many organizations for such purposes grow out of our social connections, and since those connections are largely influenced by our religious associations, it must follow that even in these matters Churchmen are often more likely to be thrown with each other, and Dissenters also. But the history of charity throughout the land plainly shows that there is no such antagonism between good men as we are told exists between Churchmen and Dissenters, and that the few cases in which such a feeling seems to have cropped out are unworthy of being introduced into the discussion of such a great question.

But even if the social separations between Churchmen and Dissenters are as great as we are told, it does not therefore follow that they are evils in themselves. For men must be divided into sets on some principle or other. Formerly it was religion, now it is politics. A great number of political clubs where those of the same party can spend their evenings together drinking and smoking, reading and playing, have sprung into being during the last few years and have been ardently supported by most of those who object to Churchmen and Dissenters being socially divided, yet no one says that politics should be abolished. But since men must be divided, that division is surely the best which is grounded upon the highest principle, and there can be no doubt that in this respect religion is better than politics. Since we cannot help having some system of social classification, let us adopt one which will have the elevation of the highest associations and the gentleness of religious feelings. Not merely does society in general gain by such a principle but politics comes in for a large share of the benefit, for it is saved from that intense bitterness which men are sure to throw into it when it is their only ground of division. Probably much of that impracticable animosity which exists between political parties in France and which has made the past of that country so disastrous, as it now makes its future so gloomy, is the result of the withdrawal in past days of the national attention from religion and its exclusive concentration upon politics. Religion, as we see if we compare the present tone of Catholicism in France with that of the old Gallican Church, has become servile and unreal, whilst politics have become selfish and unreasonable.

It is not merely foolish to complain about the people being socially divided but it is also unmanly. That sickly desire to be fraternising with everybody which seems to possess some people is unworthy the dignity of the Christian character. Life is much too short and our work in it is much too long to give us time to associate with everybody, and it is unmannerly to suppose, as we find so constantly done in social affairs, that those who do not care to associate with us are either proud or ill-disposed. We have each our own task to do and for that we shall be individually responsible. It is one of the fundamental doctrines of Christianity that men are to be judged by themselves and not in batches. We ought therefore to go on minding each his own work, being brotherly when occasion offers but not caring much about anything else except doing our duty, and certainly not wasting our strength with trying to talk to all our neighbours. This longing to do away with all social divisions is as unreasonable as would be the attempt in commerce to make everyone sail in one ship. Because others do not go aboard with us, and perhaps do not even salute us on the ocean, we should not therefore consider them as enemies, but should rather believe that all are really engaged in one service and carrying freight for one port.

But even if such social differences as we are told of actually do exist, and if these differences are as injurious as they are described, it does not follow that they are caused by the National Church and that to cure them that Church should be destroyed. If it is an evil for men to be divided into Churchmen and Dissenters, it is as reasonable to ascribe this evil to the existence of Dissent as to that of the Church, and more reasonable when we consider that the Church was here for centuries before Dissent came into being. But it may be said that there would be no Dissent if there was no Church. It is true that there could be no Dissent from the Church in such a case, but both the history of our own country and the present condition of other countries amply prove that sectarian divisions, which are the real cause of these social estrangements, are even more plentiful where there is not than where there is a National Church. Besides, even if the Church was the cause of Dissent that would not justify its destruction, for if the nation has decided to adopt a principle like that of a national religion it ought not to desist from carrying it out merely because some people disapprove of it. If this were so then every good work would have to be abandoned which a few people thought fit to oppose. But no one thinks of acting on such a principle in ordinary life; on the contrary most people believe that difficulties are meant to be overcome and not to be surrendered to. It certainly seems unreasonable to ask that because those who are opposed to the national ideal have first damaged it, we should next throw it way because it is so damaged; the wolf first muddles the stream and then wants to eat the lamb lower down the course because the water is dirty.

If the national principle is a good one, as is here attempted to be shown, but if differences are caused by opposition to it, the proper course appears to be to withdraw that opposition. No larger social entity is possible than that of the nation, and no better means can be found for uniting all classes in the bonds of an elevated union than the loyal carrying out of the national principle of religion. Then not merely would the name of Dissenter disappear but also that of Churchman, for it must be remembered that according to the national ideal all men are Churchmen who belong to the nation.

The next objection is that—

3. *Where there is a National Church Dissenters are placed in an inferior social position.*

It is said that the State, by favouring one sect and ignoring all others, confers upon that sect a social prestige which places the others at a disadvantage. We are told that this is the reason why what are called "the higher classes" are generally attached to the Church and why those who are said to be "getting on in the world" very frequently abandon the Dissent in which they have been brought up.

Even if we acknowledge it as a fact, which may however well be disputed, that Dissenters do as such occupy a lower social position, we must not therefore infer that this is a result of the national principle. When we find a phenomenon whose cause is not apparent we ought first to see if it can be accounted for by well-known causes before we ascribe it to those which are less known. Following this rule we shall find that there are ample causes to account for this alleged social inferiority of Dissenters without having recourse to the national principle.

Undoubtedly, turning first to the past, it must be acknowledged that the legal disabilities under which Dissenters suffered so long must have had a tendency to connect them with inferior social associations which would linger a long time after those disabilities were removed. For obedience to the law is most happily the strongest determining director of national feeling, and resistance to the law, even though carried on from the highest motives and with the most heroic sufferings, is almost certain in a well-ordered country to be attended with some social ignominy. The people generally accept the judgment of the State and put a stigma upon those whom the State has placed under disabilities. It is undoubtedly true that Dissenters in England were for a long time severely persecuted but it is not consequently true that this persecution arose from the existence of the National Church. The cause was not the principle of national religion but that of persecution, which was in those days universally accepted as true. No one doubted that to persecute those who differed in religion was not merely the right of the majority but was also its duty. The real question was not whether there should be persecution or not but only which party should persecute. This is shown by the case, amongst others, of those Dissenters who left England for America for the sake of what they believed to be conscience, and yet who, in their new country, subjected Quakers and all others who differed from them to persecutions far greater than those they had themselves suffered at home. It is very foolish to throw charges of persecution about in reference to times when everybody believed in it. The party which was the strongest was sure to persecute the others, and this party was sure to be that of the National Church because that must be the Church of the majority. Although we have learned to see how futile and miserable all this persecution was we cannot help acknowledging that there was after all something good in the object of it, for undoubtedly it arose in a large degree from a desire to clear religion of those differences which seem to spoil its beauty. The method was a mistake but the motive was not bad.

It is not therefore correct to say that the National Church, because it was the National Church, persecuted the Dissenters because they were Dissenters, but only that the majority, which happened to be that of the Church, persecuted the minority, as would have also been the case if the majority had happened to be that of the Dissenters. Instead of the national principle ministering to persecution it may well be maintained that it diminished it, for the reason that persecution carried on under the control of the State is sure to be less violent than that of erratic factions or of a Church to which the State is merely a servile instrument. As long as the majority will persecute the minority it is much better that it should do so under legal conditions and subject to public control. Great as were the persecutions in England there is good reason to believe that they were much less severe than those carried on in any other country similarly situated which did not possess a National Church.

Most probably considerable effect was produced on the social character of Dissenters by their exclusion from some of the means of general culture and by their voluntary withdrawal from others. Whilst they were shut out from the Universities they also shut out from themselves the influence of that literature which has so great an effect in determining social character; they tabooed Shakespeare as immoral, Bacon as profane, and Addison as frivolous. Of course we may say that it ought not to be so, but still we cannot alter the fact that social status is, and always has been, largely determined by such causes as these. If any class of men in these days chooses to withdraw itself from the means of social culture, if it is ignorant of literature, and art, and music, and the other influences which go to make up what are called the social amenities, it must be content to lose what is called social caste. Men may be quite right in doing this and their lives may consequently be simpler and purer, but they must then be judged by another standard than that which is accepted as the social one.

Undoubtedly the fact of Dissenters being in a minority must

have greatly affected their social standing, for in social matters especially the majority is always triumphant. Those who hold peculiar opinions on any subject by which public feeling is largely determined are sure to be placed more or less under a social ban, and the social obloquy of Dissent arose much more from its being the unpopular cause of a minority than because it was Dissent from a National Church. This is one of the consequences which those must be prepared to submit to who feel obliged to place themselves in a minority on a great question. Fashion chiefly rules in social matters, and fashion is governed by the majority.

Other causes for the social position of Dissenters are to be found in their own character and circumstances. The position of their ministers never has been such as could be likely to help their social standing. Having no social security, but depending upon the wills of their congregations, and generally possessing themselves neither much social position nor much general culture, it cannot be expected that they should do much to raise the social reputation of the class of which they are the leaders. The position of any religious body is chiefly determined by that of its ministers, and we need go no further to account for much of that which is complained about in respect to Dissenters, especially when we consider the poverty of many of their ministers. It may be true that poverty and religion go best together, but it is certainly not true that poverty and social position do so ; in fact as a general rule they are in inverse proportion. If Dissenters choose to adopt a system which prevents their ministers from possessing the ordinary social requisites, they cannot expect them to occupy such a social position as can only come from the possession of such requisites.

Probably the most important cause of all is the fact that the system of a National Church is much broader, both religiously and socially, than that of any other Church can possibly be. The generally narrow, and it must be said sometimes even low, type of religion taught by Dissenting bodies must give its impress to their social character, and that character must also be largely affected by their methods of exclusiveness. No self-governing, and consequently more or less narrowed, Church can possibly compete in social conditions with a National Church, which includes all classes and teaches a religion suitable to all.

In conclusion it may be said that it seems rather unreasonable for those who describe clergymen as "creatures of the State" and who talk about wishing to relieve the Church from the "shackles" of the State, to complain of the social inferiority of those who dissent from that Church. Surely those who provide for themselves in religious matters may be expected to occupy a higher social position than those who are said to depend for support upon the State. If connection with the State is degrading, then Dissenters should possess that social superiority which is involved in the exemption from such degradation. Since dependence of any kind always involves social inferiority it seems that there must be inconsistency either in the assertions about the receiving of aid from the State amounting to religious pauperism, or else in the complaints about the social inferiority of Dissenters.

Another objection is that—

4. *A National Church represses individual generosity.*

There is a general tendency in these days to draw conclusions more frequently from theories than from facts. We constantly hear opinions asserted, both in religion and politics, with all the positiveness of infallible proof, which vanish almost immediately before the test of well-known facts. The human mind has an immense capacity for being absorbed in itself and for not observing, or not heeding, the plainest phenomena. Just as it is much easier for a man to stop at home than to start away for new lands, so the mind is very prone to keep within the little circle of its own thoughts and feelings rather than to roam abroad over the great world of facts.

Thus it may seem probable, if we merely appeal to our own fancies, that a system which receives considerable external help is likely to get so much less done for it by its own adherents; we should say that of course it must be supported and that therefore if others do less for it its friends will have to do more. Thus we arrive at the conclusion that the aid which the Church receives from the State prevents its own adherents from doing as much as they otherwise would.

Apart from the fact that what the Church receives from the State is merely the fund derived from the stored-up gifts of its own previous adherents, we should ask ourselves whether, as a matter of fact, the present gifts of individuals to the Church are at all less in proportion than those which other Churches receive from their supporters, and if they are less, whether they are so much so as would justify us in inferring such a cause as this. We shrink from the unseemliness of parading statistics of religious benevolence, and happily there is no need to do this, for no one can fail to see on every side undeniable proofs that the Church is treated by its supporters with a generosity which is remarkable and almost unbounded. There is no call to go into details when every town, and almost every parish, bears witness to the fact. The amount which has been voluntarily raised, during the last twenty years, for the building and endowment of new Churches and the restoration of old ones would surprise those who have not observed what has been going on around them and would compare favourably with the best efforts of any self-governed Church during the same time. We are almost forced to believe that much of the opposition which is now being shown towards the National Church arises, not because the generosity of the laity is repressed but because it is so great as to promise little chance for the permanent success of any other system. The Church of

England is to be disestablished not because it is a failure but because its success is too great for the theories of its enemies and the hopes of its rivals.

It is unreasonable to suppose that endowments can really affect the generosity of the supporters of a vigorous institution. For unless that institution is already extended to the utmost possible limits, which no one will say of the Church, the effect of extraneous help is merely to extend it faster than could otherwise have been done. And thus endowments really in the long run promote generosity, for they extend the system so much during periods of enthusiasm that during periods of indifference more has to be given to keep up that system than would otherwise have been found. Perhaps contributions of this sort do not come strictly within the application of what we may call generosity, but in such matters we must not pry too closely into motives; besides, an organization is thus kept up which more quickly rouses generosity into action when enthusiasm returns.

Another objection is that—

5. *The system of a National Church is not adaptable to changes of population.*

There can be so little in this objection that the only justification for referring to it is that it is frequently raised. For it is plain that a Church which is under the control of the nation must be more amenable to the will of the populations which make up the nation than any other Church will be. There is nothing in the national system against its adaptability in this particular and much in its favour. We see how well the system of tithes works in this respect, for generally the number of the agricultural population and the amount of the tithes vary together according to the quality of the land. And as to towns it may safely be said that exclusive of the Roman Catholics it is upon the Church that the poor districts are chiefly dependent for whatever religious care they receive.

Another objection frequently raised is that—

6. *In a National Church the laity are not drawn socially together.*

It is said that there is no bond of union between the frequenters of the Church; that they merely go in to worship and come out again without manifesting any feelings of Christian fellowship, and that they are not brought together either for social intercourse or to take part in managing the affairs of the Church.

It must be confessed that this charge is in the main true; Churchmen do not mix together socially as Dissenters do; the fact of attending the same Church does not, other social requisites being suitable, constitute any claim to, or lead to any expectation of, personal intercourse. Of course customs vary in different districts, and between town and country, but still it is undoubtedly true that the fact of being Churchmen is not as strong a bond of social union as is that of being Dissenters. And this is no more than we should expect, for men who are exercising functions which belong to them simply as members of the nation are not likely to feel so drawn towards each other as those who have set up a separate organization of their own and who know that they are joined together in opposition to the great majority. The isolation of a small minority is very favourable to the cosiness of social fellowship.

Undoubtedly there is something very taking in the social character of a chapel. Most men are fond of exercising some authority, and the Dissenting system finds them ample opportunities; as deacons, or trustees, or members of committees, they can have something to occupy themselves and to make them feel that they are of some importance. Those who have not had any experience can hardly realise how almost completely the social associations of many Dissenters centre round their chapel; they meet at each other's houses, talk over each other's affairs, and are very partial to intermarrying amongst themselves. To be as the phrase is "one of us" is to have a claim which is readily recognised upon their sympathy and help; they even regulate their business transactions largely by these considerations, and the man who attends the same chapel has a much better chance of obtaining a situation or an order. Much as is said about social inferiority there is little doubt that many Dissenters if they went to Church would find themselves very cheerless and forlorn; their leading men would not relish losing that sense of personal importance which was so fully gratified in their own little society, and the others would not like being exiled from their circles of acquaintance and from their subjects of gossip. Most of us have a strong liking for feeling that we are somebody, and this liking is undoubtedly much more freely ministered to by the system of Dissent than by that of the Church.

But although this social friendliness of Dissenters is very pleasant, it does not follow that it is very good, or at any rate that it should be cultivated by religious organizations. For it has its dangers, and these are all the more serious because they are so subtle. Pharisaism is just as likely to be developed by fussy activity as by empty forms; the man who is so busy with official duties, who presides at meetings, and serves on committees and takes an active interest in all the affairs of his society, is in great danger of coming to think that by doing these things he is attending to his religion, whilst those who have so many social interests connected with their particular place of worship are very apt to think more of these things than of the object of the worship itself. We do not for a moment say that this is generally the case, but those who have had experience will acknowledge that it is often so; too frequently when a man feels obliged to retire from a particular religious sect, his course is judged much more by vexation at his quitting a social communion than by considerations of whether he is doing the best for his soul's good. Of course all these affairs must be attended to by some one, but few men can touch them much without risk; the voice of religion in the soul is so delicate and quiet that it is very difficult to keep it from being silenced amidst the clamour of bustling activity. It is very different with other business, but that which is connected with religion is so apt to be mistaken for religion itself because activities are seen whilst religious cultivation of the soul is not seen. Therefore that system seems best which keeps these two apart as much as possible, so as to avoid that temptation of mistaking one for the other which is too strong for so many. It is not pretended that there should be no business matters in connection with a Church, but only that the national system, which throws most of these upon the State, seems more likely to produce a really religious sentiment than those systems which leave them all to the people themselves. There is enough, and too much, of these evils in the Church of England at present, without adopting changes which would greatly increase them.

There is nothing in the nature of a National Church to prevent there being amongst its frequenters as much social intercourse as they like, but we cannot help feeling that the Church of England acts wisely in not encouraging this any more than it does now. In these days especially we need to cultivate the feeling that religion has very little to do with organizations or societies but is a matter for each individual soul.

Of course Christians as such ought to feel drawn towards each other in brotherly sympathy. Christian fellowship ought to be cultivated; it is a help to the weak, a pleasure to the strong, and a comfort to the lonely. But that fellowship ought to be based on the great unities of our common faith and not on the trivial differences which separate sect from sect; it ought to be a fellowship of Christians and not merely one of Wesleyans or Independents or Baptists. For such a proper fellowship a National Church affords the fullest scope.

Another objection is that—

7. *The clergy of a National Church have not sufficient social intercourse with the members of their congregations.*

It is often asserted that clergymen do not visit the members of their congregations as much as Dissenting ministers do, nor fraternise with them as freely.

Although such an objection seems frivolous when put forward as a detail of fact, it really deserves serious consideration because it involves a matter of the utmost importance, namely the difference between the congregational and parochial systems. It is evident that a clergyman who is expected to look after everyone in his parish cannot visit those who are the members of his congregation as frequently as the minister who visits no one else.

It is well it should be clearly understood that as far as organizations for bringing the people into contact with religion are concerned, only two are ultimately possible, namely the parochial and the congregational, and in reference to Disestablishment the nation must take its choice between these two. Speaking generally it may be said that by the parochial the country is divided into districts, in each of which is one place of worship, or more, open to the people, and over each of which is placed an organization responsible for looking after the spiritual welfare of everyone in the district. By the national adoption of the parochial system not merely is the duty imposed upon the clergyman, with his assistants, of providing the ministrations of religion for all who choose to demand them, but also the right is conferred upon him of making the necessary inquiries and seeing that no one goes without these ministrations who can be induced to accept them. Of course he has no authority to force these upon anyone but he is bound to take such measures that at any rate the responsibility of refusing the influences of religion shall rest upon the people themselves.

By the congregational system, on the contrary, the minister has no responsibility whatever beyond his own congregation. A number of people band together and form a religious body, and they then engage a minister or number of ministers to attend to their religious requirements. This minister cannot properly be expected to do anything more; of course the congregation may start some missionary effort, or the minister may do so of his own accord, but all this is supererogatory, and such enterprises, if they succeed, soon become themselves parts of the congregational system. The radical difference between the congregational and parochial principles may be illustrated by what is called religious visiting. Whilst the clergyman is bound to visit all the people in his parish to whom such visits would be acceptable, whether they attend his Church or not, the congregational minister is not bound to, and actually does not, visit anyone except those who are members of his congregation or are connected with it in some way. Undoubtedly such ministers are very glad, for they are Christian men, to give their services to all who choose to ask for them, but they are not bound to do so, and it must be remembered that there is the greatest difference between giving what is asked for and offering without being asked. If we consider a single street containing say a hundred families, five of which are connected with a certain chapel, the minister of that chapel looks after those five, and as far as he or his system is concerned, the remaining ninety-five may grow up perfect heathens, passing through life without anyone to offer them the means of religion or to try to bring them within its reach. Of course it is not pretended that the congregational minister does not care in his heart about the ninety-five, but his system gives him neither the right nor the duty to look after them; he may make some spasmodic efforts to reach some of them but such efforts arise from his

Christian impulses and are not involved in his position. As a matter of fact, if in any large town, to say nothing of the country, we were to ask the ministers of any sect, or even those of all the sects put together, whether they take upon themselves the duty of seeing that religious ministrations are individually offered to all the people in that town, they would have to acknowledge that they never even think of such a work, and that any permanent attempt of the sort would be to them impossible. It is not pretended that the Church of England always does this, but only that it is a part of its duty, as the National Church, to do it, and this duty will be attended to if only the nation properly carries out the national system. A principle is one thing and the carrying out of it is another; if there is any failure we must not at once blame the principle but must first examine whether that principle is being carried out properly, and if it is not, we must see that it is so carried out before we abandon the principle itself. No one in the ordinary affairs of life thinks of condemning, on its practical results, any principle without first being sure that it has had a fair trial. When we consider how greatly the long existence of Dissent has weakened the hold of the national principle, and how continuously it has thrown innumerable difficulties in the way of its practice, we are surprised not that the Church of England does not do its duty completely in this respect but that it does it as well as it does. Those who blame the national principle because of the shortcomings of the Church should consider how different would be the case if they themselves, instead of breaking away from that principle, had always loyally helped to carry it out. If they cannot conscientiously help the principle they ought at any rate to make allowances for the obstacles which they themselves put in its way.

It is plain that only a National Church can carry out the parochial system, for upon no other can such a responsibility be laid. Churches which are not national must be self-governing, and self-governing Churches must be their own masters; none of them can be obliged to attend to any people except those they choose to attend to. In this respect all the Churches in England except the National are congregational; Independent, Baptist, Wesleyan, Roman Catholic, and the rest. The Roman Catholic Church has not in this respect any essential character in its own nature, but it must be congregational where it is not national. It is clear that only the nation itself can oblige any Church to offer its services to everyone in the nation, and a Church which is so related to the nation is a National Church.

There are therefore far greater issues involved in this question of Disestablishment than most people seem to think of. If as a nation we believe that our religion is true, we must also believe that it ought to be spread as widely as possible. Religion cannot possibly be a neutral matter; either we do not care for it ourselves or else we wish everyone else to have it. And not merely do we wish this, but we also feel in our consciences that we are bound to do all we can to bring it about. And not only is it our duty as individuals to see that no one goes without our religion who can be induced to accept it, but it is also our interest as a nation to take care that our religion is offered to everybody in the land. For unless that religion is a sham we must believe that the more the nation is brought under its influence the better it will be for the national welfare.

It is then our duty as individuals and our interest as a nation to see that our religion is offered to all the people and that every reasonable means are taken to bring them within its influence. Of course we know that many of them will refuse it, but that only makes it more necessary for us to adopt a system which will relieve us from the responsibility of their being without it. We must first do our duty and then the people can please themselves about doing theirs. The parochial system is the only one by means of which we can in this respect do our duty, for by it alone can our religion be offered to all the people; and the parochial system can only be worked through a National Church. The destruction of the National Church thus involves the neglect of one of our greatest duties as Christians and of one of our plainest interests as citizens.

A great deal is said about the present alienation of most of what are called the working classes from the Christian religion and about the antagonism of some of them, and with truth, for the religious condition of the masses of our countrymen is such as to make any thoughtful man very sorrowful. But we must object to this being put down to the parochial system, for we are rather inclined to say that it is the result of that system being thwarted and neglected. The way to cure the evil is not to give up the attempt, not to abandon the only system which can possibly grapple with it, but to work that system more vigorously and thoroughly. Of course we know that the human mind is not naturally religious and that whatever we do there will always be great multitudes indifferent to our religion, but that is all the more reason why we should keep on offering it. Just as we persist in bringing food to a man in a trance although we do not know when he will come round, or if he will ever do so, in like manner we ought not to cease offering our religion to those who now reject it. We cannot tell how many may waken up from their worldly sleep, and how soon, but it is our duty so to provide that these may not then die of spiritual starvation.

The question, then, involved in Disestablishment is not whether a certain Church shall be separated from the State but whether the English nation shall give up the duty of offering its religion to all its subjects and shall abandon for ever the hope of bringing the masses of those subjects within the influence of that religion. All those who cherish that religion and who love their countrymen sufficiently to wish more of them were led to accept it, must be strong opponents of a change which would destroy the only system by which this can possibly be done.

Whatever may be the shortcomings of the parochial system it needs little discernment to see that the congregational system is utterly incapable of grappling with the religious deficiencies of the nation, and its adoption by Disestablishment would simply mean the abandonment of the attempt. It is easy to understand why this should be advocated by the opponents of religion but it is sad to see such a proposal supported by those who should be the friends of religion. We cannot believe that the English nation has so lost its faith and its conscientiousness as to adopt any measure of the sort.

Another objection is that—

8. *In a National Church the congregations are not allowed to choose their own ministers.*

This objection is grounded on the assumption that a congregation is the best judge of the minister most fitted for it. We venture to say that this assumption is not sound.

But in the first place it must be remarked that there is nothing in the national principle itself to prevent each congregation choosing its own minister; if the nation decided to adopt that plan it could be carried out just as easily in the national system as in any other.

But in the Church of England congregations do not generally choose their own ministers, and wisely so, for there is good reason to believe that on the whole no method could be worse. A Church, as a human organization, cannot in any respect attain perfection, and therefore it is easy to find objections against every method of choosing ministers now used by the Church, but these methods must not on this account be abandoned; before that is done we must be sure that we have something better to put in their place. Choosing by the congregations themselves is now offered as a substitute, but before we accept it we are bound to examine it carefully. When we do this we find how very undesirable it is; both the conclusions of theory and the facts of experience are against it.

In the first place, the qualities which make a really good minister of religion are not such as can be displayed at the beginning before a congregation so as to secure its vote. Before we can proceed to consider this question we must make up our minds as to what we mean by a good minister. If we want merely eloquent preaching and taking manners and professed agreement with our own opinions, then a congregation may be just as good a judge as we can find, but if we want a religious devotion and a cultured mind and a Christian character, then there could not be a worse judge than the congregation. For these are just the qualities—these solid unobtrusive virtues—which in proportion as they are real lead a man to think less of himself and make him shrink from any attempt to display them for his own advantage before the public gaze. Yet there is no doubt that it is these qualities which we most need in our ministers. It is pleasant to listen to clever or eloquent sermons but they have generally very little to do with the real work of religion. Considering the sermons preached in all the places of worship in England on a single Sunday, we should have great difficulty in finding, either in the present or the past, any parallel to the smallness of the result in proportion to the greatness of the labour. If we deduct those sermons, a large proportion, which have no effect, to say nothing of those whose effect is bad, we shall find comparatively few which really do much good in promoting the cause of religion. It is not advocated that sermons should be done away with, although they might be very considerably curtailed with great advantage, but it is maintained that the capacity of preaching well is not the primary qualification for a minister. Yet this is the only qualification which congregations can profess to test, and they are often very bad judges of that. A minister does infinitely more good by the influence of his character than by all his sermons, yet it is plain that this character cannot be known without experience, and a congregation cannot have that before election. And even as to preaching, this, however seemingly eloquent, is worse than useless without a consistent character; hence congregations too often find that the sermons which have led them away are quite hollow.

But even if the qualities which are really desirable in a minister could be displayed before the election, it would seem that congregations as such would not be good judges of them. For nearly all elections by large bodies are determined by a few individuals and turn upon party considerations. The Church, whenever it is vigorous, will always be divided into parties, and such parties would have the predominant influence in the elections of ministers. The still small voice of personal virtue would be drowned in the din of party conflict, and he would have the best chance of election who professed the opinions of the dominant faction and was most fortunate or most skilful in managing his chances. Let those who think this language extravagant watch the course of the congregations which now do elect their own ministers. Unless we knew from experience we should not believe how largely the elections of ministers in self-governing chapels are influenced by mean motives and determined by paltry considerations. Very frequently such angry feelings are roused by this act which should exemplify the highest Christian virtues that not only do congregations quarrel amongst themselves but very often they split up into two although when united they were unable to maintain one efficient minister properly.

But even if they avoid these dangers and are fairly agreed in their choice they are just as likely to be wrong as not. For even town congregations, with all their supposed superior ability, cannot be expected as a body to perform at once that feat which each of us finds it hard to do after long acquaintance, namely, to understand a man's religious character.

Either they must rely upon first pulpit impressions, confessedly most delusive, or they must be led by the reports of others, generally tutors who have only known the candidate in his unfledged youth and when he was more influenced by the spirit of his college than by his own character. As to judging by preaching, we see on reflection that the probabilities are decidedly in favour of a wrong choice, for religion is not meant to be a pleasant luxury but an unpleasant discipline and the sermons which really form part of such a religion must tell us the things we do not like to hear and not those which please us. Some people seem to think that men should in religion do what would be considered ridiculous in children, namely, keep repeating at school the same lessons simply because they know them. The man who merely goes to a place of worship to enjoy the self-soothing sentimentality of music and to hear the repetition of his own opinions and prejudices had much better stop at home. Sermons to do any good must show us our ignorance and carelessness and wickedness, but no one can suppose that such sermons will please us or win our votes.

Two great evils have resulted from this method adopted by some Dissenters of the congregations choosing their own ministers. In the first place people have come to attach a great deal too much importance to sermons generally, so that they are now spoken of as if they are the chief object in attending places of worship; it is to be feared that to speak of going to worship as going to hear So-and-so is not merely an accidental phrase but also indicates a deep-seated evil. In the second place ministers, through being judged so much by their sermons, have come to regard those sermons more as means for winning applause than for doing good. Thus the position of sermons has been unduly exalted whilst their character has been seriously lowered.

It is not pretended that many objections may not justly be raised against the various methods of electing ministers now used by the Church of England, but we are not called upon here to treat of those objections. We have merely to consider the methods which are suggested to replace those now used, and if these cannot justify themselves the case falls to the ground. The principal method suggested is that congregations should choose their own ministers, and in reference to this we have to say in conclusion that this method is not good in itself, and that if it were good there is no reason why it could not be adopted in full consistency with the national principle.

Whatever may be objected against bishops and chapters and colleges, it is evident that these are likely to be better qualified than the congregations to choose suitable ministers. And as to appointments by patrons it may be said that a man having the education and independence of a gentleman and living in intimate social intercourse with the class from which ministers are chiefly supplied will have a wider choice and be better able to make a good one. Although as a whole the system of purchasing livings in the Church must be condemned still more may be urged in its defence than is thought of at first. The clergyman who pays money must undergo the same tests as the one who does not pay, and it may reasonably be suggested that when two men are equally qualified in other respects the advantage is on the side of the one who pays money in addition, for he thus gives a pledge against the neglect of his duties and consequent depreciation in the value of that which he or his heirs will want eventually to dispose of.

As to the wide principle that the people generally ought to choose their own ministers, it may be maintained that this can only be properly carried out in the national system, for even if the separate congregations do not exercise this function, the people as a whole do. For a National Church is under the control of the people, and they can take back to themselves at any time those portions of their power which they have delegated, whether to patrons, or bishops, or organized bodies.

Connected with this objection is the one that congregations cannot remove their ministers when they are displeased with them. Although it does not follow that a minister ought to be removed simply because his congregation does not like him, for very often congregations most need that sort of discipline from their ministers which they are least likely to take kindly, still undoubtedly there should be some means of removing a minister whose unfitness can be made plainly manifest. The advantage to be named in this respect is that whilst in the congregational system there is no authority to appeal to and the plaintiffs must also be the judges, in the national system such disputes can be brought before an organized tribunal and settled publicly in accordance with the principles of law.

Another objection is that—

9. *The national system makes the clergy too independent.*

We are told that a clergyman when once he has secured a living has no such outward incentives to do his duty as most men, whatever be their position, require, and that no punishment can be inflicted upon him if he chooses to neglect it, for his congregation are powerless and the law is too uncertain, tedious, and costly to have any terrors. Whether the clergyman attends to his work well or badly, or even if he almost neglects it altogether, he still receives his income, and thus his people are deprived of one of the most efficient means of securing proper service.

It is quite true that when a minister is entirely dependent upon contributions and pew-rents his congregation, by being able at any time to deprive him of his means of subsistence, possesses a power over him such as no national system could allow. If ministers of religion ought to be servants in this sense to their congregations then we must confess the national system to be at fault, but we maintain that such ministers ought to be the servants only of the nation as a whole and not of the few people who happen to resort to the same building for worship, and that their duty is to the entire parish and not merely to those who frequent their religious gatherings. Indeed we should be inclined to say that a minister ought to pay more attention to those who do not frequent his church than to those who do, for it is the backward who need most looking after. Of course we know that whatever we do, a vast number must remain outside, still our ideal ought always to be to get humanity through the gates of heaven abreast and not to have a few a long way ahead and the rest nowhere. Religious culture, as far as the people are concerned, should have for its object to bring up as many good useful animals as possible and not merely to train a few Derby winners.

Apart from the fact that the national is irreconcilable with the congregational system, it may also be said that the state of dependence in which the minister is placed by the congregational system is in itself unsound and mischievous. For if the people will insist upon the commercial basis as giving them a hold over their minister, they must expect the minister to act upon that basis too, and therefore he will consult his interest by giving them what they like and will pay for rather than that which he knows they most need. Or if the individual minister does not so trifle with his conscience but retires, the commercial law of supply and demand brings a successor who is disposed to give the congregation what it chiefly desires. Thus both the congregations and the minister are greatly injured by this system, for whilst the ministers lose their independence, the congregations have their weaknesses and ignorance encouraged instead of reproved. A great deal is said about the clergy being bound by creeds, but the bondage to a creed plainly laid down and legally administered is liberty itself compared with the subjection to the individual whims and money control of a congregation.

It is hard enough to feel that each member of the congregation may set up a court of inquisition and drag the minister's opinions before it, but the position is rendered much more intolerable by the fact that the supplies may also be stopped, and so resignation forced on. As every one knows, such congregations are generally led by one or two leading members who give most to the funds. If the minister does not keep the approval of these, and cannot resort to the unpleasant expedient of getting up an opposition party strong enough to maintain him, he must give up his place and be often put into uncertainty even about the common necessities for himself and family. The men who are most needed as ministers of religion and who alone are fit for the office are just those who would not think of submitting even to the chance of being placed in such a humiliating position. The idea of controlling ministers in this way through their physical necessities is radically irreligious, for it is based on the assumption that money and religious capacity go together, which we know to be not at all true. Indeed if we look abroad at those who have money and at those who have not, we are inclined to think that God Himself sets little value upon it, when we see the fools to whom He gives it and the wise men from whom He keeps it away. At any rate we are quite sure that its possession was never meant to bear any ratio to the power of controlling ministers of religion.

Even if men of the right sort would submit to this uncertain dependence for themselves, they would not allow their families to be subject to it, and therefore if the Congregational system were generally adopted there would only be the choice of two alternatives—for either the ministers of religion must remain unmarried or they must be men of a lower social position. An unmarried clergy is opposed to the genius of Protestantism and antagonistic to the welfare of religion and to the liberty of the people. Unless the ministers of religion are to become a separate priestly caste they must be surrounded with social ties so that they may be in sympathy with the people and their religion may be human and reasonable. The self-governing bodies of Protestants recognise the force of this necessity, and hence they expect their ministers generally to be married. The natural consequence is that these ministers are mostly obtained from lower social classes than those to which the bulk of the clergy of the National Church belong. If Disestablishment were carried out this would become general. No one can doubt that such a consequence would have very lamentable and wide-spread results, for although gentlemanly culture is not the first requisite in a minister it is a very desirable quality, and it would be an evil day for the nation if ever the higher social classes withdrew from the service of religion and left it to the sole care of those of inferior training. It may be said that devotion to religion ought not to be regulated by such considerations, but it is, and those at any rate have no right to object who claim superiority for their own system precisely on these grounds.

The independence conferred upon the ministers of religion by the national system, and by that alone, ought not to be diminished, then, for these two reasons amongst many, namely, that their influence would be diminished and their character would be lowered.

Even judging the matter by the commercial considerations which this objection introduces we may say that the independence of the national system decidedly pays. For although some salaries may be large, if we add together the whole amount received by the body and divide it amongst the number we shall find that the clergy of the Church of England are worse paid than any other set of men of similar education and position. Many of them possess large private incomes which they devote more or less to the service of religion and most of them are willing to forego the desire of worldly abundance for the sake of the dignity and honourableness of their position. All this would cease if that position was deprived of its independence as it would be by Disestablishment. The consequence would then be that either religion would have to be served by men of a lower class or more money would have to be paid to obtain those of the same class, even if any money could compensate for such a loss of independence.

It cannot be denied that there are many drawbacks to the independence conferred by the national system, as there are to everything else of the sort in this world. Out of so large a body there must always be many clergymen who, relying upon their independence, either neglect their duties or misuse their power, but we must not on account of such cases condemn the system itself. It must first be proved that the evils of the abuse of independence exceed the benefits of its possession, and we maintain that this cannot be done.

Another objection to the national system is that—

10. *The salaries of the clergy are not proportioned to their congregations.*

It is said that many of the largest incomes of the Church of England are received by those who have only to look after little country parishes whilst the hard-worked clergy of the towns are often very poorly paid.

It might be sufficient to reply that if this is a fault it is no essential part of the national system, and since the nation is master of the Church it may if it chooses so apportion its income as to do away with this objection without interfering with the system itself. Indeed such an act would be one of the most forcible assertions of that system, for it must not be forgotten that Disestablishment itself would be the supremest declaration of the national principle, for upon no other ground could be defended such an interference with the revenues of the Church as would be involved in that change.

Since, however, great consequences are involved in this

argument it may be well to examine it more closely, and in doing so we are bound in the first place to say that this objection rests upon a false and vicious principle. The doctrine of supply and demand, from which it is derived, may do very well for trade and commerce, but it is radically bad when applied to religion. There is this fundamental difference between, calico and religion that whereas the one should only be offered in proportion as it is desired, the other should be offered in proportion as it is not desired; whilst it is pretty certain that those who need calico will wish for it, it is also certain that those most need religion who do not wish for it and will not pay for it, and that the smallness of their demand for it is the best measure of the greatness of their need.

This is one fundamental defect, and probably the greatest of all, which belongs to the Congregational system and to that of all other self-governing and self-supporting Churches. Their places of worship are like shops which can only be kept going where customers are plentiful enough and rich enough to make them pay. If one of these places of worship is opened in any district it must be either self-supporting or not self-supporting. If it is not self-supporting, but has to be helped by other congregations, then it is so far in a condition of religious pauperism the effects of which are far more injurious than any which can result from connection with the State, for what is received from the State is a right but what comes from our fellows is a favour. But if it is self-supporting, then it is plain that the amount paid to the minister, and consequently in a general way the quality of that minister, will depend upon the amount of such support. Now a congregation of poor people will not pay anything like as much as one of rich people of equal size, chiefly because they cannot, and partly also because they do not as a class take as much interest in the subject. Therefore the poor congregation, to be equal, must be so much larger as to make up the difference. But it is found impossible, except in very exceptional circumstances, to get such congregations together, and still more impossible, with the self-governing principle, to keep them together. Also, even if this could be done, it would be impossible for the minister to give proper attention to each individual member.

Thus it is an absolute necessity that self-supporting places of worship shall follow after money and shall have the quality of their ministers regulated by the worldly means of their congregations. This is not merely the result of theory but it is also the plain teaching of every-day experience. Where do we find those who are considered the best ministers of such self-governing bodies, as for example, the Congregationalists? In the country? No, but almost invariably in the towns. And in what part of the towns do we find their places of worship? In the poor quarters? No, but in the well-to-do suburbs. The simple truth, too plain to be hidden, is that self-supporting places of worship cannot live decently in the poor districts of towns, and those which do remain in such districts are almost invariably old chapels which will soon either fall into neglect or be removed into more eligible neighbourhoods. The changed localities of chapels during the last fifty years would, if marked on a map, pretty accurately indicate the shiftings of respectability during the same period. And as to poor districts of the country, such chapels cannot be said to live there at all. Unless there happen to be one or two wealthy supporters in the neighbourhood, towards whom the rest occupy such a position that it would only be satirical to speak of the congregation as self-governing, these chapels cannot maintain a minister with the barest requirements of an educated gentleman, and more frequently than not, as is shown by the recent statistics of the Baptist congregations, cannot maintain a minister of any sort at all. It is an inevitable consequence of the self-supporting system, acknowledged and regretted by its most thoughtful friends, that its best ministers must gravitate towards the towns and that the country must receive the worst or none at all. Voluntaryism as a system cannot meet properly the religious wants of the towns and is utterly incapable of grappling with those of the country. Yet we are asked to destroy the national system for the sake of this. It is true that most of the agitators for this change come from towns, and we may fairly beg these to remember that England does not consist entirely of towns and that before they can expect us to destroy the National Church they are bound to suggest some system which can meet the religious wants of the country better than the national system can. Voluntaryism at any rate cannot, and therefore we say that it is essentially snobbish, for no other word can describe this most mischievous tendency of a system which is in this respect opposed to the dictates of reason and to the fundamental characteristics of Christianity.

If wealth were a drawback to religion, which it is not or its pursuit even by individuals would be unjustifiable, there would then be some reason why those who possess it should receive the best religious ministrations. But on the contrary it is well known that, other things being equal, it is much harder for the poor man, mentally absorbed and physically exhausted by the struggle for subsistence, to keep up in himself the religious life than it is for him who can command spare energy and cultivated leisure, though probably if he succeeds the poor man's religion will be the most robust. Therefore it is the poor who chiefly need religious attention, and even intellectual power, for it is much more difficult to make the truths of religion plain to uncultivated minds than to cultivated ones. Christ recognised this duty most significantly; it was the common people to whom He gave most opportunities of hearing Him, and one of the facts which He most openly advanced to prove the divinity of His mission was that the poor had the Gospel preached to them. We need have no hesitation then in saying that a system which, like

Voluntaryism, gives most attention to those who can pay most is radically out of harmony with the essential spirit of Christianity.

Its adoption would, also, be very injurious to the welfare of the Christian religion and to the social safety of the nation. For one of the most alarming symptoms of our modern civilisation is the growing alienation between different social classes. Undoubtedly this has been greatly fostered by the enormous growth of our towns and their increased unpleasantness which have led the wealthier classes to go out into the suburbs instead of living amongst their people as their forefathers did. Thus large towns may be mapped out into differently-coloured districts, each colour denoting a separate social grade. The people from the different districts merely come into town for business and have scarcely any social intercourse except with those of their own class. Of course circumstances vary, but this is a fair representation of the tendency of modern town life.

Thus the different classes are becoming more estranged from each other, and this is probably in a great degree the cause why our modern social life is, in spite of our wealth, so dull and unenjoyable. The towns have now so much influence that this estrangement is gradually spreading throughout the whole country.

Now a nation which has really got the right spirit will not submit to this process very long but will check these social divisions either by some gradual process or by some sudden outburst. Religion is the only social solvent, and if that is not made effective we may look for communistic extravagance or military violence. The great problem now before Christian men is to bring religion to bear so that class divisions may be subdued and the brotherhood of men vindicated. But Voluntaryism, instead of doing this, would use religion to foster those class divisions and would identify it with them, therefore all Christians and patriots ought to oppose any change which would pull down the National Church and put Voluntaryism in its place. We do not say that Voluntaryism consciously encourages these evils which religion ought to discourage; on the contrary we believe that the personal sympathies of most of its supporters are decidedly opposed to them, but in considering this question we are only concerned with inevitable tendencies. Most of the mischief of this world is done by people whose intentions are right but whose judgment is wrong.

It is easy to talk about the large salaries and high positions of bishops and other dignitaries, to point out how merely by influence the sons of wealthy families receive good and easy livings, and to say that the majority of what are called "the better classes" favour the Church because it is fashionable to do so. All such assertions as these may be quite true, but they are not in themselves arguments, and we must not allow ourselves to be led away by them into believing that the National Church is the Church of the rich. Instead of judging by such accidental circumstances we must search out and weigh the fundamental characteristics of the system itself. If we do this we shall find that the National Church is especially the Church of the poor, not merely because its doors are open without charge or test, and also without any dependent feeling of favour, but also because there is no reason in the system itself why the poor should not receive as much and as good attention as any one else. If the Christian religion is to maintain its ground and to exercise its proper influence it must be in organisation, as it is in spirit, democratic, and it can only be so on the basis of the national principle; a National Church is the only one which can be properly under the control of the people.

In reference to the fact that in the Church of England there are many good livings in small country parishes, two incidental advantages may be named. In the first place by this means some of that culture is kept in the country which otherwise has always a strong tendency to drain into the towns. The evil consequences, both social and political, of this excessive predominance of the towns are plainly written on the pages alike of ancient and modern history; Greece, Rome in a still more marked manner, and the France of our own time, all tell the same tale. For we have to remember that the great majority of nearly all nations must live in the country, and that if we bestow our culture too exclusively upon the town minority, we put a gulf between the two populations; it is like throwing out of gear the governor tackle of a steam-engine. Thus we see in France that the people are divided in this way, and so are like a pair of horses which do not pull well together; for a while the stolid country animal can rule the pace but every now and then the chafing steed at its side breaks out of all bounds and sometimes dashes the conveyance to pieces. It is easy to laugh at what is called "the gentleman in every parish" argument, but laughing will not rob it of its truth, especially since this laughter chiefly comes from those who are little qualified to judge. Anyone acquainted with the general characteristics of English country life knows very well that as a class the clergy do more for the general improvement and culture of the people than all other classes put together. There is no other class which can be named except the landowners, and they could not possibly vie with the clergy, for they are mostly from home half their time and occupied with something else the other half. To say nothing of education which, in country places he alone is qualified to look after, a thousand ways could be pointed out in which the clergyman exercises an improving influence upon the people. The clergy of the Church of England are the only body of men in the land who possess the culture of gentlemen and who are bound by their office to come into constant contact with the poor and to promote their welfare.

Another incidental advantage arising from the fact that by the system of the Church of England many able clergymen have to spend their lives in comparatively obscure places is that thereby is inculcated a very important religious truth and one which needs especially teaching in these days. For although the principles of commerce are very good in their way, the world needs reminding that they must not be carried too far, for then they are at variance with the fundamental laws of God. Success in this world is a very blameless object of pursuit within proper limits, but still it must not be forgotten that this is not the Christian standard. On the contrary one of the most fundamental, and also most beautiful, principles of our religion, which is the one lying at the root of that great doctrine of the Atonement whose meaning is now often so lamentably narrowed, is that of self-sacrifice. We are taught that the highest success is often that which to us seems failure, and that in the workings of Providence the greatest ability is often doing the most good when, according to the judgment of the world, it is being wasted away in obscurity. The Bible tells us that we must not expect to occupy a worldly position and to make a display before others, in proportion to our power for good, and Nature teaches the same lesson. For all the beauties which we see there are myriads which no human eye can ever gaze upon, yet these go on repeating themselves, and we cannot but believe that in the economy of God not one of them is wasted. We are told that to lose our lives is often the only way to gain them, but the world does not believe this. In every nation, and especially in one so much devoted to business as ours, there is a strong tendency to think that every quality must find a proportionate worldly value, that the best man must have the best place and so on in proper ratio. The system of the National Church, which does not necessarily assign its positions of prominence in proportion to worth but often leaves able men in obscurity whilst inferior ones are put forward, so far counteracts this tendency and exemplifies a truth which it is especially incumbent upon religion to teach.

The last objection to be considered here is that—

11. *The Church ought to be disestablished because it has ceased to be the Church of the majority of the nation.*

It is said that even though the national system may be sound in theory it ought not to be kept up any longer in England because the majority of the nation is not now attached to the Established Church.

In reference to the assertion that the number of those, added together, who belong to all the other religious bodies exceeds that of the adherents of the Church, it may be remarked, without any intention of entering upon delusive statistics, that there is no reason to believe it is true. For it must be remembered that those who differ from the established order of things on any subject are sure to be more assertive than those who conform to it, and that there are great numbers who do not frequent the services of the Church but who are favourably disposed to the system and would come forward to defend it if its existence was imperilled.

But even if this assertion about its numerical inferiority were true, it might be an argument in favour of an alteration of the National Church but could not be one for its destruction. For it is undoubtedly true that no other single religious organization has anything like as many adherents as the Established Church and therefore that Church has the best right to national adoption.

But we reject all such pleas, for it cannot be too plainly understood that this is not a question of numbers but of principle. If the national system of religion is sound and just it ought not to be given up merely because numbers are alienated from it, but rather that alienation itself should be overcome so that all may work together for the wisest good.

Of course those who disapprove of the national system are justified in wishing for its destruction but no defence can be offered for those who are now so frequently telling us that although this system may be sound in itself we ought to make up our minds to give it up because there is no hope of maintaining it much longer. The English nation must first have fallen into second childishness before it can be persuaded to give up a good work merely because there are difficulties in the way.

We are now fast moving on to a great religious crisis; thoughtful men are growing sick and ashamed of our multitudinous and paltry sectarian divisions whilst lovers of Christianity are alarmed at the little progress their religion is making, at the smallness of the influence it now exercises even upon our own nation, and at the hopelessness of spreading it over the world unless we can work more harmoniously together and set a better example of Christian brotherhood. We do not care to pass any judgment upon our forefathers but we do say that even if they acted rightly in originating these sectarian divisions it does not follow that their descendants are justified it perpetuating them. The armies which are marching against Christianity itself are united and bold and we ought not to let the defence be weakened by isolations on account of trifling differences. The national fortress is strong and well supplied, and this alone is capable of sheltering a large force and of offering a successful resistance. Instead of bidding the garrison abandon it and form themselves into another flying column, those who are now outside ought, as did the Athenians of old when their country was attacked, to return into this fortress and to help in making from it a united struggle against the foe.

CHAPTER VII.

POLITICAL OBJECTIONS.

IT seems best to consider these objections, for the sake of clearness, separately as they relate to the Church and to the State, but the caution should here be repeated that this division of the subject must not be taken as acknowledging that there can actually be any such separation between the institutions of the Church and the State themselves. We hear a great deal concerning the union of Church and State but many of those who have most to say about this union seem to think it quite unnecessary to possess any distinct ideas of what they mean by the terms Church and State. We rarely meet, in the writings on this subject, with any attempts even to explain the sense in which these terms are used by the writers themselves, although it seems impossible to understand what should be the proper relationship to each other of two unknown quantities. It is most easy, however, to be verbose and declamatory about the vague and varying notions which people generally attach to the terms Church and State, and this is probably the reason why so little trouble is taken to get at definite ideas.

There is almost as much misunderstanding about what is meant by the State as we have seen to exist concerning the Church. Whilst the Church is commonly spoken of as a separate body although it is nothing of the sort, the term State is used as if it denoted something quite distinct from the nation, and the common way of speaking conveys the impression that this State has formed an alliance with this Church and forced it upon the nation.

It may be difficult to give any correct definition of what is meant by the State, still we may get at a negative notion by saying that the State does not, in a monarchical country, merely mean the sovereign, or his executive advisers. It includes the whole people, and we may say that whatever is the form of government, the State is the governing energy of the nation made objective.

We thus see that the Church and the State are not two different things but merely denote two different views of the same thing, for the Church is the nation in its religious aspect, and the State is the nation in its political aspect. We can understand how impossible it is to separate these from each other if we consider the twofold character even of religion itself. For unhappily Christianity is too often spoken of by its advocates, and especially in England at present, as if it was solely a plan for getting people into heaven; as if this life was a sort of mistake, a mere period of waiting like that spent by a crowd before the doors of a theatre are opened, and that all we have to do here is to secure our tickets and learn the Open-Sesame which will give us admission into the regions of celestial bliss. But the Christianity of Christ is very different from this for it teaches that true religion must make us good in this life as well as fit for that which is to come, and that earth is the training-ground for heaven.

Religion, then, as far as our existence as nations is concerned, has for its object to make us good citizens, and this process consists of two parts, the one repressing the manifestations of evil and the other curing its causes. This repression of manifestations is especially the business of the State, but the Parliamentary history of every session amply proves that the State does not profess to confine itself to this. In dealing with crime we do not merely punish criminals but since crime arises in a great degree from mental ignorance and physical depravity, the State enforces Education Acts and Sanitary Laws. As it is found that the State cannot, in these matters, neglect the causes of evil, so much the more is it impossible for it to separate itself from Religion, which is the only means of dealing with these causes completely. Education may make intelligent citizens, sanitation may make healthy citizens, but only religion can make good ones.

Thus not only does the State, and especially in our days, act upon a principle which makes it impossible that it should consistently separate itself from religion, but even nature is plainly opposed to such a separation. It may suit our little arguments to talk about religion being one thing and politics another, we may arrange our duties into classes and say that this class belongs to the nation and this other does not, but Nature will have nothing to do with our classifications; national life flows on in one unbroken stream and our divisions of it are no more lasting than lines drawn on water with a stick. In this, as in other things, dumb Nature is wiser than talking man, and we may be quite sure that she will not recognise the principle that the State, which is the organization of national life, shall be separated from Religion, which is the chief cure for the evils of that life. It is possible, though not probable, that Disestablishment may be carried out in England, but such a measure can never be final; the great principles out of which our present condition has come will again assert themselves, and the fleeting fancies of the hour, although they may for a time have ruled the conduct of the nation, will quickly disappear and take their work away with them.

It must therefore be understood that not only do we not believe that it would be advisable that the Church and the State should be separated from each other but we also maintain that it is not possible thus to separate them. We may, however, consider the arguments in favour of such a separation as they relate to the Church and to the State. The political objections relating to the Church which are most generally urged against the national principle of religion may be divided into those referring to the position of the Church and those referring to the character of the Church.

It is said that the position of the Church is lowered by the national principle because—

1. *The State has no right to choose what Religion the nation shall follow.*

As named before, the State does not, by the national principle, choose the religion of the nation, but merely gives that religion, after it has been chosen by the people, a State organization. There have been cases in which this religion has first been introduced by the instrumentality of the State, but it could not become, in our sense of the term, the national religion until it had first been adopted by the nation, and this adoption, and not the introduction, was the ground of its nationality. The national principle starts from the assumption that the people have a religion, and it says that since that religion must have an organization we ought to give it the best we have, namely that organization of the State which we use for our other highest purposes. Religion without an organization is like an unclothed man, and so, instead of theorising against the necessity of clothes and leaving the man to pick up a scratch suit for himself, we bring forth the best robe and put it on him, and we not merely provide the shoes of necessity for his feet but also the ring of honour for his finger.

Therefore we utterly deny the applicability of all that is said, so frequently in these days as to make us quite weary of it, about the Church doing better when liberated from State Patronage. It is not patronage which the Church receives from the State but an organization, and without such an organization there could be no National Church at all. It is not a matter as to which Church shall be established but as to whether there shall be any Established Church at all, and the question must be decided not by what we think most advantageous for an association which we choose to call the Church but by what is best for religion and for the nation.

2. *Religion has no right to be subservient to the State.*

It is plain that as long as religion requires an organization, that organization must in a certain sense be under the control of its own governing organ, and so far religion must be subject to restriction. But it is not reasonable to call such a relationship as this one of subserviency any more than it would be to say that the soul of a man is subservient to his body. We can imagine that religion, like our souls, would be freer if liberated from any human organization, but it is neither sensible nor religious to raise objections which call into question the fundamental conditions of our human existence.

It is to be feared that this objection has its real root in that lowering of the ideal of the State which we must confess seems to have taken place in this country during the last few years. If men believed that their State possessed the best organization which the nation could then get to work, and if they also believed that this organization ought to be used for such purposes as the highest conceptions of national duty dictated, then they would not imagine that religion could be degraded by connection with such a State. Even a State so elevated must of course have many imperfections, but it would be the best organization we could give; the widow's mite was a poor gift in itself, but it won honour for the giver because it was her all. But instead of believing that a nation is bound, as a nation, to carry out higher and more unselfish purposes than come even within the range of individual duty, many men seem to think that a nation should have no nobler object than the security and accumulation of wealth, and that therefore the State should be little else than an economical police organization. Religion would indeed be degraded by close association with such an organization, but the true course to adopt is not to acquiesce in such a demoralisation of the ideal of the State but to raise that ideal so that all complaints of degradation would be groundless. Both the State and the Church would thus be benefited.

In reference to the character of the Church, it is said that this is lowered by the national principle because—

3. *It makes religious men political.*

It is said that the political feelings of Churchmen and Dissenters, instead of being allowed free play, are both obstructed and diverted by religious considerations, and that many religious men who would otherwise be reasonable politicians are made passionate ones through opposition to, or friendship for, the National Church. This institution is blamed for making so many Churchmen Conservatives and for throwing so many Dissenters into the arms of the Radicals.

It must be remembered, in the first place, that for the good government of the State men have to be divided into political parties upon some principle or other, and therefore it seems reasonable to expect that the higher that principle the more dignified and wholesome will be that division. It is absurd to suppose that if the Church was done away with, the political attitude of Churchmen and Dissenters towards any proposed measure would be determined purely by the consideration of that measure itself, for everybody knows that most men, as the phrase is, "go with their party," and therefore the important matter is as to what determines their choice of a party. It is not here advocated that such political allegiance should be determined simply by ecclesiastical sympathies, but it is maintained that both the State and the nation have at least not been injured by the influence which these sympathies have so far exercised over English political life. This influence has at any rate given to English political parties a dignity, and to English history a consistency, which have been signally wanting wherever religion has been more largely excluded.

It is also not true to say that religion embitters political animosities. The way to subdue these animosities is to make the oppositions from which they arise depend upon some great principle and not upon trivial practical differences. Just as those are generally most violent in argument who really agree on the subject-matter but differ about the form of expression, so as a rule political animosities are the greatest where political differences are the least. Thus political feeling runs much higher in the United States of America, where the points in dispute, especially at present, seem comparatively unimportant, than in England, where we are told that religion exercises an embittering influence.

The present political condition of the United States also indicates another consideration well worth weighing in this connection. For it is there found, as it has been found in similar conditions all the world over, that the great difficulty is not how to prevent religious men from getting too political but how to keep them interested in politics at all. And this is no more than we ought to expect, for we may be sure that religion will always claim the first allegiance of the best men; they may sometimes seem to be breaking away from it, but they are certain to return before long. This supreme fascination of religion was never greater than now, although so many current theories would lead to a contrary expectation. Religion occupies the centre of the territory of mental exploration, and no matter from what side they start the most pushing adventurers are sure soon to set foot on its soil. This is no time to talk about the decay of religion when the leading men of all sorts cannot keep off it; explorers of physical phenomena, professors of physiology, doctors, chemists, metaphysicians, men of letters, politicians of every school, from the most quiescent to the most turbulent—all fly to the spider-web of religion and most of them stick fast there. The foremost knights of every arm, however different or distant may have been the regions they set out to conquer, are sure sooner or later to present themselves before the castle of religion—some to attack and others to defend, but both by their coming acknowledging its importance.

There have been many able men who do not seem to have felt this fascination, but there have been no great ones; self-satisfied cleverness can never have depth of soil enough for the growth of greatness. The men who do not feel the need of religion are not the sort which the State should most desire to attract to itself, whilst those who do feel this need are sure to acknowledge the supremacy of religion. As long as politics are united with religion these men take an interest in politics because they feel that they are thus performing one portion of that sum of duty which their religion dictates, but if separation takes place, many soon come to think that politics have lost their dignity and their only claim upon attention. Of course this is not the right course to follow, nor is it the one which the very best men of all will follow, for these will recognise devotion to the State as a distinct duty in itself and will feel well assured that though the Church may be separated from the State, religion and politics must go together, for what God has joined man may not put asunder. But in deciding on a question of this sort we have not chiefly to take into account the probable conduct of the very best men but we have to consider what religious men generally would do, and there is no doubt that if the Church was separated from the State, the majority of these would soon become more or less alienated from politics.

It is easy to say that politics could do without such men but it is not true, for however it may be taken as a symptom of weakness, there is no doubt that those who may be called religious are just the men of most real use to the State and whose influence is necessary to preserve the purity and vitality of politics. Fashion follows in the wake of religion, and when politics have ceased to be religious, it is not long before they cease also to be respectable, and when this comes to pass a crisis is not far off.

As to the complaint that many are made politically Conservative merely out of zeal for the defence of the Church, it surely seems that the easiest way to cure this evil, if it is one, would be to stop the attack.

Considering this objection as referring to the laity, the corresponding objection to the national principle is that—

4. *It makes the clergy political Conservatives.*

It is undoubtedly true that the large majority of the clergy of the Church of England are attached to the Conservative party, but it does not follow that this is an effect, whether we think it advantageous or otherwise, of the national principle. For ministers of religion, as named before, are naturally conservative both in politics and religion. Their chief concern is with the fixed principles of existence, and therefore they have little sympathy for the varying details of politics; men who are occupied in maintaining the unalterability of divine government are sure not to have much liking for changeability in human governments. There have undoubtedly been many cases which seem to contradict this theory but they do not do so when properly looked into. Ministers of religion have frequently taken an enthusiastic part in politics but their enthusiasm has had its root in religion. Dissenting ministers are now almost universally Liberals not merely from political conviction, for then such a unanimity would be inexplicable, but chiefly from past and present religious causes.

It is not asserted that after Disestablishment the ministers of religion would not take any interest in politics, but that they would not take a political interest in them; their almost sole consideration would be the welfare of their Church and they would manipulate their political influence to promote that. Then would come great danger both to the State and to politics generally. Especially would this be the case with the Disestablished Church of England, for a body possessing so much property must exercise great political influence. In its times of danger this body would feel obliged to seek the alliance of one of the great political parties, in order to protect its own interests, and in its times of power some political party would offer bribes to gain its help. In either case great injury would be inflicted both upon the Church and upon the State, for the Church would have to bate its principles to win allies, and the State would be jeopardised by the power wielded by the Church.

The sum of the matter seems to be that the clergy, whose political sympathies would remain the same, are now the servants of the State and under the control of the nation, but they would, after Disestablishment, be merely the members of an independent faction and sometimes the opponents of the State. By this change not merely would the State lose the advantage of their filial patriotism but it would be constantly liable to their factious enmity. Let those who still doubt cast their eyes to Ireland and ask themselves whether the position of the State would not be infinitely better there and its work infinitely easier if the priests were under the control of the State instead of belonging to an independent Church.

Not merely would the Church suffer from the consequent lowered tone of its clergy, but Disestablishment would also tell against freedom of opinion in the Church itself. Churches, as religious organizations, do not believe in freedom of opinion, and it is only lay influence which can introduce this. If the Church does not care for the friendship of the State it will not concede this freedom, whereas the State, to please the Church, will often, as it has frequently done in the past, lend its help to repress all such expressions of this freedom as the Church disapproves of.

As to the dignitaries of the Church being made political because their appointments are given for political reasons, we can only say that if devotion to politics has become so strong in the nation, such dignitaries would be political however they were appointed. If the people care so little for religion and so much for politics, it does not matter whether the heads of their Church are chosen by themselves in small bodies or by themselves collectively as a nation. We see the operation of this principle, although turning upon official fitness and not upon religion, in the character of the Civil Service of the United States, appointments to which are chiefly made on account not of suitability but of political partisanship.

By the national principle the clergy are led to be politicians and are yet prevented from being dangerous ones, so that the State is saved from the two evils of a large class of the most influential citizens withdrawing generally from politics and of such a class occasionally exercising their political influence in antagonism to the welfare of the State. It certainly seems unwise for Liberals to advocate that the State, of which they themselves are masters for at least half the time, should give up all control over a body of men who in any case would certainly be generally opposed to their proposals and probably often their most dangerous antagonists.

Turning next to the political objections which especially concern the State, we may divide these into those which relate to the theoretical unsoundness of the national principle and those which relate to its practical injuriousness.

We are told that the national principle is theoretically unsound because—

5. *It is not the business of the State to meddle with Religion.*

Everyone knows how frequently those who try to do anything out of the barest routine are met with the warning that they are meddling with what is not their business. If we heed this reproof our life must be merely a wearisome trudge along the dusty highway of selfish and stupid monotony; if we glance across the fields into the nooks of out-of-the-way charity, if we gaze up longingly at the heights of heroic duty, if we look down into the valleys of individual humour—everywhere the same signboard against trespass stares us in the face. But we must not be frightened off in this way; we must demand to see by what title-deeds dulness and selfishness and littleness claim to hold all the territory out of the common road. If we are told that it is not our business to go where we think we ought to go, we must ask those who object if it is their business to stop us, and we shall generally find that it is not.

It is much easier to tell people that this or that is not their business than to explain what their business is. Of course it is not possible fully to set out the whole sum of duty, but we are bound to have a general idea of the territory before we can say whether any particular spot is within or without its boundaries. Especially is this so with institutions, whose limits are more exacting and yet often more doubtful than those of individuals.

Thus we ought to have some pretty definite idea of the proper duties of the State before we have a right to say that any particular work does not come within its business. Considering the character of the State, its past history and its present policy, we may say that it is the business of the State to do that which needs doing and which cannot be done so well by any other instrumentality. Now we also say that offering the ministrations of religion to all needs doing and cannot be done so well by any other instrumentality. Therefore we conclude that this is the business of the State.

By way of objection to this, no doubt the definition of the business of the State will first be rejected, but it is not easy to see on what grounds, and especially in these days, when it is made the business of the State to take care that our children are vaccinated and sent to school, our houses healthy and our habits temperate. Many of those who are now advocating what is called the Permissive Bill are in favour of Disestablishment, yet it seems impossible to find any reason why the State should be asked to regulate our liquor and yet be told that it has no business to have anything to do with our religion, for the State is much more affected by what we believe than by what we drink. Not only now, when the interference of the State is being extended to almost everything, but also at any time it may be maintained that it is the business of the State to do whatever cannot be done as well otherwise.

It may be taken for granted that the ministrations of religion ought to be offered to everyone, by some means or other. Of course those who are opposed to religion, or indifferent about it, would not agree with this, but it is not with such persons that we have on this subject to argue, for it is very certain that the proposal for Disestablishment would not be even listened to if it was understood that it involved the abandonment of all such ministrations. The only question then to be discussed is whether this offering should be done under the control of the State or by some other instrumentality, therefore those who advocate Disestablishment have to suggest a system which will do this better than the national one can, for we cannot be expected to abandon a system which we know and have had so long for one which at best has only the chance of turning out as good.

We will however give up our claim to a better one and merely ask what is offered us which will be even as good as the national system? In reply the only suggestion is Voluntaryism, and in reference to this we not only maintain that Voluntaryism cannot offer the ministrations of religion to all as well as Nationalism can, but we also assert that it cannot do this at all. The reasons for this inability of Voluntaryism have been indicated before, and we need only here refer to one—namely, that Voluntaryism cannot help gravitating towards wealth and numbers. The statistics of every voluntary society tell the same tale; these societies spring into being from a fever of enthusiasm, and at first some of them seem as if they would be able to grapple with this primary duty of religious organizations, but gradually either their tone gets lowered or their better attentions become mostly confined to the numerous and well-to-do; no voluntary organization has ever been able permanently to offer to the poor as good religious ministrations as might be expected by any other class. As named before, the fundamental defect, which no variation of organization can get rid of, is that Voluntaryism does best for those who have least need; its ministrations are chiefly offered to those who wish for them and will pay for them instead of to those who do not wish for them and will not pay for them.

Ample proof of this incapacity of Voluntaryism to do the work now incumbent upon Nationalism can be found not only in our own country but also in the United States of America. The difficulty of estimating roughly, and the impossibility of estimating accurately, the religious condition even of our own country must here be fully acknowledged. Statistics can be made to prove almost anything, and so can extracts from books and reports; what are called facts are like witnesses whose evidence must receive little weight until they have been fully cross-examined. All these difficulties become infinitely greater when we attempt to deal with another nation, for although the people may speak the same language as ourselves and have similar customs, it is impossible for us fully to understand the phenomena of a nation without belonging to it; the messages cannot pass along the wire cut by national isolation. Still even though we can place little reliance upon statistics or assertions, we may by observing broad and fundamental phenomena often form tolerably accurate opinions, and we shall probably do this more correctly if we never visit the country, for travellers are generally taken up with superficial appearances and persist in drawing wide conclusions from absurdly limited premises.

Tried in this way we cannot help thinking that Voluntaryism in the United States has not been a success. It is not pleasant to have to say that which another nation does not like, but it would be unmanly to refrain from doing so if any good can come of it. Nations are set up more to teach lessons than to receive praise, and the relations between England and the States would have been better if the remarks they have made about each other had contained more frank criticism and less indiscriminating flattery or carping spitefulness. We do not mean to assert that what we say about Voluntaryism in America is certainly true; we merely give it as the impression produced upon foreigners at a distance, and it can be taken for what it is worth. It must also not be supposed that because other nations are criticised we think our own to be perfect, or even much better; the *tu quoque* argument is in such matters more than usually ridiculous, for nations, like individuals, must have become sadly demoralised when they dare not freely criticise each other and thus both be benefited, for we cannot so soon know of the holes in the backs of our coats if we do not tell each other.

The following characteristics about Voluntaryism in America seem to justify its condemnation. In the first place religion has been broken and its character lowered; Christ's garment has been torn to pieces and the shreds have been divided amongst a number of narrow sects. Instead of the absence of a National Church restoring unity to Christianity it has in America had quite a contrary effect, for nowhere are sects more numerous or more divided. And all of these sects, or denominations as they are called, present religion in a more or less distorted form, and all of them are what must be called religiously narrow. Not one of these denominations, nor all of them put together, teach such a Christianity as, compared with that set forth by the National Church of England, is so human and yet so scriptural, so simple and yet so dignified, so definite and yet so liberal, or so much in harmony with what is actually the religious belief of most practical and enlightened Christian men. The condition of America is such that no provision is made for the two great classes which no religious system can afford to neglect, namely, those who are above sectarian differences and those who are beneath them ; the man who wants merely to receive the simple ministrations of Christianity and who cares nothing about the differences of Independents, Presbyterians, Episcopalians, Wesleyans, Baptists or others, is in America religiously exiled. And we may depend upon it that the number of those who not only are indifferent about these sectarian divisions but who also dislike them so much that they will have nothing to do with them, is much greater than is supposed and is very rapidly increasing. The world is getting sick of such trivialities in religion. Much is said about the growing indifference both of the educated classes and of the masses to the Christian Churches, and we need not wonder if all that is said is true, for men's eyes cannot be any longer kept shut to the great discrepancy between the Christianity of the sects and that of the Bible. Only the national system can save us from the evils of Protestant Sectarianism and of Roman Papism ; Voluntaryism in America ministers to both of these evils and therefore it needs no prophetic eye to see that it cannot be abiding. It must not be forgotten that the United States, as a country, is quite in its infancy, and it is yet much too soon to predict that any of its present features will live to maturity. Population and wealth may increase with unexampled rapidity but political and religious constitutions will not on this account be hurried in their development, and we must not pronounce on the success or failure of any new attempt until sufficient time has been allowed, not merely according to our own notions but also as required by the inexorable laws of nature.

Another effect of the voluntary system in the United States is that the ministers of religion there are poor. Some of them no doubt receive large incomes but as a body they are not paid as well, in proportion to those engaged in other occupations, as their office demands. It may be said that wealth is not a proper object of pursuit for ministers of religion, and that they are better without it, but everyone knows that there is no safer test in general for the quality of ministers than the amount and security of their incomes, and at any rate the sum which the people are willing to pay is the best standard of their respect for the office and of the influence which it exercises over them. Judged in this way, the office of a minister of religion in the United States does not stand as high as does here that of a clergyman of the National Church of England, and this is confirmed by the fact that ministers of religion do not there exercise so great an influence as they do here over the general affairs of the nation. They have there no special influence of this sort belonging to their position and the social estimation in which they are held does not give them any.

But if ministers of religion in the Unites States are wanting in general influence they frequently exercise a special influence which is not at all desirable. Although the complete divorce of religion from politics would be a great calamity, which it is one of the objects of the national system to avoid, still it is not good either for religion or for politics if the pulpits of the churches are used as political platforms. Religion should elevate the motives and purify the tone of politics, but it becomes degraded when it lends itself to the promotion of merely party interests. The Dissenting chapels of England have always been very liable to become in times of excitement schools of political propagandism, and this is the case with most of the places of worship in the United States. Complaints are sometimes made that the clergy of the Church of England preach political sermons, and undoubtedly they do, but there is this fundamental difference—that whereas there is nothing to prevent voluntary ministers being as political as their congregations will submit to, national ministers cannot go farther than the nation allows, and can be stopped at any time from officially opposing such political measures as the nation desires.

Another feature in the United States is the prevalence of religious extravagance. Of course considerable allowance must be made for the peculiarly mixed character of the people and for their general temperament; still, the fact that so many wild systems of belief and practice spring into being and gain numerous adherents is not creditable to the dignity of Voluntaryism, and does not at any rate say much for its unschismatic tendencies.

The fact must also be noted that although Voluntaryism is recommended to us because it allows free play to all the sects, it has not practically this effect in the States. For there certain sects get possession of certain States or districts and in these the other sects are in a position of inferiority or helplessness quite as depressing as any effect of the national system. And in such a case Voluntaryism has this drawback that the dominant religion comes from the sectarian dictation of the majority upon which the minority can use no influence, whereas in the national system each individual can exercise the control belonging to him as a member of the nation.

One of the most serious results of Voluntaryism is already making itself seen in America, for although the stage of cultivation and the abundance of new land should spread the population over the country, it is undoubtedly true that the places of worship are gravitating to the towns. We hear about every village having its spire but we are told on much more reliable authority that nearly two-thirds of the people are out of the reach of the ministrations of religion. These spires, where they exist, too often belong to miserable edifices which possess no settled or efficient ministers, and even such ministrations as many of the people can get at are more calculated to promote ignorant and injurious excitement than to do any lasting good. Grand city churches and highly-paid city preachers say very little in favour of the religious condition of a nation, for that depends upon the influence of religion being extended everywhere, and operating just as much upon the poor labourer as upon the rich tradesman. It may be very pleasant to hear clever sensational sermons on topics of the day but the enjoyment so derived is often of that sort which should be sought in a theatre and not in a church. The American Dives may especially be surprised to find how in the next world that Lazarus is preferred before him who could not here get near him in a church of which the pews were let by auction to the highest bidder.

After all, the value of any religious system, so far as we have any concern with it, must be tested by its effect upon the nation. This is a matter, however, to be treated with great hesitation and delicacy, for it is a very difficult one to estimate. Whilst fully and very painfully conscious of the dreadful indifference and heathenism of our own people, we cannot help believing that the general religious and moral tone of the United States is lower, or at least not higher, than that of England. In whatever direction we turn, whether to the quality of the religion taught, to the neglect by the people of that religion, to the state of political and business morality, to the exaggerated social tone, or to the character of the general ideals and aspirations of the people, we are forced to the same conclusion. Englishmen are almost precluded from drawing adverse inferences about American affairs through fear of being accused of unworthy feelings, but we may quote the opinions of Dr. Döllinger respecting the condition of Christendom in America. In his *Kirche und Kirchen* he says that it is "a great and serious warning." He pronounces the American theology to be shallow and the tone of the religious press to be "a scandal to the cause of Christendom;" indeed we fear he might make the same charge against what is called "the religious press" of our own country. He asserts that under the so-called freedom of the sects extreme intolerance prevails. "The whole present condition of North "America in religious relations is such as to awaken grave "anxieties among the thinking men of the land." "Want "of every feeling of reverence is, as American theologians "mournfully acknowledge, a predominant trait of national "character."

It may be said that the Episcopal Church flourishes in America without State alliance, but why does it flourish? Because it has inherited the dignified traditions of a National Church and because by not being national it is relieved from the obligation of attending to religion except where it can do so with success to itself. But our true duty is not to organize prosperous and selfish churches in particular districts but to spread religion broadcast over the whole land.

Considering its culture and power America has contributed surprisingly little during this century to religious knowledge, and now exercises scarcely any influence upon religious development. These facts are very eloquent respecting the tendency of Voluntaryism to impoverish the resources and paralyse the spirit of religion.

We have thus dwelt upon the religious condition of the United States of America not to draw any invidious comparisons but merely to show that Voluntaryism has not been so successful there as to justify its adoption here. In this matter we must not be beguiled into acting upon hasty conclusions. We may take a warning from the change of feeling which has during the last few years come over this country respecting the political system of America. Not long ago those who call themselves "advanced" politicians were never tired of singing its praises, but at present even these think it best to be silent, whilst moderate politicians, who at one time were half inclined to acknowledge its superiority, are now coming to believe that this experiment seems likely to turn out a failure and that its collapse is not far off. The gloominess of the political prospect in America must be acknowledged with regret, for it is a great disappointment to those who had hoped that a political constitution would have been established there which more than any other would have afforded free play for the powers of humanity and would have raised their character. But we cannot alter facts and we may infer from the fate of the political system of the United States what is not unlikely to become of its religious system. It must be borne in mind that America has never tried the national system of toleration and that it is just as likely that this system will have to be adopted there as that Voluntaryism will obtain the mastery here.

Since, then, Voluntaryism, which is the only other likely means suggested, has not proved itself capable of offering the ministrations of religion to all, we conclude that this is the business of the State.

The next theoretical objection is that—

6. *A National Church is contrary to the rights of citizenship.*

The rights of citizenship may in this connection be considered as divided into particular and general, the particular arising out of the definite laws and conditions of each separate State and the general depending upon what are considered the fundamental claims of humanity in respect to all States. Of course an institution like a National Church existing by law cannot violate any such particular rights of citizenship but it is asserted that it does violate several general rights.

The most important of these rights, as lying at the root of nearly all others, are those which relate to opinions, and we are told that the national principle especially violates these.

It is said that the State has no right to make any arrangements which repress the free formation, promulgation, and reformation of opinions, and that the National Church is such an arrangement.

And first as to the formation of opinions it is said that the National Church creates a bias in favour of certain opinions which is too strong for private judgment; the religious doctrines thus adopted by the State receive an unfair advantage which is equivalent to the handicapping of all other doctrines, and which is adverse to freedom of thought generally. This complaint is undoubtedly true, but it does not follow that it is therefore just. Every institution creates a bias in favour of the opinions upon which it is founded, or the institution itself would not be called into existence. This is just as true in politics as in religion, and we might as reasonably ask for the destruction of monarchy, or parliamentary government, or popular representation, merely because these institutions exercise an influence adverse to the opinions opposed to them, as say that the Church should be done away with because it gives an unfair advantage to the doctrines which it inculcates.

To meet this objection consistently we must not only abolish all institutions founded upon any opinions but we must also put down these opinions themselves, for opinions which are generally held receive by being thus held an advantage which is quite apart from any depending upon their intrinsic worth. Little experience of life is needed to teach us that very few people think for themselves, and probably there are fewer than ever in times like these when by the immense extension of printing so many opinions are furnished ready-made upon every subject that nobody is put to the necessity of forming any for himself. As far as thought is concerned most people are merely retail dealers, and if we had the requisite knowledge we could point out the foreign source of all their mental stock; the manufacturers are an exceedingly small number, and even these can only produce a very little themselves, and must depend upon importation for the rest. Not merely do very few men think out opinions for themselves—which is undoubtedly a great advantage, for much of such thinking would bring on chaos—but very few also ever think over the opinions which they obtain from others, but pass then on like coins which receive no stamp from their own mint. It is too much to expect that many men can be wells of living water, but we may ask each man to pass the water through his own filter before he presses it upon others to drink. When, however, we come to name the objections which first suggest themselves to prevalent opinions we soon find that although almost everybody professes these opinions scarcely anybody takes the trouble to examine them. This evil increases in proportion to the rapidity of life, and consequent want of time, therefore an age like this may be favourable to the diffusion of knowledge and to the increase of information, but cannot be to the creation or solidity of thought.

Since we thus come by our opinions, it is plain that what may be called fashion in its widest sense is the strongest force in determining the opinions which prevail in any nation, and fashion depends upon the opinions which already prevail. Thus quite apart from institutions, which are but one form of embodiment, opinions by being general receive an advantage which by the principle of this objection may be considered unfair to other opinions and to freedom of thought. Opinions which are widely adopted receive thereby a momentum which helps them in the race against new opinions. This is one of the difficulties through which such new opinions must inevitably struggle, and which providentially kills off most of them and so leaves only those of some vitality for the world to trouble itself with. If we are to destroy the Church because it is unfair to other doctrines, we must not only do away with all institutions about which there can be any difference of opinion, but we must also repress all such opinions themselves and annihilate all influence of majorities.

As to the promulgation of opinions, the objections which used to be so frequently urged have now no weight, for the present condition of England amply proves that a National Church can exist and flourish where the freest promulgation is allowed of opinions different from those which it inculcates. There are now no restraints in this country, beyond the essential ones of decency, to the promulgation of any opinions whatever. As far as religion is concerned, this freedom of promulgation is involved in the recognition of the right of Dissent. This right we would most amply acknowlege and most emphatically insist upon. Whilst we say that the State has the right to organize the religious opinions of the majority in a National Church, we also say that the minority has just as good a right to organize and promulgate its own opinions in any way it chooses. Men have exactly the same right to dissent about religion as about anything else, but they have not the right to expect that their opinions, as long as they are merely those of a minority, shall receive the same advantages as if they were those of the majority. Thus we would entirely object to the invidious use of the word "toleration" as describing the actual position of Dissenters in England. To "tolerate," in this sense, is to allow a thing to exist which we might put down, but no one has a right to put down Dissent. The State has a right to provide the water-trough, but it has not a right to make every horse drink.

Not merely has the State, whilst offering the appliances of religion freely to all, no right to prevent those who wish from providing for themselves, but it ought not to desire to do so. For although there would be many advantages in the national principle being universally adopted there are also many in

Dissent existing by its side. For a rivalry of this sort, if it is not carried too far, and does not involve fundamental doctrines, is often a benefit to the Church. Dissenters, even from the partial character of their religious systems, often uphold and re-establish doctrines which the Church might allow to fall behind, and the abuses which will creep into all Churches are sometimes got rid of more quickly by the help of those who are without. In this world all institutions of this sort are better for having some opposition, and the Church of England, whilst defending and loving its own system, ought not to forget the great benefits which it has received from the Dissenters. Often has the influence of the Dissenters helped the Church to clear itself of abuses in doctrine and practice which had crept upon it, and in this connection we need only refer to the services of the Puritans.

As to the reformation of opinions it is said that a National Church, being a State institution, cannot be adapted to changes of opinion as readily as self-governing Churches. But history does not confirm this idea, and the reasons have been named before. From amongst these we may here repeat the following, namely, that the doctrines of a National Church are publicly defined and are subject to open criticism under the protection of the law, and also that Churches under lay control are always more amenable to change than those which are under clerical government. It is true that the inertia of a State Church is not readily overcome, and thus it is saved from adopting fleeting eccentricities or half-formed ideas, for these break down before they can produce any effect upon it. But since the Church is under the control of the State there is no reason why reforms which have commended themselves to the nation should not be carried out in this as readily as in any other department.

In reference to these reforms of religion, about which we hear so much in these days, it would be well for us to ask ourselves soberly whether we really think that there are any fixed verities in religion at all. It is quite open for any man to believe that religion must keep changing and that none of its fundamental doctrines are immutable, but we must plainly declare that such a belief is quite inconsistent with Christianity. Either Christ was not what He professed to be, or else the doctrines of His religion must be accepted as eternal truths which cannot be altered by any changes of civilization, by any improvements of education, by any discoveries of science. It is said that Christianity is giving way before modern enlightenment and that no one can tell how greatly it will be changed before long, but when we come to sum up calmly the achievements of its opponents we are surprised to find how little they amount to; going over the field of battle for the last twenty years, during which the fight has been the hottest, we see that it is not in the ranks of the Christian religion that the carnage has been greatest; numberless newly-sprung-up adversaries, who once boasted that they were going to carry all before them, are now lying helpless or dead, whilst all the leading champions of religion are still standing bravely, and few even of its smallest supporters have fallen. Christianity in its duels generally fights a waiting battle; its opponents are allowed at first to carry off popular applause by their bold attacks, but they ultimately come to the ground, either through their own exhaustion or from a well-delivered blow.

If the changes which are likely to be required in the Christian religion cannot alter its fundamental doctrines it would seem that these changes can be carried out by the national system at least as well as by any other, and the objection is not sound which asserts that this system is opposed to the reform of religion.

As far as theory is concerned it seems that after all there must be State supremacy over religion, for even amongst self-governed Churches disputes must frequently arise which can only be settled by the law. Where property is involved there must be some authority to decide the conditions of its possession, and to vindicate what may be called religious rights. Such an authority can only be the State. Some Churches escape State control by their weakness and some by their strength, but all others must eventually be more or less subjected to it.

Turning next to what may be called the Practical Objections to the national principle we come first to the one that—

7. *It obstructs the business of the State.*

We are asked why the time of Parliament should be taken up in discussing questions with which it has rightly no concern, and in which most of its members take little interest, and also why the functions of some of the heads of the Government should be complicated by duties so different from those which properly belong to their positions and for capacity in which they have been chosen.

As to the time of Parliament one is inclined to think that it would be better if more of this was taken up with great subjects, so that less would be left for those ignoble details and trivial personalities which are now so continually coming forward and the prominence of which must tend to lessen the dignity of Parliament in the eyes of the nation. But even if less time than now was given to these little considerations and more to what are called "great measures," it does not follow that religious affairs would be any injurious hindrance to State business, for such great measures cannot, and must not, be at any one time too numerous. It is worse than useless, it is mischievous, for Parliament to pass these great measures until the nation is prepared for them, and this preparation is for each such measure a very slow process. A Parliament which is too far ahead of its people is like a parent who keeps putting his child into clothes which are too big for him, so that both the child and the clothes are spoiled.

But Parliament must be occupied with something, and it

would be well if the nation understood better than it seems to do at present that after all the chief duty of Parliament is to carry on the affairs of the nation, and not merely to keep making organic changes in the constitution. A man who in business gives his chief attention not to the general conduct of his affairs but to the planning of alterations in his system, will soon come to grief even though all such alterations may be good in themselves. The old dictum that the King's government must be carried on may be taken in a wider sense as indicating the first duty of Parliament. The business of the nation must be carried on and its religious affairs constitute one of the most important parts of this business. It is therefore the duty of Parliament to attend to these, and we ought not to be asked to relieve it from this duty unless it can be shown that something must be struck off and that religion ought to be the first to go.

If Parliament is not able to manage its business that is a reason not for lessening that business but for improving the capacity of Parliament. A man would be considered a fool who in packing a statue knocked off its head or feet instead of getting a larger box.

But even if Parliament is getting so enfeebled that, like an old man, it must be relieved of some of its work, we would ask why must religion first be given up? If the ship of State is now so creaky that it cannot carry all its cargo, we may still demand why we are first of all to throw religion overboard? But no explanation of this sort is offered; we ask in vain what are the matters which are more important than religion and which will absorb the whole energy of Parliament. If some things must be given up the least important should go first, and we maintain that religion, instead of belonging to these, is one of the greatest and most vital with which a State can concern itself; it is connected more or less with almost every political measure and exercises the strongest influence in determining the political character and destiny of the nation. Every citizen, whether he knows it or not, is intimately concerned with religion and it is hard to believe that any man qualified to be a member of Parliament can help taking an interest in it.

Of course the duties of those ministers of State upon whom the national principle makes demands would be simplified if that principle were abandoned, but it is not clear that such a simplification is desirable. These offices would be simplified still more if there were no duties at all attached to them, but of course no one proposes that. Since there must be some duties it would seem best that these should be dignified and varied. For the first object of every form of government ought to be to get the best men of the nation into the highest posts, and such men will not accept positions concerned merely with official monotony or with secondary interests. Whatever the State may decree, the ablest men are sure to continue to believe that religion is the strongest force in politics and that to cut off a position from religion is to lower its dignity and to lessen its power.

It is acknowledged that the management of religious affairs is the most delicate and difficult part of the State's business, but this is an advantage to the State, for not only are inferior men thus disqualified for the highest positions, but also those who do occupy those positions receive thus a training which makes them more capable for all their other duties. This holds good for Parliament also, and the management of religion may be regarded as a sort of tuning-fork by which we can test whether the general tone of the State is up to what it should be.

Another objection to the national principle is that—

8. *It arrays Religion against Political Reform.*

It is said that as long as the Church is one of the institutions of the State it is interested in keeping all the other institutions as they are, from fear lest it may be itself interfered with, like a schoolboy who is opposed to flogging in general out of consideration for his own shoulders. It is asserted that the Church has always resisted reforms in the State, and that this is the reason. Not to go back farther than the time of this generation, we are repeatedly asked what was the attitude of the Church of England towards Free Trade and Parliamentary Reform, and also what is its attitude now towards any new measures which are proposed for the good of the people.

In the first place we would reply that in these respects the Church can have no attitude at all, because there is no such body as the Church. People often speak of the Church doing this or that without having any definite idea of what they mean by the term. Except as indicating the organization for religion under the control of the State, the word "Church" has no proper meaning when used in the expression "The Church of England." Most people, however, when speaking of the Church mean the clergy of the Church, and perhaps there would be some truth in the charge that the clergy generally are opposed to political reforms—or it would be more correct to say political changes, for every change is not necessarily a reform. It has been before explained that opposition to change is the natural attitude of the clerical mind, whether in the Church or out of it. Partly because those who have to do with the fixities and greatnesses of religion are not likely to think so much about the variablenesses and littlenesses of politics, and partly because those whose office is to make authoritative declarations are not so disposed to be open to conflicting arguments, or whatever may be the reason, it is certain that ministers of religion are nearly always conservative in politics. It does not follow that they must necessarily be "Conservatives," for they may be conservative of radicalism. Getting at good government is rather like finding a way across a country; for a while we ought to keep along the high road of tradition, but sometimes we must take the short field-paths of change, and afterwards come into the road again. Those who will not return into the road when they should are just as unwisely conservative as those who previously refused to venture into the fields. Sometimes when a number of people are walking along a road, only those who are behind take the right turn, whilst those who are in front keep along the wrong road, boasting that they are still the leaders, until they find at last that they must retrace their steps and come up in the rear. So it is with many politicians; the principles they inculcate may be true at first, but they become false when insisted upon too long or carried too far.

As long as there must be such a class as ministers of religion and as long as this class will be conservative in politics it is much better that it should be conservative of preservation than of change. If we must have a weakness one way or the other, it is much better that it should be towards keeping too much to the road than towards venturing too much into the fields; the road is likely to come right at last, though it may go a good way round, but the field-paths may lead nowhere. It is much safer that the ministers of religion should be the allies of the State and the defenders even of its abuses than that they should be its opponents; as long as the State has control over the ministers of religion it can take good care that they do not impede any reform which the nation desires.

But such precautions are not needed against the clergy of the Church of England, for history can tell of no body of ecclesiastics which has shown such sympathy with the people's needs and such willingness to acquiesce in their wishes. Individual clergymen—and surely they have as much right as other people to form opinions of their own—have frequently been opposed to proposed political changes, but they have always acquiesced in these changes when once they have been carried out, and loyalty to laws which they have disliked as well as to those which they have liked has always been a striking characteristic of the clergy of the Church of England. This advantage must chiefly be ascribed to the national principle, for those who are thus connected with the State must necessarily be in favour of anything which will promote its welfare and must at any rate have the strongest interest in setting an example of that obedience to the laws of the State which is essential to its continuance. The national principle not only preserves the State by securing it from the thwarting opposition of a most powerful class but it also preserves the clergy from themselves, for each clergyman is perfectly safe from intimidation by his fellows. The clergy, although their social training and position naturally lead most of them in a similar direction, take no political action as a class and probably are more independent in this respect than any other ministers of religion. We may appreciate this by considering the position of a Congregationalist minister who chooses to be a Conservative in politics or to set himself prominently against the Disestablishment movement.

Sometimes the word "Church" is used to include that portion of the laity which attends the services, or is attached to the system, of the Church. In this sense it is not true that the Church of England is, or ever has been, hostile to political reform. The old acts of persecution so often referred to were not passed by the people as Churchmen but as Englishmen, and they were repealed by Parliaments consisting almost exclusively of Churchmen. And if we come to our own times we find that all the reforms which have been passed and have proved themselves good have been more or less supported by those who were strongly attached to the Church, and have not been opposed on Church grounds. Since every proposal for a change must first come from a minority, or the change would have already been made, and since the Church must be that of the majority, it is plain that this Church cannot as such adopt these proposals at first, but we maintain that it is not an obstacle to them when they have commended themselves to general approval. It is absurd to say that the Church, meaning the laity, is an enemy to political reforms when no reform has been passed which has not been carried out by a Parliament containing an immense preponderance of Churchmen, and no reform is now proposed which, if it is reasonable, Churchmen are not as ready as others to support. Undoubtedly those who are attached to one ancient institution are likely to feel tenderly towards others, and this is an advantage to the State, for the tendency in these days is not to go too slow but too fast, and our conveyance is in danger of dashing itself to pieces at the bottom of the hill unless we regulate its speed with a brake. The three great classes of politicians are like three gardeners called in to consult about a tree; one advises nothing to be done to it, another that its branches should be trimmed and its roots nourished, and another that it should be torn up altogether and a fresh one planted. In the present condition of the tree called the British Constitution, the middle treatment is the right one, and this will be best administered by those who are fond of this tree.

But there is another sense in which the word Church is used in this connection, namely as an organization, and we maintain that in this meaning the Church is not only not an obstacle to political reform but that it is also one of its greatest helps.

There is an idea prevailing strongly on the Continent at present and also widely accepted in England that somehow religion and freedom are naturally opposed to each other, but this is not true. The political condition of a nation is the result of its moral principles; physical circumstances and intellectual capacities are the material upon which these moral principles operate and out of which they mould political character. Looking back over history we find that repeatedly certain political relationships, as of monarchs to their subjects, or of some portions of those subjects to others, have for long periods been almost universally accepted which appear to us manifestly unjust, and numberless acts have been committed of cruelty and oppression, even in the name of religion, which were at the time sanctioned by the best of men but against which it seems to us that any ordinary conscience must have revolted. If we ask ourselves why it is that certain things which seemed right at one time seem wrong now, we must acknowledge that the cause lies not in our own improved ability or honesty but in the change of our moral principles. Although these principles regulate their conduct, the people themselves probably are little aware of them; the leaders develop them and the rest unconsciously obey them.

If we want to get at the forces which determine political condition we must find out what it is which forms these moral principles out of which that condition comes. According to the methods of thinking generally prevalent here at present there are two rival claimants for this position, namely, religion and philosophy, and we are commonly told that philosophy is the mother of political freedom whilst religion is its enemy. But a little thought will show us that this is just the reverse of the truth, especially when by religion is meant the Christian religion. For political freedom is mainly the result of knowledge of, and attachment to, our own rights and respect for the rights of others. But philosophy, and particularly that utilitarian philosophy which is now put forward as the especial rival of Christianity, can give us no rights at all, for by no principle of that philosophy can we be expected to do anything which is unpleasant to us or to refrain from anything which is pleasant. It is pleasant for those who have power to exercise it and it is unpleasant to allow others to share it, therefore by this philosophy tyrannical conduct in those who have the power is, as long as they think it to their interest, perfectly defensible and we have no right to expect anything else. Utilitarianism is therefore the ally of force, and force and political freedom are antagonistic to each other.

But this last assertion may be denied, for we may be told that we can oppose force to force and so secure our freedom. We must however bear in mind that political condition always naturally gravitates towards force. It may seem reasonable to expect that as a general rule the many will be able to master the few, but as a fact it is not so. It is not the place here to try to explain the reasons, but history unmistakably teaches that although the many may for a while maintain their rights, in all countries and times power inevitably tends into the hands of the few. With nothing but our ordinary circumstances, and only utilitarian philosophy to help us, tyranny must be our normal political condition.

We must then seek for some other cause why in Christian countries political freedom more or less exists and why there are such things as political rights. This cause we shall find can alone be the Christian religion, for from religion alone come the principles which modify the brute operation of force. Man must be either selfish or religious, using the words in their broad sense, and general selfishness and political freedom cannot go together. Mere selfishness, although it were twice as enlightened as any which the most civilised nation has ever been capable of understanding, would be insufficient to account for such a measure of political freedom as exists even in the least civilised Christian country. Outside the Christian religion the very word "rights" as applied to politics has no meaning at all.

Not merely is the dependence of political freedom upon the Christian religion a conclusion of theory but it is also a matter of fact. Those who talk of certain political rights as being the natural heritage of every man quite apart from religion must consider that all through the past, and throughout the world at the present, most of these rights have no existence whatever outside the boundaries and influence of the Christian religion. Slavery except for Christianity is perfectly defensible, and Christianity is the only capable foe which it has ever had. Even if slavery has been discouraged amongst some nations not under Christian influence, this has been due to the religion of those nations. And this is in confirmation of all that we have here to maintain, namely, that political freedom derives its existence from religion.

And not merely is religion the only source of political freedom but it is also the principal means of political progress. For such progress must chiefly be won by self-sacrificing effort and this will not be given at the dictates of selfishness or philosophy. Men will not submit to the sufferings needed to gain political freedom, they will not go to the battle-field or the scaffold, merely for the sake of utilitarian calculations or philosophical theories; such sacrifices can only come from high, inspiring, unselfish principles, and such principles can only come from religion.

Those, therefore, are acting an inconsistent part who profess themselves the friends of political freedom and yet are arrayed amongst the enemies of religion. The more "advanced," as it is styled, a man's political opinions are, the more strongly he insists upon what are called "political rights," the more rigorously should he champion that religion from which those rights are derived and upon which alone they depend. Yet it is undoubtedly true that many of such politicians in England, and still more on the continent, are either indifferent about religion or actually opposed to it. The reason seems to be that they make the mistake of confounding the Churches with the Christian religion. It cannot be denied that many Church organizations have at different times strongly opposed political freedom and reform, and many such do so now. But if we examine carefully we find that such conduct has not been in any way the result of religion itself, but has arisen because the Churches so acting have been left too much to the control of their clergy and have thus ceased to be national. We find that this is

A A

especially true of the Roman Catholic Church, which is at present the chief clerical opponent of political freedom in Europe, and the chief cause why so many of the friends of that freedom have become the enemies of religion. The Catholic Church which in the past has done more than any other institution for the advancement of political freedom, has, since it became distinctively Roman, gradually shut itself out more and more from lay influence until now it has become merely a clerical self-governed organization. Such an organization is sure to be more or less opposed to political freedom and political changes, but the fault lies not with its religion but with its clerical self-governedness.

We must not be beguiled by superficial appearances into believing that religion is opposed to political freedom or ought to be separated from it, but since there can be no true political freedom which is not based upon religion, our object should be to hold fast to that religion and yet keep ourselves free from such organizations as would use its influence to oppose what we desire. Since the political condition of the nation must be so largely determined by religion, the true course is for the nation to bring itself into the closest connection with that religion, so that the influence of the nation may freely act upon it. This can only be done by the national principle, which has in this connection these two great advantages, that it preserves religion as the basis of political freedom and also prevents the influence of religion from ever being exercised in opposition to that freedom.

Another objection raised against the national principle is that—

9. *It lowers the dignity of the State.*

Gibbon tells how Julian the Apostate used to summon to his palace the champions of the hostile sects and beguile himself by listening to their disputings with the dignity of amused indifference. We are told that this is the sort of attitude which the State should now assume towards religion, and that even though it does not derive amusement from religious disputes, it should leave them to settle themselves and ought not to meddle with religion at all. As Gibbon would give us the idea that Julian would have lowered the imperial dignity by taking any part in such matters, so we are now told that the State, by having any connection with religion, is degraded to the position of a combatant in controversial quarrels, and receives the ill-will which meddlers generally get from both sides. It is represented that the State when it takes a part in religious disputes is like a person who tries to settle a quarrel between a husband and his wife, and who generally comes in for the enmity of both. Thus it is said that the State by interfering with religion not only lowers its own dignity but also draws upon itself such ill-will as weakens its power and increases its dangers.

Even if all this were true it would not follow that the State ought to keep its hands off religion, for states, like individuals, do not exist to make themselves pleasant to everybody but to do their duty in the world. The organization of a state is not meant to be passively admired but to be actively employed, and there is hardly any State employment of much good which does not stir up the enmity of some one. Criminals do not like prisons, careless parents do not like school-boards, publicans do not like policemen, and in fact no class likes the restrictive interference of the State with itself, but we do not on this account suppose that the State should refrain from anything of this sort. On the contrary we believe that this is what the State is for, and that it ought not to be restrained from doing what is right by any fear of being disliked in consequence.

Thus even if all the consequences would follow which are asserted, these ought not of themselves to deter the State from being connected with religion. But these consequences are greatly exaggerated. It suits the purposes of the enemies of religion, and serves as an excuse for those who neglect it and as a subject of pleasantry for those who ridicule it, to describe the quarrels of Christians as so intense and numberless, but such language is for the most part a gross exaggeration. Confining ourselves to one nation, as we do in the national principle, and speaking for example of England, it is not true that Christians are so much divided amongst themselves as we are often told. They differ considerably amongst themselves, as men in earnest always do, for there is nothing like indifference for promoting unanimity, but those who think and feel keenly about one object are sure to pull different ways in trying to help it. Christianity is no half-and-half religion; either a man is enthusiastically its friend or, enthusiastically or not, its enemy; he who is not with it is against it. Christians when they become such do not cease to be men, and one of the inevitable conditions of men is that when they feel strongly on such subjects as religion they must differ amongst themselves, and sometimes break out into downright quarrels, and often persecute and punish each other. Bigotry and persecution are not amiable things in themselves, but they seem more or less necessary to earnestness, and intolerance with earnestness is far better than tolerance without it. Thus it is granted that there are frequent differences even amongst the Christians of the same nation, but it does not follow that these lead to such quarrels as we are so often told of. For the impression is frequently given to us that these Christians differ amongst each other so much about everything that it seems there is really nothing certain about their religion on which they agree. But the fact is that all Christians differ far more widely from those who are not Christians than they do amongst themselves, and that compared with the differences between Christians and non-Christians, those between Christians themselves amount to a practical unity. Indeed it is this practical unity which is largely the cause of their quarrels, for those who agree about the main points are sure to differ most keenly with each other.

If it followed that the State by being connected with religion was called upon to participate in these quarrels, it would then be less out of sympathy even with those Christians against whom it had to take part than if it had no connection with Christianity at all. But the national principle does not require the State to participate in these quarrels to such an extent as can arouse any dangerous enmity. For by this principle the State embodies only those fundamentals of religion which have been generally adopted by the nation, and awaits the issue of disputes in the arena of public opinion before touching the subjects about which these are concerned. Apart from the Roman Church, an essential principle of which is the rejection of State control, the religious faith now upheld by the Church of England is such as can be accepted in the main by the Christians of nearly all denominations.

Thus the national principle confers upon the State the sympathy of the Christian character, and also exonerates the State from participation in such controversial disputes as would lessen its dignity or imperil its welfare.

Not only is connection with religion uninjurious to the State in the respects stated in this objection, but we may go further and maintain that it is positively beneficial—and for the following reasons amongst others:—

In the first place this connection raises the tone of the State. The welfare of a State depends much less than people suppose upon those political measures which create so much excitement, and much more upon that tone about which scarcely anybody seems to think. The particular form of the Constitution of a State is of small importance compared with the character of its people, and is indeed but the outcome of that character. If the people are good and sensible and brave they may be trusted to get a suitable Constitution for themselves, and if they have not these qualities the most perfect Constitution in the world will do little to make them better. The chief law of hydrostatics holds good in politics, for no organization can make a nation rise above its own level; Snug the Joiner was not made a bit more leonine by having a lion's head upon his shoulders. The tone of a State is determined by the character of the people, and that character is determined chiefly by religion. Of course many other causes, such as origin, physical surroundings, and state of civilization, exercise a great influence upon character, but these causes are chiefly such as are fixed for us and upon which we can exert little effect. Of the causes which lie within our own control, religion is by far the strongest, and therefore he who governs the religion of a nation may be said in the truest sense to make its laws. This is one reason why mere politicians, who are so large in their lives, soon look so small; in reading political memoirs we are surprised to find how many men whom their contemporaries believed certain to cut a great figure in history, have become almost entirely forgotten in a single generation. Practical politics are like a glass which magnifies the near present but minifies the more distant past. Only those who influence first causes can hope to live long in history, and politicians can rarely be of this sort, for most of them are mere followers of public opinion, and even those who help to lead it seldom exercise much influence upon the character which chiefly determines that opinion. He who makes the songs of a people may be more powerful than he who makes their laws, but he who influences their religion, especially when they are a serious people like the English, is the most powerful of all.

It may be said that even if that elevation of tone which is so essential to the well-being of a State can only be derived from religion, it does not follow that this religion ought to be taught by the State itself, for men combine into various societies for purposes which require such a tone, yet these societies do not think of concerning themselves directly with religion. But this proves that such societies are indebted to the influence fostered by the State rather than that the State ought not to foster that influence. Undoubtedly religion is needed in other associations than those directly concerning the State. We do not however maintain that it should be taught in all these associations, but only that it should be taught in some way or other, and the greater the number of these associations the stronger appears this necessity. As explained before, the organization of the State is the only effective means for doing this, and therefore it ought to be so used. It must be remembered that the State is the only organization which can affect every part of man's outward life; other organizations end with the specific purposes for which they exist but the State never takes its fingers off us from the day it registers our birth until the day it ensures our burial. Men form various organizations which could not be carried on without the rudiments of education, but the State alone has the responsibility of seeing that these are given—and so with religion.

Besides, the State has infinitely more at stake than any other organization, and therefore has the strongest motive to take care that the necessary influence of religion is brought to bear. It cannot delegate this duty to any other organization upon which it can rely, and it dare not leave it to chance, therefore it is bound to attend to it itself.

We can scarcely over-estimate the importance to the State of its tone being determined by religion, using the term not with the narrow meanings given to it by theologians and schoolmen but in the broad sense of the New Testament. As determining the State ideal, there is no choice except such a religion or selfishness, and who can tell how vast is the difference between these? Many members of our own Legislature are often led by weak and unworthy motives, but that Legislature itself cannot be charged with being as a whole selfish, and the best proof is the confidence placed in it by one of the most hard-headed of nations. Although Parliament has the disposal of such great interests, and so many public undertakings involving vast property are subject to the decisions of its Committees, we scarcely ever hear of a single member being bribed and never of anything like systematic corruption. The fact is that the State of England is surrounded by those high associations of duty which come from religion, and we can see in other countries the lamentable effects which follow from the absence of such associations. Therefore it is the duty of patriots to hold fast by every influence which can help to keep their country above the corruption of selfishness, and no better exhortation can be given to young men than that they should form and cherish a high ideal of their State and of their own duty to it, not considering power as an opportunity for personal gain but as a means for general good.

The State also gains instead of losing by its connection with religion, because thereby respect for the law is increased. We are so accustomed to the law being obeyed simply because it is the law that we seldom examine into the causes of such obedience. But if we do this we find that such obedience can only come either from fear, or from a conviction of utility, or from such a sense of duty as has its origin in religion. It is not possible for fear to be the sole, or even principal, motive amongst a free people, and even if it were possible, obedience so grounded would be the most difficult and costly to exact and the most imperfect when exacted. Neither can conviction of utility be a sufficient motive, for it is impossible to give this to vast numbers of those whose obedience is necessary, and the acknowledgment of this basis would convey to most minds the impression that obedience might be refused where such conviction could not be established, or at any rate where a contrary conviction was held. Undoubtedly cultivated minds can perceive, quite apart from religion, that it is much better that bad laws should be obeyed than that the supremacy of law itself should be jeopardized, but this is a belief which the majority cannot be made to understand, and which will not serve as the sole basis of obedience. Political order could not be maintained if it had to wait for obedience until the people were convinced of the utility of each particular law or comprehended the philosophical necessity of obedience to law in general.

The fact is that this supremacy of law must have a firmer basis than force or utility, and such a basis it can only find in religion. This necessity has been discovered, more or less, by all States, both civilized and uncivilized, in all times, and this is the reason why every State of consequence, and certainly every one of long duration, has found it necessary to connect itself with religion. For it must be remembered that this idea of the Church and the State being two separate institutions is quite a modern one, and finds no warrant in history. In those nurseries of civilization the ancient kingdoms of the East, in pagan Greece and Rome, amongst the sturdy nations of the North and the tropical tribes of the South, in every country and age of which history gives us knowledge, we find that amidst all the varieties of political organization and religious belief, the State and the Church have always more or less gone together. The cause of a phenomenon so universal must lie in some deep and fundamental principle, and that principle is the necessity that obedience to the law must be associated with religion. It may be, and often is, that that religion is mostly false, but it serves its purpose in this respect so long as it raises the religious emotions and is the best which can then be got. It is futile to try to account for such a fact as this by saying that States have called in the help of superstition to make up for the want of ability and justice, for this connection with religion has been maintained most closely by those States which were strongest in themselves and therefore least liable to such a motive, and the relaxation of this connection has generally been contemporary with the decline of those States.

A State which professes to have no connection with religion cannot claim from its subjects that sort of obedience to which religion is essential, but without such obedience a State cannot have a safe and long existence. A State which is not built upon the rock of religious sentiment must rest upon the sand of utilitarian convenience, and will fall as soon as the rain of misfortune descends, and the flood of opposition comes, and the winds of discontent blow and beat upon it.

We may illustrate by the criminal laws the effects of this religious connection. Without religion the State is merely an instrument for repressing evil, and can only endeavour to restrain the criminal, whilst with religion it becomes a means for promoting good and can seek to reform him; in the one case we teach the criminal only that he must not dare, in the other also that he ought not to desire, to violate the law. A State cannot exist without "reverence for the law," and such reverence can only be based upon religion.

It may here be mentioned that religion is the most powerful help in lightening the duties of the State, for if every person was religious those functions of the State which are now its most important ones, of maintaining order, would become unnecessary. If the argument urged for prohibitive liquor legislation, that it would diminish taxation by lessening the expenses of prisons and workhouses, has any force, it holds much more fully in regard to religion, for religion strikes at the root of all evil whilst teetotalism only touches one of its offshoots. No one pretends that the absence of drink will cure indolence and cheating, but the presence of religion will do more than anything else not only to keep back all these other offences but also to check intemperance itself. Especially is this true of a religion such as that taught by the Church of England, which is simple and practical, and endeavours to make men fitted for this world as well as qualified for the next. Probably much that has been said about the advantages derived by the State from connection with religion would have to be modified if that religion was such as is taught by some sects and seems most in favour amongst those who conduct what are called "religious revivals." The State can get little benefit from the spread of a religion which conveys the impression that this life is of little consequence and that it does not much matter what we do on earth so long as we accept the plan offered for getting into heaven. But the State can receive immense benefit from the promulgation and acceptance of a religion like that taught by Christ Himself, which whilst it gives the assurance of blessedness to true believers, also emphatically teaches that none can be such who do not do justly, and love mercy, and walk humbly before God.

It is not pretended that any State can by connection with religion obtain all the advantages which are theoretically possible from this connection. Therefore it is unreasonable to ask how it comes that the nation is no better than it is, if the national principle confers all these benefits, unless we can also prove that the nation would not have been worse without that principle. After having convinced ourselves that this connection must be beneficial, we must not abandon it because its results do not come up to our desires. Since religion has a tendency to confer upon the State such advantages as have here been named, it is unreasonable to suppose that the State should give up its control of that religion or its means of helping its promulgation.

The last objection here to be considered against the national principle is that—

10. *It endangers the safety of the State.*

It is said that since the fiercest conflicts are generally waged about religious disputes, if the State mixes itself up in these and espouses the side which loses, it is liable to the calamities which often follow defeat in such conflicts, and may itself become a sacrifice to victory. And even if the side taken by the State is victorious, those who have been defeated become the enemies of the State because it has been the friend of their opponents. Also the State may be destroyed although it does not become a partisan but is merely like a fortress which both combatants are striving to gain possession of, for in their struggles it may between them get knocked to pieces like the farmstead of Hougomont, fought over by the English and French at the battle of Waterloo. Therefore we are told that the State had better keep out of these risks and have nothing to do with such a dangerous subject as religion.

In the first place it is evident that if conflicts of such magnitude do arise in a nation, the State cannot afford to be indifferent to them and yet retain its supremacy. The safest course in respect to a battle is to keep away from it, but a safety so secured implies the abdication of all sovereignty; a State, like a soldier, which did this would be drummed out of its position. It is not pretended that the State should interfere in every religious dispute, and the national principle prevents this, but only that the State cannot afford to ignore disputes of such magnitude as, by involving the risk of the destruction of the State as a consequence of its participation, could come within the scope of this objection. A State which did this would be like one which allowed, without interference, its people to be torn by civil war. If the State should be merely an instrument for defending persons and property and for conducting the commercial business of the nation, it probably should have nothing to do with religious disputes, however important or universal, but such a conception is not what the English people generally mean by the State, and the whole idea of the State will have to be altered, and not for the better, before we can be made to believe that the State ought to be indifferent to such disputes from fear for its own safety. The State may sometimes be shaken, although it can never be destroyed, by participation in such disputes, but it is certain to be destroyed if it keeps out of them altogether. When an earnest struggle is going on, the man whom both sides most dislike is he who will take part with neither. In such conflicts those who are defeated may for a time be irritated with the State, if it has been against them, but they will ultimately respect it all the more, whilst both sides will be sure to despise that State which in cowardice has kept away altogether. Indifference is far more dangerous to a State than participation; Englishmen look to their State as the organization of their highest ideal and the embodiment of their national supremacy, but it cannot remain such if it holds aloof from those conflicts which are thought to be of the supremest national importance. And in fact it cannot possibly so hold aloof, for the State is but the nation in its organized form, and therefore it must be affected by everything which moves the nation. A nation rocked by religious convulsions must have a centre of stability, and that should be the State. When conflicts arise which stir a nation to its depths and absorb its energy, the State cannot choose whether it will take part in them or not; if it does not act as the directing embodiment of the national will, it will either be trodden out under the feet of the combatants or will remain a mere mechanical organization shorn of all the dignity and power of a State.

Besides holding that the true safety of the State is not imperilled by the national principle, we also maintain that this principle adds to that safety, and for the following reasons, amongst others.

It subdues class antagonisms. The danger from the consequences of such antagonisms is one of the greatest to which States are subject. The most difficult task in political organizations is to get the different classes to work together in proper proportions. The plains of history are strewn with the bones of such failures. Almost every attempt at national organization seems to result in placing the control of the State almost exclusively in the hands of one class; if the aristocracy rule, the others are excluded and oppressed, and if it is under the democracy, the aristocracy will take no part. England has, with the exception of one or two short intervals, been ruled by the aristocracy up to this century; the middle class, that growth of modern civilization, has had a short reign of less than half a century, and now it seems that the lower class is coming into power. The working class has developed into great strength during this generation, and numerous changes have been made to give it more political power, yet it seems as if no contrivances, no Reform Bills or readjustments, can make this class blend fairly with the others in the government of the nation. There is plenty of legislation for the working man but none by him, and it is felt that if he actually took such a share in legislating as seems to be now his right, probably most of that class which has hitherto governed the country would gradually withdraw from political life.

The reason why a truly representative team will not pull together in drawing the national car is that the classes are so separated from each other that they will not run side by side. But it is evident that an ideal State must blend all these classes in a proportion such as fairly represents their power in the nation, and therefore such a State must possess some influence by which it can so subdue these class separations as to make such a blending possible. This influence is found in religion, and in that alone, for if we put away the mile-standard measurement of religion and come to the yard-stick of the world, the differences between the classes appear so enormous as to be irreconcileable. If this world is all we have to think of, the rich must despise the poor, and the poor must hate the rich, too much for harmonious partnership to be possible between them. Political equality can only be based upon human brotherhood and this has no existence apart from religion; it was not merely a noble religious sentiment but it was also a deep political truth which the angels revealed when in their song they coupled glory to God in the highest with peace on earth and good-will towards men.

The State alone can so administer religion as to make its influence most effective in subduing the natural alienation of classes. It is plain, at any rate, that a State which refuses to have anything to do with religion has no right to expect to benefit by the influence of religion, and a State which does not so benefit cannot be either efficient or lasting. It is not necessary here to explain how the national principle works in this respect, but we may illustrate one feature of its operation by pointing to the social position of the country clergyman. He is the only link between the two extreme classes, being the neighbour and associate of the labourer and the companion and equal of the squire, and being also the only man entitled to remind both of their mutual obligations and ties.

Another advantage of the national principle is that it is a refuge when serious calamities come upon the State, as they must some time or other come upon every State. In times of great danger most men fly to religion, and often those soonest do this who have hitherto professed to disbelieve in it. If the citadel of religion is not included within the territory of the State, that territory becomes then deserted and the magic of its supremacy is lost. If the State has no connection with religion, it can then only defend itself by those principles of political expediency which its calamities prove have failed in its own case—but if it rests upon religion, it can appeal to those higher motives which are at such times the only sure stay.

The last reason to be named is that unless the State controls the Church the Church will control the State. The Church and the State cannot be separated from each other, for it is impossible to draw a boundary-line between religion and politics. The phrase "A Free Church in a Free State" may sound attractive, if only because there is always something taking in such a word as "Free," but it speaks of a condition which cannot possibly in any country be permanent, and one which would be more correctly described by the words "An Indifferent Church in an Ignoring State." But Churches will not always remain indifferent and then States cannot afford to remain ignoring. The Church, meaning thereby the organization for religion, may be broken up into a number of separate Churches, as it has been by Dissent in England and America, and these separate Churches may none of them be powerful enough to rival the State, but such a fragmentary condition as this cannot long continue. Unless they grow to disbelieve in the religion itself, and then a new religion must be on its way, men eventually become sick of impotent isolations and paltry sectarian divisions. This is the condition into which Englishmen are getting at the present time, and when such a condition comes they will either break quite away from religion or will long for the dignity and unity of a great Church. Such a Church will then be revived, either in connection with the State or separated from it. But a great Church cannot long remain separated from the State. Such a Church will possess property, and the State, unless it is to abdicate its position of being the supreme guardian of property, will be called upon sooner or later to interfere in the disputes of that Church in order to decide as to the rights to this property. But still more, such a Church must acquire power, great political power, and then the State can no longer ignore it. It may be said that there is no reason why the Church, simply because it becomes a large organization, should exercise political power, for there are many such organizations, as Friendly Societies, Labour Unions, and business Companies, which do not become political. But it must be remembered not only that great efforts are needed, which are frequently unsuccessful, to keep even such organizations from becoming political in times of excitement, but also that the Church, besides being concerned with the whole purpose of man's being instead of with one particular object merely, likewise exercises control over feelings and interests which cannot be separated from those which determine political action. Supposing that such a Church desires, and feels bound in conscience to do its utmost to obtain, some object which the State does not think it wise to grant. That Church then becomes an organized body in opposition to the State, and by controlling a religious system can bring forces into play against which the State is powerless. We can get an example if we consider the question of burial. The State is bound to see that bodies are properly buried and the people insist on this being done with certain religious ceremonies, but those who are alone qualified may refuse to perform these ceremonies over any who in life had espoused the cause of the State against the Church or had offended them in any way. The State must then either submit to be defeated or must assert its authority over the Church and so adopt the national principle. And numerous other examples could easily be given.

This difficulty is not got over by saying that it arises from ignorant superstitions to which the State should pay no attention, for the State must pay attention as it is the State of the whole people and not merely that of the few philosophers. Such feelings as these, whether we consider them superstitions or not, have more influence in ruling even political conduct than all arguments put together, and when they are allied with religion they are, until changed, irresistible. Excommunication, or some equivalent, is also another power with which the State has to deal. This power is at present almost exclusively claimed by the Church of Rome, but the others only hold it in abeyance, for Churches will not readily allow their decrees to end with this life when their objects are chiefly concerned with the next. In times of excited conflict with the State, Churches make principles of the points of dispute and elevate these into cardinal doctrines of orthodoxy. It is not pretended that this is done strategically, for it is plainly a natural consequence of that feeling which to the earnest believer makes everything connected with his Church religious. The Roman Catholic Church has recently embodied this feeling in the doctrine of Papal Infallibility, which requires every declaration of the Church, that is of the Pope speaking *ex cathedrâ*, to be implicitly believed and obeyed, whether it concerns some great principle or some trifling detail.

An instance of this conflict between the Church and the State may be found in the O'Keefe case in Ireland, in which the State was called upon to deprive a priest of certain secular offices because he had been deposed by the mere authority of the Church from the religious position with which these were connected, and that simply for appealing to the State on a matter which properly belonged to the State's jurisdiction. In England the Roman Catholic Church has recently become so strong in some of the large northern towns that by compelling all its members to vote one way it can and does control political affairs, and more than one member of the present House of Commons owes his seat to this influence. And now we hear of the "Nonconformist wing" and the "Nonconformist revolt," and there is no doubt that if the Nonconformists had an organization sufficiently complete to be called a Church, we should have another irresponsible Church dictating its terms to the State. As it is, Liberal candidates are told that, however qualified in other respects, they will be excluded from Parliament unless they can adopt the last crotchet on ecclesiastical policy of the Nonconforming minority, and we are threatened even with the ordinary balance and influence of political parties being interfered with, and the direction of the State consequently changed, unless this crotchet is conceded. If this can happen with Churches which are comparatively weak, we can imagine how it would be if the Church of England, possessing its enormous influence, was left to its own control. That Church would then have interests apart from those of the State, and whenever its enthusiasm was properly roused on behalf of any of these interests which conflicted with those of the State, that Church could and would exercise such a control over its members as to make the State submit. If the State would not do this, we should then have another Reformation, and with all our boasted modern advancement, we should find ourselves fighting over again precisely the same battles which have been fought for us long ago by the heroic and far-seeing Tudors.

We need not confine ourselves to our own country to prove the impossibility of permanently disconnecting the Church and the State. Unless they are united, they are opposed, and when opposed the relationships which are possible between them are only those which can exist between combatants, for either the State must rule the Church, or the Church must rule the State, or both must be lying on the ground recovering for another struggle. France and Italy are just now in this last condition, for their people are in a state of indifference to religion which cannot, and ought not to, be permanent; Germany and Belgium, are in the throes of the conflict to keep down the mastership of the Church, whilst the only countries in Europe which enjoy religious peace are those in which the national principle is adhered to.

Therefore the people of England ought clearly to understand that in this question of Disestablishment they have to decide, not whether the State and the Church shall be separated from each other, but whether the Church shall remain under the control of the State or the State be ultimately placed under the control of the Church. The Church and the State cannot be disconnected, and they cannot both be rulers; the experiment of two kings resulted, in Japan, in one becoming supreme, and in Sparta, in both being merely commanders under an oligarchy. So it must be always, for supreme power must lie somewhere, and there is no doubt that in this world it ought to be with the State. As shown before, it is not pretended that the State ought to interfere with the consciences of its subjects or frustrate in any way the free operation of that religion which should exercise the strongest influence over their lives, but only that the State cannot afford to leave to itself any organization which may imperil its own independence, for the independence of the State is essential to the preservation of political freedom and to the development of national progress.

But we must not let this argument lead us into supposing that the true relationship between the State and the Church ought to be one of submission or of antagonism. If we rise to proper conceptions of what the State and Church should be, all such ideas vanish immediately, and we perceive that the union of the Church and the State is equally honourable and necessary to both, and that he who would break up that union is, though perhaps unwittingly, an enemy to the Church no less than to the State.

In concluding these remarks about objections, we cannot help saying that in this respect the Church of England is not fairly treated by its opponents, for they use both failure and success as arguments for its Disestablishment. If deficiencies are revealed, they point to these as showing that the Church ought to be disestablished because it is not doing its duty, but if prosperity is manifested, they say that this is a proof that the Church ought to be disestablished because it could evidently get on very well without being connected with the State. It seems much more reasonable to infer that failure shows that the national principle is not being carried out properly, and that success is a proof of how much may be done by the help of that principle.

CHAPTER VIII.

CONCLUSION.

IT is not necessary to enter into any lengthened positive explanation, for enough has already been said to give a sufficiently clear idea of the chief purpose of this book. Undoubtedly many persons will consider that some of the objections which have been referred to are frivolous or beside the question, whilst many more will hold the opinion that some of the objections which are pertinent have not been sufficiently answered. It must be understood that not merely have those objections been introduced which are perceived by the many, but also an attempt has been made to recognise those which can suggest themselves to the few who consider this matter more fully and curiously. The strong consciousness must also be acknowledged that many of these objections have been very imperfectly dealt with, and that some of them, as well as others which have not been introduced, could not possibly be perfectly answered. For it is not pretended that a National Church is, or can be, a perfect institution, and it would be well if this evident fact was more borne in mind by those who take up the discussion of this question. It may seem foolish, although it is really necessary, to keep repeating the truism that no human institution can be so perfect that valid objections cannot be raised against it. Those, and they are many, who, because they can show up one or two flaws in the Church, jump to the conclusion that it ought therefore to be destroyed, forget that they are acting upon an assumption which not only involves an irreligious denial of the confessedly imperfect character of this life, but is also directly opposed to their own constant practice. No form of house has ever been designed which has not had some faults, but no sensible person has ever been found to say that on this account mankind should, where climate seems to require them, give up having houses at all. And so with almost everything else we can think of, and it may be confidently said that if men will only judge the National Church as they judge other things, most of the objections raised against it will fade away, and we need have little fear for its safety.

As with a dwelling-house, so with a National Church, we must first make up our minds whether we need one at all, and afterwards we may set about to see whether we have got the best we can. The main purpose of these pages has been not even so much to set at rest certain specific objections, or to persuade that the National Church of England should be allowed to remain merely because there are not sufficient reasons for its destruction, but their object will have failed if they have not done something towards making it clear that this Church is based upon a principle which is sound and good. It is not pretended that the Church was originally consciously formed upon this principle; it would be absurd to suppose that its founders first convinced themselves of the truth of the national principle and then built up a Church in accordance with it, but nevertheless it is true that no great institution can long continue which is not, however unconsciously, based upon some principle, and that it is to this national principle that the Church of England owes its long existence in the past and upon this it must depend for its future. The question of unconsciousness has nothing to do with the matter, and indeed tells in favour of the principle, for those principles are generally the truest upon which we act without thinking, or even knowing, anything about them. Consciousness marks the beginning of decay and error, for self-inspection is a symptom of sickliness. No constitution which has been formed upon a theory has ever lasted long; all great and durable institutions have grown out of the unconscious spontaneousness of nature, and the National Church of England is one of these. It is what the necessities of human nature have made it, and its best defence is that it is what it is. As long as people were content to take it in this way there was no need to go further, but now that its anatomy is being so keenly discussed and we are told that it has no root, we are compelled to try to show that it has a root, and a very good one too. That root is the national principle.

Sufficient has already been said to explain the nature of this principle, but one feature of it may here be referred to, and this is perhaps one of the greatest advantages derived from a National Church, namely that it secures Regulated Liberty. Religion, at least such a religion as that held by the people of this country, requires liberty. This word liberty has become so vague from its associations that it scarcely conveys any idea at all, but we may understand its meaning in this connection if we consider what is the nature of Protestantism. As opposed to Roman Catholicism, against which it protests, the fundamental characteristic of Protestantism is its belief that each soul may go direct to God and does not for this require the intervention, although it may welcome the help, of Church or priest. A condition like this involves such liberty as is inconsistent with the dominion of any priestly caste.

But if Protestantism requires liberty, Christianity also requires a Church, for religious liberty does not mean that men can differ amongst each other as much as they like in belief and action and yet all belong to the same religion. Christianity teaches plainly, with all its simplicity, that however large the liberty it allows, there are certain fundamental doctrines and sentiments in which its followers must agree. Indeed such a condition as this is of the very essence of a religion, for a religion without definiteness is no religion at all. Also a religion must have an organization, for in the simple fact of its acceptance a demarcation is set up which is the beginning of an organization. If the religion is worth anything it is subject to these two necessities, namely that its own followers shall be able to receive its continuous ministrations, and that its acceptance shall be pressed upon those who are not its followers. Thus every religion requires an organization which is both ministering and missionary.

In choosing a basis for such an organization we ought to be guided by two wishes, namely, to get the largest which is practicable and yet not one so large as to be inconsistent with our other conditions. For these two reasons we hold that the national, basis is the best. If we take a larger basis than the national, we get an organization which cannot be worked except under such an autocracy as is inconsistent with religious liberty. The necessities of language alone involve this, for language is a fundamental requisite of religion, and yet it is impossible to express the same idea with exact identity in two languages. A single organization must have a single means of communication, and if this organization comprises several nations, that means must be a learned language. But such a language implies the undue subjection of the unlearned to the learned, which subjection is opposed to the spirit and teachings of Christianity and to the freedom of Protestantism.

If we choose a smaller basis than the nation, we do not take the largest practicable. For, in the first place, the national organization is the largest of which we have any experience, and it is the one of which we have the most experience. We have no practical conception of any larger basis than the national one, and hence the difficulties in the way of what is called international arbitration. In the second place, the national organization is, for such purposes, the best of which we have any experience; the smaller we go from this the worse we get. Even in trifling matters, people are coming to believe that large organizations are better than small ones; gas and water and other companies are being swallowed up by large corporations, and so with innumerable other connections, yet we are told that a change which would split up the National Church into a number of little organizations is required by the spirit of the times. It seems as if men do not care as much about religion as about gas and water.

But it must most of all be insisted upon that any organization which is adequate to the requirements of the Christian religion, must offer its services as widely as possible. The barriers of language and locality must be acknowledged, and though the Church is bound to overcome these as far as possible, it is manifestly not bound to attempt the impossible feat of making them disappear altogether. But a true Christian Church is bound to be open to all those within the largest reasonable area, and that area is the nation; such a Church is bound to be truly missionary to all those who speak the same language and live under the same legal and social conditions. Such a Church must be a national one.

If we take a smaller basis than the nation we let in, as pointed out before, amongst many other evils, two most serious ones, namely exclusiveness and dependence. For the next basis we are driven to is that of agreement in belief, and this gives us a Church which ministers only to those who least need it and does not minister to those who most need it. If such a Church is missionary as well as ministering, it can only be so very partially. We see this in the present condition of the self-governing Churches in England. Not one of them shows any possibility of being able to minister to the whole nation; to think of Independents or Baptists doing this is plainly absurd, and though the Methodists seem the most likely, it must be remembered that we ought not to measure the abiding possibilities of their system merely by what it has done under the influence of its initial enthusiasm.

No religious systems have ever attempted to grapple with this difficulty of ministering to all except such as have been founded on the national lines; Methodism arose out of the National Church and Presbyterianism was built on its pattern. And indeed these self-governing Churches seem, so to speak, to be unconsciously conscious of this difficulty, for none of the supporters of Disestablishment consider, as they ought to do to be consistent, how it would be if the system of the National Church was entirely abolished. They say that they would leave to the Church its buildings, and parishes, and complete organization apart from State control, but they must reflect that all these things are the natural result of the national principle and must come to an end, though it may be gradually, with that principle. Holding, as it does, substantially the same creed, the Church of England differs from the other Churches, Methodist, or Congregational, or Baptist, only because it has always been, and is, national; and those Churches have no right to denationalise it until they can show that their systems are equal to doing, and doing at least as well, all the work now done by the National Church. Not their most ardent admirers, if capable of judging, will maintain that they have yet made any near approach to success in this.

Even if self-governing Churches could do equally well this, which may be called, in the wide sense of the word, missionary work, the effects upon those receiving the benefit of their labours would not be so good, for their sense of independence would be weakened. Every member of a nation may unhesitatingly make use of a National Church because it is his own, but for the services of other Churches he is indebted to the members of those Churches themselves. A National Church is the only one which has the right to offer itself fully and which all men of the nation have the right to accept freely.

We say, then, that we cannot take a larger basis for a

Church than the nation, and that we ought not to take a smaller one, and that therefore the national principle is theoretically the soundest. Therefore instead of begging that the Church of England may not now be disestablished merely because it is doing a useful work, whilst acknowledging that of course no one would think of setting up such an institution now, we plainly assert that the principle of that Church should be maintained even if the Church itself was now doing no good, and that if there was no such Church existing, it should be the object of wise statesmen to establish one. The benefits which the State derives from such a Church would be a sufficient reason for its establishment, though it is not pretended that statesmen everywhere should attempt this immediately. A good institution is bad if set up at the wrong time, and National Churches, like other valuable permanencies, must grow rather than be made, but we maintain that wise statesmen should direct their policy towards the eventual adoption of the national principle as the soundest basis for a religious system. A National Church can alone properly give regulated liberty in religion ; Romanism gives regulation without liberty, and Congregationalism gives liberty without regulation. It is not asserted that all Churches belong exclusively to one class or the other ; it cannot be denied that the Methodists, for instance, although a self-governing Church, have a good deal of regulation, as also have the Presbyterians, but that regulation is of the character of what we here call Romanism and is obtained at the sacrifice of liberty. A National Church gives the fullest measure of regulation which is possible with the fullest measure of liberty.

The national principle as here inculcated does not, as is often asserted, place the individual conscience in subjection to the State. It is assumed that there are certain fundamental doctrines of religion which commend themselves to the consciences of the majority of the nation, or at least to the consciences of those who lead that majority, and these doctrines are made the religious basis of the National Church. The consciences of all are left free to accept or reject these doctrines, with their consequent practices. Those whose consciences reject, are perfectly justified in dissenting, for the national principle as here laid down recognises the right to dissent, subject to the condition that the advantages, taken altogether, including the claims of conscience, seem likely to outweigh the drawbacks of such a weakening of the national principle. In a world like this, in which in all things we have to compromise more or less to make life with each other practicable, no men have a right to make any differences they like, however trivial, matters of rigid conscience. Those who persuade themselves that they ought to hold out, at any cost, for their own way in secondary matters respecting which enlightened Christianity inculcates a spirit of mutual concession, are not to be credited with martyric heroism but only with intellectual narrowness or spiritual stupidity. The national principle recognises the full rights of conscience within all reasonable limits, and no sound principle of any sort, if it is a principle at all, can be expected to do more.

Neither is it true that this principle places religion under the control of the majority, for that would imply that national affairs generally should be under such control. But this is not a necessary belief. It is true that during the last thirty or forty years there has been a growing tendency, fostered by the character of the political changes which have been made, to encourage a vague theory that there is some particular virtue in mere numbers and that the first object of a constitution should be to make all men equal in political power. But this theory is rapidly exploding itself, and we are coming to acknowledge that the best constitution is that which leads the nation to follow the best men, and that the most important thing about a government is what it does, and not how or by whom. In a free country the government cannot go against the will of the majority, but everyone knows that in most matters that majority has no will of its own, and merely acquiesces in what is recommended by those whom it trusts as its leaders. If mere counting of heads is the best method in national affairs of one sort it is the best in those of another. The national principle does not express any opinion on this matter, but merely asserts that it is best for the outward organization of religion to be under the same control, whatever that may be, as is the national organization generally.

Neither is it reasonable to speak of a National Church as being "a creature of the State" any more than it would be to apply such language to any other part of the national organization. It is not professed that the national principle should be put into force until the nation has already adopted a religion. The State may help the spread of such a religion, as it did when Christianity was introduced into England; such help, however, is not based upon the national principle but depends upon the relationship existing between the State and the people. This principle can only come into play when the religion has been adopted, and its operation then is to provide that religion with the best organization which the nation can offer. A National Church is not a creature of the State but is a creation of the people, governed by themselves through the same organization which they use for carrying out all their other wishes as a people.

Having thus called attention again to a few of the chief features of the national principle, we have next to consider how far the National Church at present existing in England is in accordance with this principle. If we do this we find that this Church conforms to this principle with more accuracy and completeness than we are justified in expecting. In the first place, it is under the government of the nation; Parliament, which controls other national affairs, is complete master of the Church also, and can, if the nation so wishes, make any change it likes in its doctrines and arrangements, and can also, as is shown by the agitation for Disestablishment, do away with that Church altogether. Parliament, including under that term, for the sake of shortness, the three Estates of the Realm, has no rival in its government of the Church, and since Parliament is supposed to be the best means of carrying out the national will, it is plain that the Church is under the control of the nation.

In the second place, the Church is open to all the nation. There is not a single acre in England the spiritual responsibility of which is not placed upon some officer of the Church, neither is there a single person in England who has not the right to claim the offices of the Church. Although there is a tendency to introduce the congregational idea into the Church itself, this tendency, which must therefore be resisted, is alien to the nature of that Church, which, being national, is and must be parochial. The clergy are bound by the theory of their position not only to give the offices of religion to all who ask for them, but also to offer them to all who may be induced to accept them. If there is any person in a district upon whom reasonable means have not been brought to bear to bring him within the influence of religion, the responsibility lies upon the clergyman of that district, although this may of course be greatly modified by the existence of rival systems, by the deficiency of support, or by numerous other circumstances. Those who speak so strongly of the shortcomings of the Church should think also of its possibilities, and should consider how greatly those possibilities have been hindered by the alienations and oppositions of its enemies. In spite of these shortcomings, it may safely be said that the Church of England at the present day carries the influence of religion to a larger number of the population than any other Church, or probably even than all the other Churches put together, and if we compare the areas over which this influence is spread, there can be no doubt that the Church is far ahead of all its competitors. Indeed it embraces the whole land in its arms; there is not a secluded village, not a moorland hamlet, not a solitary farm-house, which is beyond its care; no man, however poor or far away, is too remote for its fellowship; there is some Church whose bell calls him to his prayers, whose door is open for his welcome, whose minister is ready to speak to him and his the words of comfort and of hope, and whose sacred soil receives his body at the last. In spite of all the theories which are begotten of congregational commercialism and town civilisation, we must feel in our hearts that this all-pervading system is in theory at least most in harmony with the spirit of the Christian religion, yet this system can only be carried out by a National Church. The Church of England, however far it may fall short of perfection, is the only religious organization in England which makes any attempt to carry out this system.

With respect to the work performed by the Church, apart from that which is specifically religious, it is done so quietly, and we are so accustomed to take it for granted, that we could hardly estimate it until we came to lose it. In towns, the organizations of the Church are the only ones which attempt to look after the welfare of all in their districts, and in the country, the Church is the bond of social union and the centre of philanthropic activity. The part taken by the Church in the education of the people is sufficient to indicate the extent of its usefulness. It is easy to attribute this to proselytising partisanship but it is absurd to suppose that such a motive can account for a phenomenon so great and general; and at any rate the ability to have done so much, from whatever motive, indicates the greatness of the possibilities of influence which the system of the Church affords. If we were to take all the organizations now existing in the country for moral and intellectual improvement, for social usefulness, and for brotherly charity, we should find that the majority, at any rate in influence, depend directly or indirectly upon the system of the Church. With all its weaknesses and shortcomings, the Church of England does more than any other institution in the land to keep up that sentiment of universal brotherhood which is so essential to the sound continuance of national unity.

With respect to the *personnel* of the National Church, it cannot be denied that its clergy are socially and educationally superior to the ministers of any other Church in the country. There is no use in disguising the fact that the ideal called up in our minds by the word "clergyman" is that of a man who is much more of what the world means by a gentleman than is he whose ideal corresponds with the words "Dissenting minister," and no people more readily recognise this in their actions, although they might not acknowledge it in their words, than the Dissenters themselves. It is true, no doubt, that this gentlemanliness is not the first requisite, but it is likewise true that it is a significant symptom, and is also a great advantage, for he who is a gentleman and pious is much better fitted for the office of minister than he who, being equally pious, is not a gentleman. And there is no reason to suppose that the piety of the clergy of the Church of England is not as real and good as that of others, although it may be less sensational and demonstrative. This may not be, and indeed is not, a pleasant subject to dwell upon, but when we are asked to deal with such a patient as the Church of England we are bound to consider all the leading symptoms, and this is one which cannot be overlooked but must be accounted for. Both parties attribute it to the connection between the Church and the State, but those who support Disestablishment maintain that if that was adopted, all ministers would rise to the social position now occupied by the clergy alone. There is no evidence, either from theory or practice, to support such a presumption, whilst all that we know and all that we can infer lead us to the conclusion that after Disestablishment all ministers of religion would fall to the social level now held by Dissenting ministers. That religion would be greatly the loser there can be no doubt, for as much good can be done out of pulpits as in them, and the minister should be looked up to by his people as their adviser and friend, but they will not do this as a rule unless he possesses corresponding social qualifications. Those who are best acquainted with Dissent will acknowledge that its ministers exercise comparatively little personal influence over their people outside the sphere of their traditionally professional duties. It may be mentioned, as a fact which has nothing to do with the advisability of perpetuating the institution under the circumstances, but which illustrates the effect of the national principle in this respect, that undoubtedly the National Irish Church gave to Ireland a body of clergymen who won the respect, if they did not effect the conversion, of its people, and whose social equals that country is not likely to receive from any other religious organization.

As to the character of the Church of England, it may be said that it teaches the religion which is approved by the majority of those in the country who care about religion at all. Undoubtedly there are differences of opinion in the Church, as there must be both in it and out of it on this subject, but confining ourselves to such fundamentals as it is necessary to consider in this connection, we may say that the religion of the Church of England is that of the great majority of Protestants both in that Church and out of it, including nearly all those who are called "orthodox Dissenters." Yet the National Church, whilst teaching this religion with greater fullness and definiteness than any other Church, teaches it also with greater liberality. There is no religious organization in the world which combines the same definiteness of belief with the same liberty of thought. This Church is the chief storehouse of religious learning, and from it have sprung most of the movements which have from time to time revived the enthusiasm of Christianity.

c c

Such being a few of the principal features of the Church of England, we have next to consider what is the proper course to adopt with respect to this Church. We are told that on every side the question is being asked, "What is to be done with the Church of England?" that theologians are puzzling themselves about it and that politicians will soon have to deal with it. Although undoubtedly those who are in favour of a change greatly exaggerate the amount of interest which is really taken in this matter, still since the question has been so far raised, we had better make up our minds about an answer whilst we can do so calmly. If we want to examine our boat we must do so as it is gliding through still waters, for all chance will be gone when it gets into the rapids of party rivalries.

It is clear that with such an institution we have only the choice of three courses, for we must either leave it as it is, or destroy it, or attempt to improve it.

It would perhaps be well if the first course received more attention than seems to be given to it at present. For like frightened soldiers who excitedly run about asking if they must go here or go there without thinking that it may be best for them to stop where they are, so nearly everyone who talks about the Church of England seems to take it for granted that some change must be made with it. But why? Is this Church in such a condition of decay—is it being so faithless to its opportunities and so injurious to religion that it cannot be put up with any longer as it is? It is not pleasant for its friends to have to talk about the good qualities of this Church, but they must overcome their backwardness when duty requires the plain facts to be stated. And although it is not agreeable to make comparisons, we must not shrink from them when they are forced upon us and can be of any use, and therefore we may ask where there is another religious organization in England which is effecting more good, or doing its duty better, than this

Church. Is it the Methodist? Is it the Independent? Is it the Baptist? Is it the Roman Catholic? Let us say if we should like the Church of England to be replaced by any one of these, and there can be no doubt about the answer which would be given by the great majority of the people. It is no part of the object here to speak disparagingly of any of the self-governing Churches, but we are compelled to declare that at least none of them excel the Church of England in the requisites, taking them altogether, of a religious organization. Therefore on this ground there is no reason to do anything at all with that Church, nor will there be until its rivals have first got rid of some of their own defects. But the test of comparison is not one which would be upheld here, and it is only mentioned because of its suggestiveness to the opponents of the Church.

The second course open to us is that of destruction, and this is now advocated under the name of Disestablishment. Nearly all its supporters assert, and undoubtedly also believe, that the Disestablishment of the Church of England would not mean its destruction but rather its restoration; they say that it would merely free it from the control of the State and leave it untrammelled to march forward with renewed vigour; they tell us that they admire the character and learning of the Church, its liberal-heartedness and liberal-headedness, its venerable associations and extensive usefulness, but that they cannot tolerate its connection with the State; if we will only get rid of this defect, they assure us that the Church will be far more successful and will have their sympathy instead of opposition. They might as well tell us that they admire the growth of a tree, its rich fruit and pleasant shade, and would let it remain just as it is only that the graceless thing called the root must be cut away. For the Church of England is what it is because it is a National Church; such Churches do not of course obtain their religion from the State, but all Churches holding the same religion differ from each other only in the principles of their organization, and the principle of the organization of the Church of England is that it is national. Churches exist as Churches, in the sense in which we can speak of them in this connection, on the bases of their organizations, and we cannot change these bases and yet leave the Churches the same.

Unless a National Church has become so effete that no successor is ready, its Disestablishment means not merely its own destruction, but also the creation of a new Church. We see that this was so with the disestablishment of the Church of Ireland. By that act the existence of the National Church of that country was terminated. The Episcopal Church which exists there now is called the Church of Ireland, but it can only claim that name by courtesy as inheriting the traditions and *personnel* of the disestablished Church. This new Church stands to the other in a relationship like that of a commercial association which has taken over the buildings and staff and name of a retiring firm, but which will conduct its business on a different system; the edifices, and organizations, and clergy, remain with the new Church, but the old master has gone, and it is the master who determines the character. There are, and will probably continue to be, archbishops and bishops, but these, although the same in name, will henceforth hold a position quite different in character from that of their predecessors, for instead of being placed over the Church they will be chosen by it. And the admission that there can be such a Church to choose them, that there can be certain men who are entitled to vote as Churchmen and certain others who are not, is a clear proof that this Church has become in its essence a sect. The present Church of Ireland, although it resembles the National Church of England in its episcopal titles, is in its nature much more nearly related to the self-governing Presbyterian Churches.

Without claiming any of the gifts of prophecy we may tell pretty accurately what will be the leading features of the future history of this Church. For a time it will go on much as if nothing had happened; the same clergymen will go on ministering in the same churches and the same bishops will go on superintending the same districts. But nature will have its way, and gradually those Churches which do not yield income enough will be given up, or come into the hands of inferior clergymen, and the Church of Ireland, becoming congregational instead of parochial, will find itself obliged, like all other sects, to confine its energies to those parts where it can pay its way. This destiny cannot be avoided by violent repudiations of such irreligious commercialism, for no sentiment, however elevated, can get rid of the fact that in self-supporting Churches, where the support, taking it altogether, falls short, the supply must be either stopped or lowered in quality.

Another effect will be that the character of those seeking office in such a Church will be gradually lowered. Of all methods of election, that by a body of voters is the one from which, in religious affairs, the best men most shrink. Besides, no emoluments can make the position of a congregational minister as attractive as that of a national clergyman. The statistics since the disestablishment of the Church of Ireland prove that these effects are already being felt, and they will be seen much more markedly in the next generation.

As to this Church itself, although the fact that it has to face a rival numerically much stronger and distinguished from it by very wide differences, will help to keep it together, still when a time of religious intenseness comes upon it, as come it will, it will be almost certain to split up. For those who are outvoted on some matter about which they feel strongly will see no reason, now that the national ideal has gone, why they should not set up for themselves, and why there should not be another self-governing Church, especially when that would be one in which they could have their own way. There are signs that this process is already beginning, and it only needs a gush of religious fervour to complete it. But Churches, like stones, are much more easily broken than pieced, and we can readily picture what will be the fate in Ireland of Protestantism, whose forces are already too much divided, when its sole remaining corps of strength has split up into independent bands.

From what has been said about the Church of Ireland it is easy to conjecture what it is believed would happen to the Church of England in consequence of its Disestablishment. Indeed there is no necessity to cross the water for analogies, for the history of the self-governing Churches of our own country furnishes sufficient. When we know the similar fate which has befallen the various pieces which have from time to time broken away from a rock in a stream, we can form a good idea of what will become of the remainder when it is loosened from its bed. The Church of England, if once it was disestablished, would become merely one amongst the religious denominations, as they are called, and would be subject to the same necessities and dangers. It is idle for those who are in favour of Disestablishment to say that they do not wish to make the Church of England merely a sectarian body, for, whether they wish it or not, that would be an inevitable consequence. Most of the mistakes of this world come, not from wrong wishes but from bad judgments, and this would be, for those who really have this feeling, another instance. To say that we admire the learning and catholicity of the Church of England, the universality and openness of its system, the character of its clergy, the dignity of its associations, the freedom of its thought, the wide effects of its charity, and that we will not by Disestablishment injure one of these qualities, but will do nothing more than separate that Church from the State, is as absurd as it would be to say that we like the elegant outline of the poised flamingo and would not disturb it but merely knock away the solitary leg on which it stands. It must not be understood to be asserted that all the good qualities of the Church of England are due to its connection with the State. On the contrary, many of these qualities, and some of them infinitely the most important of all, are due to the character of the religion itself, and are possessed by the self-governing Churches as well as by the Church of England. But what is here maintained is that those qualities in which the Church of England differs from the self-governing Churches holding the same religion must in general be attributed to that which is the chief difference between this Church and the others, namely its being National. Some people may not care much for these distinguishing qualities of the Church of England, its universality, its dignity, its liberality, or may think that it is worth while to sacrifice them for the sake of the advantages which belong peculiarly to self-governed Churches. For it is freely confessed that all the advantages are not on the side of the Church of England ; a Church loses as well as gains by connection with the State, and it is our duty to try to estimate these relative advantages. Those who believe that the qualities of sectarianism are better, in themselves and for the country, than the qualities of nationalism, are justified in supporting Disestablishment, but no people have a right to pretend that they will retain the qualities of nationalism whilst they denationalise the Church. Those who enjoy travelling but do not like its inconveniences and expenses have, before undertaking a journey, to weigh one against the other, and it would be as reasonable for them to say that they will have its pleasures without its drawbacks, as it is for those who admire the characteristic qualities of the Church of England to profess that they will retain these qualities whilst destroying that upon which they chiefly depend.

In speaking of the probable consequences of Disestablishment we must consider them as they would affect the Church and the nation, for these are the two parties to the divorce which would thereby be carried out, although it must be understood that the Church thus spoken of is not the present Church of England but that which would be its successor.

As to the Church, the first difficulty which would arise would be as to what should be done with the property of the present Church, for in times such as these money is generally a principal consideration. The State would not dare, for its own safety, to leave an institution in perfectly independent command of resources so vast as those of the Church of England, and yet public feeling would not allow all these resources to be taken away from the service of religion and to be appropriated to secular purposes. Most probably some compromise would be come to, so that the present holders of livings should continue to receive the same incomes as long as they lived, and that afterwards a certain proportion of the resources should be left in the hands of the self-governed Church which would be erected in place of the National Church, the remainder being devoted to other uses.

It is easy to see what would be the consequences of such an arrangement. For a time everything would go on pretty much as before, and most people would say that the fears about the effects of Disestablishment had been proved to be groundless. But it would before long become manifest that great principles are not settled by the experience of a single generation. The State could not hand over such property to be expended by an independent Church for the teaching of any religion of which that Church might from time to time approve, but would be compelled to lay down certain conditions as essential to the enjoyment of this property. Thus the new Church would become to all intents and purposes a richly endowed sect subject to what is called a "close trust," that is a trust specifying certain doctrinal conditions as necessary to the possession of the endowments. Such trusts are still very common amongst the different bodies of Dissenters and undoubtedly, although the unreasoning sentimentality of the times seems to be running against them, they form the only sensible basis upon which endowments can be given to self-governed Churches. For those who leave money for religious purposes wish it to be used for the teaching of that religion in which they themselves believe, and not of any religion, or of no religion, according to the changing fancies of some committee of trustees. Those who are enamoured of what they call the development of religion should reflect that after Disestablishment the chances of such development would be greatly diminished, for then the chief endowments of the country would be attached to the promulgation of a defined creed which neither the State nor any other body would have power to change, whereas now the conditions of these endowments are under the control of the nation.

As the clergy gradually died out no adequate successors would come forward for those places of which the incomes were to lapse or be greatly diminished. It may be said that the generosity of Churchmen would make up for such deficiencies, and undoubtedly a great impetus would be given by Disestablishment to such generosity, but there is no reason to believe that the generosity of Churchmen would in proportion exceed that of the adherents of other self-governed Churches, and none of these have been able to avoid the evils pointed out. The Disestablished Church would be forced gradually to withdraw itself from the poor and sparsely-peopled districts and, like all other Churches, to concentrate its energies where they could have the most effect. So the scattered country poor, who now chiefly depend upon the National Church, would be put off with inferior attention or left without any attention at all. Thus, although in a different degree according to the amount of property made over to it, the Church would in such matters go in the same course as that which is now of necessity followed by the various sectarian bodies. It is for those who are hesitating on this subject to consider whether such a result would promote the religious welfare of the nation.

Not only would the Disestablished Church become sectarian in the distribution of its ministrations, but also in the character of its religion. For the conditions necessarily laid down by the State would of themselves create a distinction between those who could claim to be Churchmen and those who could not, and the Church, instead of being open to the nation, would be made a distinct body apart from it. And, subject to these conditions, the religion of such a body would be under the control of its own governing organization; and it is pretty clear what sort of an organization that would be. Since the supreme power over every institution must lie somewhere, the State would at Disestablishment be compelled to find or form some body to which it could hand over its functions. Convocation would most probably be chosen for this, and would be extended by the introduction of more clergymen and by the infusion of a lay element. But however its arrangements might be manipulated, everybody knows what sort of a body this would eventually become. Two things about it are certain, namely that it would be under clerical domination, and that it would carry out the will of a party. As to the first, reasons have already been given why all combined clerical and lay organizations for Church government must eventually come under clerical domination, the lay element becoming, as far as its representation of real lay feeling is concerned, merely a delusion. The struggle between the clerical and lay in such assemblies is one between professionals and amateurs, between those to whom the matter is the greatest business of life and those to whom it is of secondary importance, between those who have the gifts of education and speech and those who have not, between those who are intensely in earnest and those who are not.

Reason cannot hesitate in deciding which element must eventually predominate, and history confirms the decision.

Not only must such an assembly come under the rule of its clerical portion but also under that of a party of that portion. For all legislative assemblies, whether over Churches or States, are governed by parties; this is a necessary condition of their existence. The English House of Commons is thus divided and its preferments are distributed by this division, although it is certain that in the most important matters of government the sensible men of all parties are much more nearly allied than all the men of any party; but however qualified he may be, no man whose party is out of office can hope for power, whilst the party in office is bound to give its favours to its own supporters, although they may be fools. This system works tolerably well in politics but it would not do in religion, for whilst politics depend upon material facts and considerations of practical convenience, religion is based upon spiritual beliefs and is subject to the rule of conscience. Hence it is that religious divisions are infinitely so much more rigid and lasting than political ones. Thus if we take successive maps of Europe, we find that its political divisions have constantly been changing whilst its religious have remained unmoved for centuries.

But it may be said that if the State is governed by a party, the Church, when under the State, must be governed by a party also. This, although technically true, is not really so, for the sovereign assembly is divided by political and not by religious lines, and therefore those divisions which constitute parties in politics do not do so in religion. Besides, through the constant alternations, the Church is frequently governed in turn by both these political parties, and thus considered as a permanent body, receives the impress of both.

It does not follow that the Church will always be divided as it is now, for the subjects of division are frequently changing, and generally the more trifling they are in themselves the more vehemently are they quarrelled about. But at present, if the Church was disestablished and placed under a remodelled Convocation, it would evidently be divided into the two parties of High Church and Low Church, the few who constitute what is called the Broad Church sitting below the gangway on one side or the other. Not only would the predominant party, whichever that might be, feel bound in conscience to distribute the power amongst its own supporters, but it would also mould, as far as it could, the doctrinal and ceremonial regulations of the Church according to its own opinions. But no one can suppose that the weaker party would quietly submit to this, for although both parties now yield to a third power neither of them would be governed by the other. Thus if, for example, we suppose that what is called the Low Church party was the strongest in the governing body of the Disestablished Church, it cannot be believed that those attached to High Church principles would contentedly acquiesce. Those who are ready, as is done not unfrequently now, to set at defiance the commands of the State even when such defiance implies rebellion against the principles of law in general, would not hesitate about disobeying the decision of a Church Assembly, especially when such disobedience involved nothing more than the setting up of a new Church for themselves. Although probably the Church, when flung alone into the ring of public competition, would at first pull itself together, this would not last long; gradually the different parties would pull away from each other, and before a generation had passed, we should see the Church split up into three or four Churches. Whilst the body of the old Church of England, drowned in a high tide of excited sentiment, was lying dead and stripped on the sands, numerous Churches would go about claiming her name because they had got possession of one or other of her scattered garments. Let those who imagine that this picture is overwrought and that the Church would hold together when separated from the State just as well as it does now, consider the fate of Methodism. There does not appear to be in this system any causes for differences at all comparable with those in the Church of England yet, although it is not a century and a half since its first establishment, Methodism is already divided into more Churches than most people even know the names of.

Some people may consider that even if the Church of England did so split up, no harm would be done, for such divisions would promote energetic rivalry. It would be useless to try to argue here with those whose highest Church ideal is based upon the principles of commercial competition. If it be not one of the great objects of Christianity, not to separate men but to bring them together, not to put up more walls of partition but to break down those which are already standing and to spread abroad a sentiment of universal brotherhood, then it is not the religion which the best minds of every age have taken it to be, and we cannot feel that it is worth while to trouble ourselves about any particular form of Church for its sake. But if the ideal of Christianity be not division but union, not the promotion of still greater isolation but the gathering into one fold from the north and from the south, from the east and from the west, of barbarian, Scythian, bond and free, then those have much to learn who can contemplate with indifference, to say nothing of helping, the splitting up of the Church of England into several Churches.

It cannot be too plainly understood that Disestablishment would inevitably give a great impetus to the spread of Roman Catholicism in England. It is at present one of the common charges against the Church of England that it is a nursery of Roman Catholicism, for it sanctions practices which inoculate its people with doctrines and feelings inconsistent with the true spirit of Protestantism. We are told that those who minister at, and those who attend, many of the places of worship belonging to the Church of England are familiarised with that which they should be taught to avoid, and so are easily led over at last to the Church of Rome. In consequence it is said that the Church of England is a bridge over which numbers of the clergy and laity pass who would otherwise have remained on this side, and that therefore it is for the interest of Protestantism that this bridge should be broken down.

Even if this representation be allowed, it must be remarked in the first place that the extent of the traffic over this bridge is greatly exaggerated. If we take the total of the clergy of the Church of England, and then compare with this the total of those who during the last twenty years have gone over to the Church of Rome, we shall be surprised to find how very small this number is, and as to the laity, the whole changes of which we have any evidence, much less those traceable to the influence of the Church of England, are comparatively unimportant.

But truth requires this figure of the bridge to be carried out a little further. It must be acknowledged that the Church of England has always chiefly occupied that portion of the territory of Protestantism which on one side lies nearest to the borders of Catholicism; in fact, this Church has always claimed to be thoroughly Catholic and to differ from the other only in not being Roman. The Church of England is essentially a moderate Church, not in the sense of being weak or indefinite but with the moderation of that *via media* in which the truth almost invariably lies, the moderation which is founded not upon compromises but upon the freedom from extravagances. Those who at the Reformation gave this Church its present character, insisted that it should be kept clear from the extremes of bigoted denial on the one hand and of slavish credulity on the other, and there is no doubt that at the present time it is in the Church of England that those, and they are many, are chiefly to be found, who object both to the servility of Romanism and to the narrowness of sectarianism. The Church of England is in this country the only Church in which moderate men can find refuge, and which, whilst holding firmly the simple fundamentals of Protestantism, allows great latitude in what must be considered secondary matters, whether of doctrine or ritual.

We have next to ask ourselves whether the destruction of such a Church would ultimately help the cause of Protestantism. It must be remembered that when that which is in the middle breaks up it does not follow that all its component parts will go to one side; it is not clear that when the middle territory between extreme Protestantism and Roman Catholicism is depopulated, all its people will run over to the extreme Protestantism. If it was announced, as it would be by Disestablishment, that the bridge before referred to was to be broken down and that henceforth there could be no connection across the gulf, it is not improbable that there would be such an exodus from Protestantism as would make all previous traffic seem insignificant.

Those who pronounce upon Disestablishment are required to take into their calculations not merely the ecclesiastical forces of their own connection but likewise all those of their time and country. From these Roman Catholicism must not on any account be omitted, indeed it is one of the most important factors. We have no right to close our eyes to the fact, too evident to be denied, that the Roman Catholic Church is steadily gaining ground in England; we must not allow any bigoted belief in the impossibility of such a fact, or any fear of being stigmatized as alarmists for calling attention to it, to keep us from frankly acknowledging that which ought to give us serious warning. No doubt we do not like it, for there is in most Englishmen a nervous dread of Roman Catholicism which perhaps is not often expressed, or even acknowledged, by those who feel it, but yet is none the less real and strong. Besides, through so many generations we have had a settled conviction that Roman Catholicism was, in so far as it differed from other Christian Churches, little else than a system of ignorant superstition which must inevitably give way before advancing freedom and knowledge; we are therefore naturally much surprised to find that, in spite of all our boastings of how greatly freedom and knowledge have advanced during this generation, we are told that Roman Catholicism has also advanced in England during the same time with greater rapidity than ever before since the Reformation. But this is quite true nevertheless, as is plain to anyone who carefully feels the religious pulse of the nation. There is no necessity to produce statistics, but one symptom may be understood if we compare the present general feeling towards one who goes over to the Roman Catholic Church with that which prevailed about thirty years ago. Then most people felt that such a man must be a fool, or under some hallucination, whilst now he is looked upon without surprise and not seldom even with a sort of half-admiration. We can also compare the indifferent, sometimes even contemptuous, attitude of politicians in those days towards this Church, with their present respectfulness, and sometimes even toadying, to it. Whether we like it or not, the Church of Rome is a great power in England; it is better organized and better disciplined, more extended and more united, animated with stronger hopes and larger ambitions, than ever before. If all this contradicts our favourite theories, we must revise the theories, for the facts will not move.

Attention is not here thus called with the hope of reviving some old " No Popery " cry or of stirring up angry feelings. We ought to remember that by the measurements of Heaven the differences between Roman Catholics and Protestants will probably seem very small, and that as such these two should feel themselves spiritually joined in a brotherhood infinitely closer than any which can exist between either of them and those who reject altogether the Christian faith.

But whilst acknowledging this sympathy of the inner spirit, we cannot forget that we have here to do merely with outward polity, and that in this respect Protestantism and Roman Catholicism are essentially opposed. This is not the place to enter into the arguments between them, but it is the place in which we may be reminded that, before pronouncing on Disestablishment, we ought to come to a definite conviction as to whether we believe that Protestantism is better than Roman Catholicism, and whether we believe that Disestablishment will strengthen or weaken Protestantism.

As to the first, there is no doubt that the vast majority of the people believe that Protestantism is better for the nation than Roman Catholicism. Ignoring altogether their theological disputes as not coming within the subject, everyone must acknowledge that there is a vast difference between these two systems in their effects upon the nation. Some may prefer one set of effects and some the other, but no thoughtful person can be indifferent between them. We must remember that the terms Protestant and Roman Catholic involve far more than the differences between two Churches, for they imply two widely different forms of civilization. The religion of England is only one manifestation of that Protestantism which gives the tone to almost the whole of English social and political life. Nearly all our national institutions, nearly all our political axioms and social principles, our freedom of thought, our freedom of speech, our freedom of action, derive their character from this Protestant spirit, and the proper acceptance of Roman Catholicism would involve a complete revolution, and the abandonment of most of that of which Englishmen are chiefly proud. That such a change is undreamt of is a clear proof that the vast majority believe that Protestantism is better for the nation than Roman Catholicism.

It follows then that Disestablishment, if it helped Roman Catholicism, would be inimical to the national welfare, and that it would so help it cannot be reasonably doubted. For, as pointed out, one of the first effects of Disestablishment would be to split up the National Church into a number of Churches, and so to leave the Protestant religion to the exclusive care of a multitude of isolated and scattered sectarian bodies. Against such a disorganized condition of the forces of Protestantism, Roman Catholicism would be easily and inevitably triumphant, and for the following reasons amongst others :—

In the first place, the natural tendency of human nature is, in religion, towards large organizations. During times of exceptional excitement men may break away into little separate bodies, but their permanent inclinations are sure to eventually reassert themselves, and these are always in the direction of large union. Especially is this so with Christianity, whose spirit of genial fraternity is opposed to sectarian isolation.

Besides this natural tendency, which is chiefly unconscious, most men come eventually to have a strong conscious dislike to these sectarian divisions. When that excitement of conscientious enthusiasm which led to these divisions has passed away, perhaps with the disappearance of the generation which was stirred by it, those who come after begin to ask themselves whether the points of difference are really as important as they were thought to be, and so gradually they lose interest in such sectarian divisions and finally grow disgusted with them. Those who doubt the truth of this process should look around and they will find that the Christian public of England is just now coming into such a temper as this; we can hardly believe that our fathers struggled and suffered as much as they certainly did, over disputes which seem to us so trifling and yet which caused many of the divisions still remaining amongst us. Sensible men on all sides are beginning to think that these innumerable schisms have been more or less of a mistake, and it is now generally acknowledged that they have lowered the dignity of Christianity and retarded its extension. It may be said that such a spirit will heal these divisions of itself without the help of the national principle, but this does not follow. For a National Church is the only possible centre of union; it is the only queen round which the other bees will swarm, and therefore it ought to be preserved even though temporarily the majority of the bees may be elsewhere. Without such a Church, however strong may be the desire for union it cannot, consistently with Protestant freedom, lead to the creation of a united Church except upon the national basis. Besides, it must be remembered that the moods of mankind are intermittent, and that a period of aversion to divisions will probably be followed by one of strong disposition towards them. Only a National Church can keep such a disposition within reasonable limits, and therefore without such a Church, Roman Catholicism is in both moods the gainer, for in times of aversion to divisions, it offers a ready-made Church of union, and in times of disposition towards them, it gains by the consequent weakening of its opponents' forces and reputation. Only a National Church can compete with the Roman Catholic one in gratifying that desire for union which in most men is ultimately predominant.

In addition, it must also be acknowledged that human nature has a natural liking for authority in religion. Christianity is essentially authoritative in its character, and most men look for a similar authoritativeness in the Churches which uphold it. Roman Catholicism gratifies this desire to the uttermost, and has the additional attraction of relieving its followers from the trouble of thinking for themselves, but

Protestantism can find no such element of authoritativeness apart from the national ideal. All of us are acquainted with the national authority, and this is the largest and most impressive conception of authority of which we have any experience. The national principle does not teach that this authority should over-ride those rights of private judgment and of direct intercourse with God which form the marrow of Protestantism, but it merely claims that this national authority, whilst preserving us from prelatical domination, preserves us also from that absence of all valid authority which ultimately favours such domination. This desire for authority may be merely a sentiment but it is none the less powerful, and unless we give it a worthy conception round which it may cling, it will take to some unworthy one. Most of the adherents of Roman Catholicism yield to the Papal claims not through conviction of their Scriptural truthfulness, for the evidence of this sort is both very slight and very little understood, but from this longing for authority. We may not like this longing, but we must reckon for it if we mean to compete successfully with Roman Catholicism, and Protestantism can only do this by association with the conception of national authority.

We see then that as far as the Church is concerned, two of the probable effects of Disestablishment would be the disintegration of the Protestant Church, and the increase of Roman Catholicism.

Turning next to the nation, one of the most certain effects of Disestablishment would be the lowering of the national tone. To see this we must not merely look at this or that particular work done by the National Church, but we must go deeper and we shall find that the national principle exercises a strong influence in keeping religion associated with the daily concerns of national life. As long as religious authority comes through the same channel as all other national authority, it is like a clear stream flowing into a river often muddy of itself, and making the whole body of water purer. And even if the effect at any time is not particularly perceptible, the national principle at any rate keeps the thought of religion always before the minds of the whole nation, and not merely before those of the people who are themselves religious. As long as Parliament is called upon from time to time to consider religious questions, the attention of the whole nation is then directed to religion itself, and this implies a great deal, especially in times like ours. For the peculiar danger of our state of civilization is not that people are prone to disbelieve in religion so much as merely to do without it. The progress of science, the extension of printing, the increase of locomotion, the development of commercial and industrial enterprise, indeed all the changes which go to form what we call our improved civilization, tend to make life so busy and full that few have the leisure, and still fewer feel the necessity, to turn to religion. A life full of occupation, a state of civilization full of excitement, are not favourable to religion, and require that religion to be kept with increased persistence before the public mind. The political changes of late years have all worked in the same direction, for as grievances are abolished, the unselfish enthusiasms which divide men into political parties die away, and politics tend to become a mere scramble for personal aggrandisements or class gains. A condition which socially is so full of worldly interests and politically so empty of high motives requires religion to be kept all the more resolutely prominent. But the tendency of Disestablishment would be to separate religion from politics and withdraw it still more from popular attention. If we look into the causes which go to form what we call the tone of a nation, that quality upon which its political character depends, we shall find that religion is infinitely the best and ought to be the strongest. Religion has always been the formative force in English politics, but after Disestablishment that force would be ostensibly withdrawn and the national tone would consequently be eventually lowered.

Another reason for the lowering of the national tone has been spoken of before, namely that Disestablishment would ultimately lead to the domination of some Church, or of such a combination of Churches as might be called the Church generally. For however contrary appearances at any particular period may be, and however long it may take to come about, the ultimate supremacy of religion is certain; unless the nation rules the Church, the Church will rule the nation, and a ruling Church is a natural enemy to political and social freedom. Loss of such freedom means loss of tone, from which a nation can only recover by such a struggle as that which gave us our completely National Church, and the results of which would in a great degree be abandoned by Disestablishment. If the National Church is done away with, we may rest assured that, unless the character of the English nation is to sink, our descendants will some day have to fight over again the greatest battles of their forefathers.

Disestablishment would not merely injure the character of the Church and lower the tone of the nation, but it would also diminish the reputation and influence of religion itself. It is not from any inherent weakness of its own nor from any remarkable opposition of its enemies that religion is now suffering, but its chief danger lies in the tendency, so strong and widespread, to look upon it as of little practical importance, as a matter which may concern theologians and enthusiasts but with which sensible men of the world need not bother themselves. It seems plain that this separation between religion and life would be greatly aggravated by a change which would withdraw religion from connection with the nation and from the realm of politics. Our greatest problem in this life is to harmonise the claims of religion with the necessities of our earthly existence; Religion and the World are the two combatants who have to fight for the dominion of the mind, and the best result is that which drives neither quite away, but leaves the World to exercise its own proper functions under the strict supremacy of Religion. But instead of this, Disestablishment would mean the surrender of Religion; by that change Religion would be striking its flag to the World and giving up its crown of empire; henceforth it would be declared that the spiritual was divorced from the practical, that those who thought should not act and those who acted need not think. Not merely would the world be impoverished by the withdrawal of its best and only saving spirit, but religion would also suffer by the loss of its material influences, for its tendency is always towards the impracticable, and it needs the alliance of practical necessities to keep it from becoming impossible.

But, happily, we are not compelled either to leave the Church of England just as it is or to disestablish it, for there is another course open to us, and that is to develope it. And this is by far the best of all, for having convinced ourselves that the national principle is right, we ought not to give it up nor be contented with its present half-hearted form, but we should feel bound to try to get it carried out more fully and justly. This principle, instead of being a dreamy conceit or a decayed idea, may be made one of the greatest instruments for good which it is in the power of this generation to get hold of, and such a one as is best able to cure the special evils from which we suffer. One of these is the increase of social alienations. The rapid growth of population has separated the different classes of the people far more widely from each other than was formerly the case or than is socially healthy. Every large town is divided into districts, each of which is inhabited by people of a similar social standing who have next to no means of exercising any influence over the people of the other districts, and this evil has been greatly aggravated by the modern habit, so general with the middle classes, of going to live in the suburbs. No Christian man can walk through our large towns without a sad heart as he sees how the poorer classes are either left in utter neglect or treated with a patronising charity which is almost as bad. No amount of civic enterprise in erecting fine buildings and opening parks and museums, no amount of private benevolence in founding institutions for intellectual culture and societies for charitable distribution, no amount of patriotic philanthropy in passing laws for the repression of vice and the restriction of temptations, not these, nor all the means put together which are now being tried for what is called "the improvement of the people," can compensate for the loss of the natural play of social influence. All classes suffer from this loss, for the rich need the influence of the poor as much as the poor do that of the rich, but this influence must operate so that each can accept it manfully.

The increase of population is not the only cause which is producing these caste divisions. The great development of trade, with the consequent supremacy of commercial ideas, has killed out all the old spirit of feudalism which bound men together, and has put in its place a spirit which divides rather than unites. Society, instead of being a unit, is split up into a number of organized classes each of which is almost exclusively seeking its own selfish advantage, and all of which are more or less animated with a feeling of antagonism to the rest.

Now undoubtedly our great commercial prosperity is meant to be a blessing, but it will ultimately prove a curse unless we find some means of stopping these growing class divisions and isolations. These barriers must melt away into the sentiment of universal brotherhood, but there is only one solvent to which they will yield, and that is religion, which must act through an organization as wide as the evil, and that is national. Here is a glorious field of work for the National Church of England, but before she can acquit herself in it properly she must be better equipped, for whilst fully conscious of, and deeply thankful for, the great strides which have lately been made, we cannot forget that there is much still to be improved. The organizations of the Church must be made more vigorous and comprehensive, its places of worship more free and public, its services more hearty and attractive, its parochial offices more real and beneficial. But, after all, the great need is not so much that any part of the machinery should be reformed as that the whole tone should be raised. The Church is like a warrior whose armour and strength would be all right if we could only get his spirit properly roused. The clergy, and all those who have anything to do with it, must realise more fully than they have ever yet done, that the Church of England is a national and not a sectarian institution, and that therefore its theology ought to be simple and its spirit sympathetic.

A simple theology does not mean an indefinite one, and those are not the best friends of the Church who encourage that amiable vagueness which is so much cultivated by some of its best-disposed supporters. A Church without a creed is like a body without bones, and nothing can be more alien to the spirit of Christianity than the tendency, now so prevalent, to suppose that all creeds are pretty much alike, and that therefore it does not greatly matter what is a man's religious belief, or whether he has any at all. As being merely a Church, the Church of England must have a creed, and as being a Christian Church, this creed must be definite, whilst as being a National Church, it must be simple. And this is what is here meant by a liberal theology, which is thus the reverse of a vague one. Let the simple statement of the plain fundamentals of our religion be our only necessary creed, and let the simple requirements of this creed be our only necessary forms, and then let us outside of these allow the utmost possible liberty. By thus acting the Church of England will not merely be promoting its own welfare, but it also will be doing such a service to Christianity as it now stands sorely in need of. For these are anxious days for religion, such as shake the faith of its timid friends, and even make those sad who have unswerving confidence in the omnipotence of God and in the ultimate and universal triumph of a religion which has always come victorious out of dangers which seemed infinitely greater. The old, simple, practical, manly Christianity which the Bible teaches and which has been the faith for so many generations of the best of our forefathers is going out of fashion, and the Christian world seems to be dividing itself up between priestly domination on the one hand, and on the other, worldly indifference or antagonistic scepticism. The torch of pure religion, lit by the Lord Himself with the fire of heaven, is being trodden out under the contending feet of fanatics and unbelievers. It can only be picked up and borne onwards by the hand of a Church which is practical as well as spiritual, human as well as divine, National as well as Christian. Protestant Revivalism, like Roman Catholicism, sets the other world against and above this, and to Nationalism is reserved the task of properly reconciling the two; of joining practicality with spirituality, life with religion, earth with heaven; of making Christianity a sensible reality as well as a devout enthusiasm. Can there be a nobler work, or one more needed, than this which now lies especially before the National Church of England? No better motto can be chosen as a guide to success than that which is attributed to Baxter—" In necessary things unity, in doubtful things liberty, in all things charity."

This Church must not only be simple and liberal and practical in its creed, but it must also be sympathetic in its spirit; it must have a national heart as well as a national name. Those are the most dangerous enemies to the Church of England who would make it the friend of any particular class or the ally of any particular party. If there is any class with which this Church may be especially friendly, it ought most decidedly to be the poor, for a National Church alone can offer its ministrations to all and invite the poorest to claim its services as their right. And if Protestantism is to live and grow, it must get hold of the poor far more thoroughly than it has ever yet tried to do. Wherever we go, whether to Church or to Chapel, whether in town or in country, the same question is forced upon us—" Where are the poor?" We see everywhere the places of worship frequented by the same classes of the people, the upper and the middle, but nowhere do we find in any numbers that class which seems most of all to need religion, namely the poor. So patent is this fact that we may as well frankly admit, although we must do it with deep sorrow, that the poorer classes do not as a body seem to care about our religion; no stirring revivals, no evangelistic enterprises, seem able to reach them. Probably much of this is due to that character of coarse indifference which so often accompanies poverty, but much also must be attributed to the want of the proper means and of the proper spirit. The national principle, if rightly carried out, can find such means, and it is for the Church of England, having got these means, to use them with the proper spirit. The first requisite is that this Church, even if it cannot get the adhesion of the poor, should at any rate win their confidence. There is no use in disguising the fact that large masses of the poor regard the Church of England with suspicion; in spite of all its efforts to extend education and foster charity, they look upon it as peculiarly the friend of the rich and as the enemy to political and social progress. Unhappily there is too much reason for this feeling; the Church has too often opposed what it ought to have supported, and remained silent when it ought to have spoken out. Its first duty now is not merely to atone for such errors in the past but also to renew within itself such a right spirit as shall make them impossible in the future. A truly Christian

Church should be the friend not so much of the rich and powerful, who are well able to take care of themselves, but of the poor and weak, of the widow and fatherless and of him who hath no helper; a truly National Church should never be the defender of oppressive privilege or unjust exclusiveness, but should always be found fighting in favour of the social and political improvement of the masses of the people. If the Church of England will act in this spirit there is no fear for its Disestablishment; nay, it must have before it a future whose glories will make its greatest achievements of the past grow pale. Let the Church once win, as it easily can, the honest confidence of the people, and it may then carry the message of salvation throughout the length and breadth of the land, into thousands of houses whose doors have hitherto been always shut to it; then the glad tidings of great joy shall run along our highways and hedges and through our streets and alleys; then the ears of the deaf shall be unstopped and the eyes of the blind shall be opened; then, and not till then, shall the English nation become Christian in fact as it now is in name.

And when we think of our gifts as a people, a still more glorious vision rises before us; we see that the Church of England may not only win over its own nation but may also become the chief instrument in Christianizing the world. With nations as with individuals, gifts imply responsibilities; as he who is born to a great estate and noble name is expected to regard these not as means for pleasure or pride but as obligations to a useful and worthy life, so a nation which is especially endowed is called upon to fulfil a proportionately higher destiny. We in this country have a heritage such as has never fallen to the lot of any nation before; not only does our rule spread into all parts but it also includes all races and states of civilization; we have a colonial empire girdling the earth and peopled by men of our own blood whose achievements are yet in their infancy; we are the masters of the greatest country of Asia and also the arbiters of Africa, whilst our race holds the undisputed headship of the Western Hemisphere. And our power is far more extensive than our rule, for what we may call English civilization is penetrating everywhere and is undoubtedly now the predominant influence of the world.

We ought seriously to ask ourselves what all this means. It surely cannot be that this power is put into our hands merely, or chiefly, that we may extend our trade and increase our wealth. Nay, we must rather believe that our wealth and trade are not to be objects in themselves but are meant to be instruments for some greater purpose. And as we have received the highest gifts, so we are called to the highest task, which can be no other than the regeneration of the world.

We must not be frightened away from this conception of our duty because so many may put it down as an arrogant assumption or a youthful dream, but we must do our utmost to get it established in the minds of the English people, and then, even if we do not benefit the world as we may wish, we shall at any rate confer a great blessing upon our own country. For the tone of English politics is now becoming so local, and selfish, and mean, that corruption must inevitably increase, and degradation and decay soon follow, unless we can bring in the purifying influence of a great aim. Such an aim, and such alone, can be found in this lofty conception of our destiny.

But we cannot fulfil this destiny, we cannot hope to regenerate, in any degree, the world unless we make religion our chief motive power, for religion and regeneration must always go together, and as we are to carry out this work as a nation so our religion must operate nationally.

Before we can properly start upon this crusade abroad we must first heal our divisions at home, for we cannot dare to march forth under a banner of the Cross which we have ourselves already torn into ribbons. Our plain duty therefore is not to support Disestablishment but to build up a still greater and truer National Church. So shall we be most faithful to our responsibilities as Englishmen, and most helpful in bringing nearer that time, for which all Christians should strive, when the kingdoms of this world shall become the kingdoms of our God and of His Christ.

THE END.

www.ingramcontent.com/pod-product-compliance
Lightning Source LLC
Chambersburg PA
CBHW030551300426
44111CB00009B/939